Granny Square Patchwork

40 Crochet Granny Square Patterns To Mix And Match With Endless Patchworking Possibilities

By Shelley Husband

UK TERMS

Copyright © 2021 by Shelley Husband

All rights reserved. No part of this publication may be reproduced or transmitted by any means, electronic, photocopying or otherwise without prior written permission of the author.

ISBN-13: 978-0-6451573-0-7

Charts made by Amy Gunderson

Email: kinglouiespizza@gmail.com
Ravelry ID: AmyGunderson

Graphic Design by Michelle Lorimer

Email: hello@michellelorimer.com

Project Photography by Jo O'Keefe

Email: jookeefe@hotmail.com
Instagram: missfarmerjojo
Photos taken at Longmeadow Estate
longmeadowestate.com.au

Other Photography by Shelley Husband

Technical Editing by SiewBee Pond

Email: essbee1995@yahoo.com

First edition 2021

Published by Shelley Husband
PO Box 11
Narrawong VIC 3285
Australia

shelleyhusbandcrochet.com

0824

Contents

Welcome / 5

What you need / 6
    What you need to have **/ 6**
    What you need to know **/ 6**
    Design your own projects **/ 10**
    Joining your squares **/ 12**

Patterns / 13
    Size 1 Patterns **/ 14**
    Size 2 Patterns **/ 24**
    Size 3 Patterns **/ 40**
    Size 4 Patterns **/ 64**
    Size 5 Patterns **/ 88**
    Size 6 Patterns **/ 112**
    Extension and Border Patterns **/ 138**

Projects / 147
    Summer Fiesta Necklace **/ 148**
    Dessi Cowl or Headband **/ 149**
    Bloom Scarf **/ 150**
    Shine Tote **/ 152**
    Panache Poncho **/ 153**
    Envelop Baby Blanket **/ 154**
    Rapier Blanket **/ 156**
    Marvin, the Blanket **/ 158**
    Medley Blanket **/ 160**
    Manderley Blanket **/ 163**
    Pastiche Blanket **/ 166**
    Conglomeration Blanket **/ 170**

Glossary / 174

Yarn / 176

Project Planner / 178

Helpful Links / 181

Thank You / 182

About the Author / 183

More Books / 184

Welcome

Welcome to my world of granny squares! In this book, you will find endless inspiration to create your own crochet patchwork projects from granny squares.

But why Granny Square Patchwork? Well, the definition of patchwork is:

noun

1. something made up of an incongruous variety of pieces or parts; hodgepodge: a patchwork of verse forms.

2. work made of pieces of cloth or leather of various colours or shapes sewed together, used especially for covering quilts, cushions, etc.

And that is what you will find in Granny Square Patchwork. I have designed 40 granny squares of various sizes for you to put together your own crochet patchwork creations.

I will guide you through the multitude of ways you can construct your very own granny square patchwork pieces, showing you how to adjust all the patterns in this book to be the size you need for your projects.

I hope this is the start of a grand love affair for you with granny squares.

What you need to have

If you have a hook, scissors, and a yarn needle, all you need is some yarn to get started. How much and what kind of yarn depends on what you want to make. Every granny square pattern and project tells you how much yarn I used to make it. You are, of course, not bound by that and can use any yarn type and weight you like.

This book is all about you creating your own Granny Square Patchwork creations. Let's get some of the housekeeping out of the way before we jump into the fun.

What you need to know

You need to know how to read crochet patterns and charts. It helps to know a bit about both as sometimes, it is hard to show the detail in multi-layered patterns in charts, and sometimes, a chart can show you what exactly is happening in a pattern if the words are not making sense to you.

Pattern Information

Every pattern page has all the information you need. Here is what you will see and what it all means.

Symbols

   35 m / 39 yd

Difficulty rating - 1 ball and hook is easy, 2 is intermediate, 3 is more advanced.

Yarn requirements - the amount of yarn needed to make one square using 8 ply/DK/light worsted yarn and a 4.5 mm/7 hook. You will find the approximate amount of yarn needed for other yarn weights on page 177.

Infinity symbol - this means that some rounds of the pattern can be repeated endlessly, increasing in size to create a square as large as you desire.

Notes / Special Stitches / Tips

If there is anything unusual about a pattern or if a special stitch or technique is used, it will be explained at the top of the pattern page. Some rounds will have notes within them.

Colour play

Each pattern is written for and shown in one colour. Your colour choices are only limited by your imagination. Each pattern shows just 2 examples of alternate colour schemes, some made by me, most made by some fabulous helpers. These are a guide only. You can do what you like colour-wise.

How to read the written patterns

The abbreviations of all the stitches and techniques used in the patterns are explained in full in the Glossary on page 174.

Here's an excerpt from the Quarter pattern on page 36:

> **R7:** ch3 (stch), tr in same st as ss, *tr in next 7 sts, (dc, 2dtr, ch1, 2dtr, dc) in 2-ch sp, tr in next 7 sts**, 3tr in next st*, rep from * to * 2x and * to ** 1x, tr in same st as first st, join with ss to 3rd ch of stch.
> {20 sts, 1 1-ch sp on each side; 4 3-st cnrs}

And another from the Flourish pattern on page 52:

> **R12:** dc over joining dc, *2x [dc in next st, 2dc in 2-ch sp], dc in next st**, dc in 2-ch sp*, rep from * to * 14x and * to ** 1x, join with ss to first st. {128 sts}

After the beginning of round instructions, the first single asterisk indicates the start of a repeat and the second single asterisk indicates the end of a full repeat. The double asterisks indicate the end of a partial repeat. Ignore the asterisks and follow the instructions until you get to "rep". That is your cue to go back to the first single asterisk and redo the pattern repeat as many times in full and partially as instructed. After the repeats, I tell you how to finish off the round.

Brackets

(xxxx) are stitches and/or chain spaces that are either to be all worked in the one stitch or space as indicated, or a set of stitches and/or chain spaces to be skipped.

[xxxx] indicate a small set of stitches and/or chain spaces to be repeated within a full pattern repeat. These brackets will be preceded with a number and x to indicate how many times to work the small repeat.

{xxxx} contain the stitch count for each round. For a square shape, it states how many stitches are along each side between the corners and describes the corners. If the pattern begins as a shape with no corners, then it describes how many stitches in total make up that round.

Things to note

If there are a number of chains at the beginning of a round not followed by (stch), these chains are not included in the stitch count.

If there is a slip stitch at the beginning of a round, it is not included in the stitch count. However, if there is a slip stitch within a pattern repeat, it is included in the stitch count.

If the instructions don't specify a round to work into or skip, it is assumed you work into or skip the stitches of the previous round. If you need to work into or skip stitches of rounds other than the previous round, it will be stated in the instructions.

Charts

Charts are visual representations of the written patterns and every pattern has one. For the larger or more complex patterns, the charts have been broken up to show things more clearly. Each stitch is represented by a symbol on the chart. You will find a key for all the symbols used in the Glossary on page 174.

Seamless tips

To avoid having a visible seam where the rounds begin and end, I end each round in the middle of a corner. In the case of a square with 2-chain corner spaces, the round will end with the instruction to chain 1 and join with a double crochet. That double crochet takes the place of the second chain and places your hook in exactly the right spot to begin the next round, with no need to slip stitch or work backwards. Depending on the pattern, you may be instructed to work a stitch over that joining stitch.

Treat the joining stitch as the second chain of the 2-chain corner space and work over it as if it were a chain space. If the corners of the pattern are longer chain loops, the final number of chains to be worked and the joining stitch will be different. For example, if a round has corners of 4-chain spaces, it may end with chain 1, join with a treble crochet. A round with 3-chain spaces may end with chain 1, join with a half treble crochet. Check the Helpful Links on page 181 for a more detailed explanation of this technique.

Another trick to make your crochet look seamless is to work a false stitch instead of a starting chain. While I state the standard starting chain at the beginning of rounds, (e.g. ch3 to take the place of a treble crochet), I rarely use starting chains when crocheting. Instead, I use a false stitch. You can find a video of it on my YouTube Channel linked to on the Helpful Links page.

Blocking

Blocking is a way to make your crochet sing. Some patterns require a good blocking to sit flat and square. It is part of the process and does not take long to do.

You do not need anything fancy to block. A folded towel works well. I use foam mats intended for temporary flooring. These are handy to block large blankets too.

Block each square by pinning it out and squirting it with steam from your iron. Some squares will only need a pin in each corner, while others will need some all along the edges and in the centre to correct any swirl or distortion. Some fibres will block best after washing according to yarn label instructions and pinning out while wet to dry.

Design your own projects

The goal of this book is to give you endless possibilities to create your own crochet patchwork wonders.

For ease of calculation in designing your own layouts and explaining how the patterns fit together, all measurements for the granny square patterns are noted in inches.

To design your own project, follow these steps.

Decide what to make

Things to consider are who it is for, how big it needs to be and what shape you want to make.

Decide your layout

Once you know what you are making, you can move on to the next step and begin to choose the patterns you want to make. You can use anything from one-to-many patterns in one project.

I have given you patterns for squares that are six different sizes. Each size up increases by the same increment. For example, if you are using an 8 ply/DK/Light worsted yarn, the size goes up by 3 inches for each size. If you are using 4 ply/sock/fingering, the size increment is 2.5 inches for each size. If you are using 10 ply/aran/worsted, the size increases by 3.5 inches.

But that is not all you have! I have also given you six patterns that you can use to add one increment to any of the patterns, extending them to the next size up if you need to for your layout. These extensions can also be used as borders for your projects.

If you need small filler squares of one increment, there are four patterns you can use to make small squares by making only the first 3 or 4 rounds. They are Melbourne (make Rounds 1 to 3) and Bushel, Foundation and Kim (make Rounds 1 to 4).

On page 178 you will find a project planner page you can copy to help with your layout ideas. Alternatively, you can download it from the Helpful Links page.

You will see sections of the grid are labelled with the six sizes of the patterns in this book. Each one has gridlines that represents one increment. Cut them out and play around with possible layouts. There really are endless options, as you will see when you start to play. I have created a couple of variants for the projects I made as follows:

- Use more than one size squares as they appear in this book. Examples of this can be seen in the Medley Blanket, Bloom Scarf, Pastiche Blanket and the Manderley Blanket.

- Use more than one size with an extension to make them the same size. Marvin, the Blanket is an example of this.

- Extend as much as you need one of the patterns suited to that as seen in the Envelop Baby Blanket.

- Use just one pattern as shown with the Dessi Cowl, Shine Tote, Panache Poncho and Rapier Blanket.

Here are some other suggestions for blankets:

- A size 3 square surrounded by size 1 squares, then use an extension as border for a smaller blanket.

- Four size 5 squares, each surrounded by size 1 squares, then joined and with an extension as border for a medium blanket.

- Six size 6 patterns for a large rectangular blanket.

Once you have decided on your layout, write down how many of each pattern you need, including details of any that you are extending. Decide on a border to finish it off with.

Work out your yarn needs

Things to consider for yarn choice are, is the yarn fit for purpose? Do you need to work within a budget? What are your environmental thoughts on yarn sources and fibre? Are there allergies to consider? What colour or colours will you use?

The amount of yarn needed for all patterns is stated in metres and yards in 8 ply/DK/light worsted on the pattern pages, or in other yarn weights on page 177.

Compare the metres or yards per gram of your yarn of choice to the weights listed. If it is less metres or yards per gram, you will need more, and if it is more, you will need less.

If using many colours, use the overall yardage as a guide. To be more precise, make a sample square of average size for your project in your yarn and colour choice. Weigh either the yarn balls or square as you go, to work out how much of each colour you will use. Work out rough percentages of each colour used and use those figures to work out how much you will need overall. My tip is to add extra of the colours used most at the end of patterns, particularly if you are using the larger sizes patterns.

Using your layout plan, work out how much yarn you need. Add 10-15% more for joining and the border. The larger your project, the more you will need for the finishing.

Before you begin • 11

Joining your squares

There are many possible ways to join your squares. These are the joins I have used in the projects included in this book.

All of these joins can be used regardless of stitch counts. If stitch counts differ, use the same stitch on the edge of the square with the smaller stitch count twice, while using a new stitch on the edge of the square with the larger stitch count as many times as needed to make up the difference.

dc on back join

Hold squares right sides together, attach joining yarn with a standing double crochet to both 2-chain corner spaces of each square at the same time. Work a double crochet into both loops of both squares all the way along, end with a double crochet in both 2-chain corner spaces. Fasten off.

dc on back though blo join

Worked the same for the dc on back join, but when working along the edges of the squares, use the back loops only.

Zipper join

Place two squares right sides up, next to each other in front of you. Beginning in the chain stitches, slip stitch through the back loops only of stitches of both squares from the front, working from the bottom of both squares to the top, ending in the chains.

Joining order

Join the squares into strips, then join the strips as the squares were joined but when you reach the 2-chain corner spaces, work one stitch in each, ignoring the join if the joins meet. If the joins do not meet, use each 2-chain space, and join with individual stitches of the opposite edge.

How to join lots of different sized squares

If you are making a project with a lot of different sized squares, like the Conglomeration Blanket on page 170, it can be a bit daunting knowing where to start.

The thing to do is look for smaller blocks of squares or rectangles within your layout and join them. I find it best to lay the squares out on the floor and join in small sections, looking for straight lines, then joining those smaller sections into larger ones. Doing it this way limits the number of the more fiddly sections to join at right angles.

Patterns

And now the fun begins. Here is where you will find all forty granny square patterns, as well as the six extension and border patterns.

Each pattern size is in its own section. While each section has patterns of one size, any can be made to the next size up by adding one of the extension patterns.

There are four patterns that can be extended indefinitely by repeating Rounds. They are Foundation, Quarter, Bushel and Melbourne.

If you need small filler squares of one increment, there are four patterns you can use by making only the first 3 or 4 rounds. They are Melbourne (make Rounds 1 to 3), Bushel, Foundation and Kim (make Rounds 1 to 4).

Some patterns will be ruffled, warped or cupped at some stages of their construction. Trust that all will be well. If it is extreme, it is noted in the pattern.

A note about size

You may find that some of your squares end up a little different in size to mine when using the same yarn weight and hook as me. When you consider all the possible chances for variation – the stitch sizes, our techniques and tension, yarn and hook combinations, well I'd be surprised if there weren't some variation.

If you find a square is larger than you need it to be, leave off the last round or so. Most of the large patterns have simple last rounds to make that easy.

If you need to add a little size to any square more than what you can gain by blocking, then adding a round of double or treble crochet will be all you need to do.

Size 1 Patterns

I love small granny squares! They are so portable, and you can usually complete a square in one sitting. They are so satisfying to make a project from.

Below are the approximate sizes you will achieve with 3 different yarn weights and hook sizes. The amount of yarn listed on each pattern page is for the middle yarn weight and hook size. The amount of yarn needed for the other yarn weights is on page 177.

hook	3.5 mm hook	4.5 mm hook	5.5 mm hook
yarn	4 ply/sock/fingering	8 ply/DK/light worsted	10 ply/aran/worsted
square	5"	6"	7"

Bellis
page 16

Blossom
page 17

Danvers
page 18

Floret
page 19

Foundation
page 20

Millpond Mini
page 21

Nosegay
page 22

Valance
page 23

Size 1 Patterns

Colours by Shelley

Colours by Jenny Hebbard

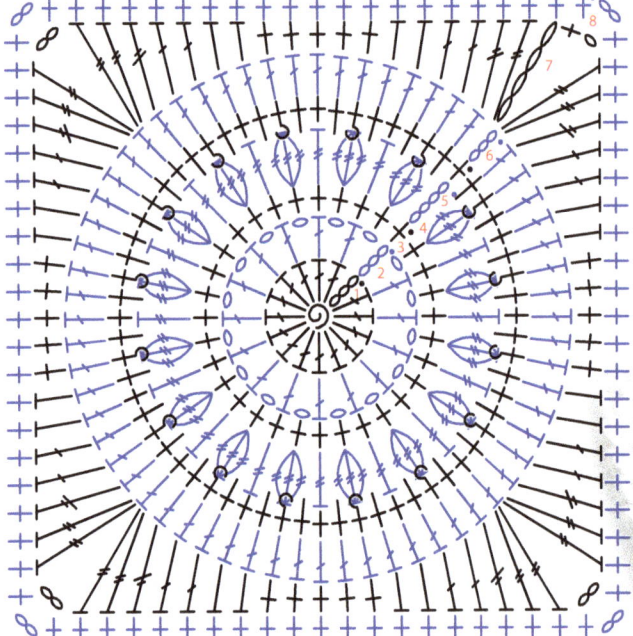

Bellis

The scientific name for a daisy is Bellis Perennis. As this design is very daisy-esque, Bellis it is.

 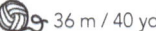 36 m / 40 yd

Begin with mc.

R1: ch3 (stch), 15tr, join with ss to 3rd ch of stch. {16 sts}

R2: ch3 (stch), *ch1**, tr in next st*, rep from * to * 14x and * to ** 1x, join with ss to 3rd ch of stch. {16 sts, 16 1-ch sps}

R3: dc in same st as ss, *dc in 1-ch sp**, dc in next st*, rep from * to * 14x and * to ** 1x, join with ss to first st. {32 sts}

R4: ch4 (stch), *3dtrcl in next st**, dtr in next st*, rep from * to * 14x and * to ** 1x, join with ss to 4th ch of stch. {32 sts}

R5: dc in same st as ss, *dc between last and next sts, fpdc around next st, dc between last and next sts**, dc in next st*, rep from * to * 14x and * to ** 1x, join with ss to first st. {64 sts}

R6: ch3 (stch), tr in next 63 sts, join with ss to 3rd ch of stch. {64 sts}

R7: ch4 (stch), dtr in same st as ss, *hdtr in next st, tr in next 2 sts, htr in next 2 sts, dc in next 5 sts, htr in next 2 sts, tr in next 2 sts, hdtr in next st**, (2dtr, ch2, 2dtr) in next st*, rep from * to * 2x and * to ** 1x, 2dtr in same st as first sts, ch1, join with dc to 4th ch of stch. {19 sts on each side; 4 2-ch cnr sps}

R8: dc over joining dc, *dc in next 19 sts**, (dc, ch2, dc) in 2-ch cnr sp*, rep from * to * 2x and * to ** 1x, dc in same sp as first st, ch2, join with ss to first st. Fasten off. {21 sts on each side; 4 2-ch cnr sps}

Blossom

The explanation for this name is pretty obvious – it's a flower and so Blossom it is.

  47 m / 52 yd

Begin with mc.

R1: ch3 (stch), tr, *ch1**, 3tr*, rep from * to * 4x and * to ** 1x, tr, join with ss to 3rd ch of stch. {18 sts, 6 1-ch sps}

R2: fpdc around same st as ss, *ch2, skip 1 st, 3tr in 1-ch sp, ch2, skip 1 st**, fpdc around next st*, rep from * to * 4x and * to ** 1x, join with ss to first st. {24 sts, 12 2-ch sps}

R3: dc in same st as ss, *ch2, skip 2-ch sp, 2tr in next 3 sts, ch2, skip 2-ch sp**, dc in next st*, rep from * to * 4x and * to ** 1x, join with ss to first st. {42 sts, 12 2-ch sps}

R4: *fptr around fp st of R2, ch5, skip (2-ch sp, 6 sts & 2-ch sp)*, rep from * to * 5x, join with ss to first st. {6 sts, 6 5-ch sps}

Pull petals through to the front of the ch sps.

R5: ch3 (stch), *6tr in 5-ch sp**, 2tr in next st*, rep from * to * 4x and * to ** 1x, tr in same st as first st, join with ss to 3rd ch of stch. {48 sts}

R6: ch4 (stch), 3dtr in same st as ss, *skip 3 sts, dc in next 4 sts, skip 3 sts, 4dtr in next st**, ch2, 4dtr in next st*, rep from * to * 2x and * to ** 1x, ch1, join with dc to 4th ch of stch. {12 sts on each side; 4 2-ch cnr sps}

R7: ch3 (stch), tr over joining dc, *2tr in next 4 sts, skip 1 st, dc2tog over next 2 sts, skip 1 st, 2tr in next 4 sts**, 3tr in 2-ch cnr sp*, rep from * to * 2x and * to ** 1x, tr in same sp as first sts, join with ss to 3rd ch of stch. {17 sts on each side; 4 3-st cnrs}

R8: dc in same st as ss, *dc in next 9 sts, fpdc around next st, dc in next 9 sts**, (dc, ch2, dc) in next st*, rep from * to * 2x and * to ** 1x, dc in same as first st, ch1, join with dc to first st. {21 sts on each side; 4 2-ch cnr sps}

R9: dc over joining dc, *ch2, bptr around last st of a 3-st cnr of R7, bptr around next 8 sts of R7, skip 1 st of R7, bptr around next 9 sts of R7, ch2**, dc in 2-ch cnr sp*, rep from * to * 2x and * to ** 1x, join with ss to first st. {18 sts, 2 2-ch sps on each side; 4 1-st cnrs}

R10: dc in same st as ss, *dc in 2-ch sp, dc in next 18 sts, dc in 2-ch sp**, (dc, ch2, dc) in next st*, rep from * to * 2x and * to ^^ 1x, dc in same st as first st, ch2, join with ss to first st. Fasten off. {22 sts on each side; 4 2-ch cnr sps}

Colours by Evangelia V Katsafouros

Colours by Jenny Hebbard

Blossom - Size 1 Patterns • 17

Colours by Shelley

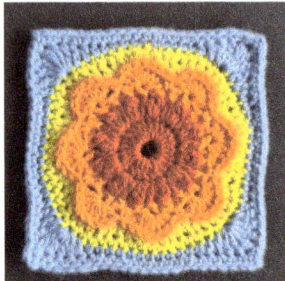

Colours by Cheryl Shields

Danvers

Danvers is one of the 3 patterns named after characters in the book Rebecca by Daphne du Maurier that make up the Manderley Blanket.

  36 m / 40 yd

Begin with mc.

R1: ch3 (stch), 23tr, join with ss to 3rd ch of stch. {24 sts}

R2: ch3 (stch), *ch1, 3trcl in next st, ch1**, tr in next st*, rep from * to * 10x and from * to ** 1x, join with ss to 3rd ch of stch. {24 sts, 24 1-ch sps}

Will be ruffled.

R3: fpdc around same st as ss, *dc in 1-ch sp**, fpdc around next st*, rep from * to * 22x and from * to ** 1x, join with ss to first st. {48 sts}

R4: *Don't work a false st.* ch3 (stch), 6tr in same st as ss, *skip 2 sts, dc in next st, skip 2 sts**, 7tr in next st*, rep from * to * 6x and from * to ** 1x, join with inv join to first true st. {64 sts}

R5: Attach with stdg dc to lbv of the 4th st of any 7-st group, dc in lbv of next st, *htr in lbv of next 2 sts, tr in lbv of next st, htr in lbv of next 2 sts**, dc in lbv of next 3 sts*, rep from * to * 6x and from * to ** 1x, dc in lbv of next st, join with ss to first st. {64 sts}

R6: dc in same st as ss, dc in next 63 sts, join with ss to first st. {64 sts}

R7: ch4 (stch), 2hdtr in same st as ss, *tr in next st, htr in next st, dc in next 11 sts, htr in next st, tr in next st**, (2hdtr, dtr, 2hdtr) in next st*, rep from * to * 2x and * to ** 1x, 2hdtr in same st as first sts, join with ss to 4th ch of stch. {15 sts on each side; 4 5-st cnrs}

R8: ch3 (stch), *tr in next 19 sts**, (tr, ch2, tr) in next st*, rep from * to * 2x and * to ** 1x, tr in same st as first st, ch2, join with ss to 3rd ch of stch. Fasten off. {21 sts on each side; 4 2-ch cnr sps}

Floret

A floret is a small flower that makes up a composite flower head. There are petal-like sections in this one that made me think of florets.

  38 m / 42 yd

Begin with mc.

R1: ch3 (stch), 11tr, join with ss to 3rd ch of stch. {12 sts}.

R2: ch3 (stch), tr in same st as ss, 2tr in next 11 sts, join with ss to 3rd ch of stch. {24 sts}

R3: ch3 (stch), tr in same st as ss, *tr in next 2 sts, ch1, skip 1 st, tr in next 2 sts**, 3tr in next st*, rep from * to * 2x and * to ** 1x, tr in same st as first sts, join with ss to 3rd ch of stch. {4 sts, 1 1-ch sp on each side; 4 3-st cnrs}

R4: ch3 (stch), tr in same st as ss, *tr in next 2 sts, skip 1 st, dtr in skipped st of R2, ch1, 3trcl in 1-ch sp, ch1, dtr in same skipped st of R2, skip 1 st, tr in next 2 sts**, 3tr in next st*, rep from * to * 2x and * to ** 1x, tr in same st as first sts, join with ss to 3rd ch of stch.
{7 sts, 2 1-ch sps on each side; 4 3-st cnrs}

R5: dc in same st as ss, *dc in next 4 sts, dc in 1-ch sp, fpdc around next st, dc in 1-ch sp, dc in next 4 sts**, (dc, ch2, dc) in next st*, rep from * to * 2x and * to ** 1x, dc in same as first st, ch1, join with dc to first st.
{13 sts on each side; 4 2-ch cnr sps}

R6: dc over joining dc, *dc in next 13 sts**, (dc, ch2, dc) in 2-ch cnr sp*, rep from * to * 2x and * to ** 1x, dc in same sp as first st, ch1, join with dc to first st.
{15 sts on each side; 4 2-ch cnr sps}

R7: ch3 (stch), tr over joining dc, *ch2, tr4tog over next 4 sts, ch2, tr in next 3 sts, fpdtr3tog over next 3 R4 sts, skip 1 st, tr in next 3 sts, ch2, tr4tog over next 4 sts, ch2**, 3tr in 2-ch cnr sp*, rep from * to * 2x and * to ** 1x, tr in same sp as first sts, join with ss to 3rd ch of stch.
{9 sts, 4 2-ch sps on each side; 4 3-st cnrs}

R8: dc in same st as ss, *dc in next st, 2dc in 2-ch sp, fpdc around next st, 2dc in 2-ch sp, dc in next 3 sts, fpdc around next st, dc in next 3 sts, 2dc in 2-ch sp, fpdc around next st, 2dc in 2-ch sp, dc in next st**, (dc, ch2, dc) in next st*, rep from * to * 2x and * to ** 1x, dc in same st as first st, ch1, join with dc to first st. {21 sts on each side; 4 2-ch cnr sps}

R9: dc over joining dc, *10x [ch1, skip 1 st, dc in next st], ch1, skip 1 st**, (dc, ch2, dc) in 2-ch sp*, rep from * to * 2x and * to ** 1x, dc in same sp as first st, ch1, join with dc for first st. {12 sts, 11 1-ch sps on each side; 4 2-ch cnr sps}

R10: dc over joining dc, *11x [dc in next st, dc in 1-ch sp], dc in next st**, (dc, ch2, dc) in 2-ch cnr sp*, rep from * to * 2x and * to ** 1x, dc in same sp as first st, ch2, join with ss to first st. Fasten off. {25 sts on each side; 4 2-ch cnr sps}

Colours by Chelsea Butler

Colours by Miranda Howard

Colours by
Kim Siebenhausen

Colours by
Kim Siebenhausen

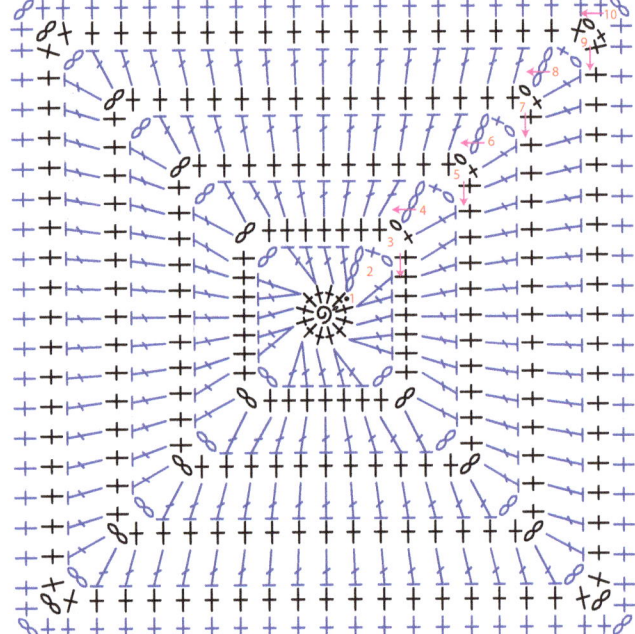

Foundation

This pattern is a basic one that forms a good foundation for starting out with granny squares.

  35 m / 39 yd

Foundation can be extended easily by repeating Rounds 8 and 9 as many times as needed, before ending with Round 10.

To combat the swirl, this pattern is turned at the end of each round from Round 3 on.

Begin with mc.

R1: ch1, 12dc, join with ss to first st. {12 sts}

R2: ch3 (stch), tr in same st as ss, *tr in next st, 2tr in next st**, ch2, 2tr in next st*, rep from * to * 2x and * to ** 1x, ch1, join with dc to 3rd ch of stch.
{5 sts on each side; 4 2-ch cnr sps}

R3: Turn, dc over ch1, *dc in next 5 sts**, (dc, ch2, dc) in 2-ch cnr sp*, rep from * to * 2x and * to ** 1x, dc in same sp as first st, ch1, join with dc to first st.
{7 sts on each side; 4 2-ch cnr sps}

R4: Turn, ch3 (stch), *tr in next 7 sts**, (tr, ch2, tr) in 2-ch cnr sp*, rep from * to * 2x and * to ** 1x, tr in same sp as first st, ch1, join with dc to 3rd ch of stch.
{9 sts on each side; 4 2-ch cnr sps}

R5: Turn, dc over ch1, *dc in next 9 sts**, (dc, ch2, dc) in 2-ch cnr sp*, rep from * to * 2x and * to ** 1x, dc in same sp as first st, ch1, join with dc to first st.
{11 sts on each side; 4 2-ch cnr sps}

R6: Turn, ch3 (stch), *tr in next 11 sts**, (tr, ch2, tr) in 2-ch cnr sp*, rep from * to * 2x and * to ** 1x, tr in same sp as first st, ch1, join with dc to 3rd ch of stch.
{13 sts on each side; 4 2-ch cnr sps}

R7: Turn, dc over ch1, *dc in next 13 sts**, (dc, ch2, dc) in 2-ch cnr sp*, rep from * to * 2x and * to ** 1x, dc in same sp as first st, ch1, join with dc to first st.
{15 sts on each side; 4 2-ch cnr sps}

R8: Turn, ch3 (stch), *tr in next 15 sts**, (tr, ch2, tr) in 2-ch cnr sp*, rep from * to * 2x and * to ** 1x, tr in same sp as first st, ch1, join with dc to 3rd ch of stch.
{17 sts on each side; 4 2-ch cnr sps}

R9: Turn, dc over ch1, *dc in next 17 sts**, (dc, ch2, dc) in 2-ch cnr sp*, rep from * to * 2x and * to ** 1x, dc in same sp as first st, ch1, join with dc to first st.
{19 sts on each side; 4 2-ch cnr sps}

R10: Turn, dc over ch1, *dc in next 19 sts**, (dc, ch2, dc) in 2-ch cnr sp*, rep from * to * 2x and * to ** 1x, dc in same sp as first st, ch2, join with ss to first st. Fasten off.
{21 sts on each side; 4 2-ch cnr sps}

Millpond Mini

The centre of this square and the larger Millpond Squared on page 57 are from a large circular baby blanket I designed a couple of years ago.

  41 m / 46 yd

Begin with mc.

R1: ch3 (stch), 11tr, join with ss to 3rd ch of stch. {12 sts}

R2: ch3 (stch), tr in same st as ss, 2tr in next 11 sts, join with ss to 3rd ch of stch. {24 sts}

R3: dc in same st as ss, *fptr around next st, 3tr in next st, fptr around next st**, dc in next st*, rep from * to * 4x & * to ** 1x, join with ss to first st. {36 sts}

R4: dc in same st as ss, *fptr around next st, tr in next st, 3tr in next st, tr in next st, fptr around next st**, dc in next st*, rep from * to * 4x & * to ** 1x, join with ss to first st. {48 sts}

R5: dc in same st as ss, *fptr around next st, tr in next 2 sts, 3tr in next st, tr in next 2 sts, fptr around next st**, dc in next st*, rep from * to * 4x & * to ** 1x, join with ss to first st. {60 sts}

R6: ch3 (stch), *fptr around next st, bptr around next 7 sts, fptr around next st**, tr in next st*, rep from * to * 4x & * to ** 1x, join with ss to 3rd ch of stch. {60 sts}

R7: ch3 (stch), tr in next st, *htr in next 2 sts, dc in next 3 sts, htr in next 2 sts**, tr in next 3 sts*, rep from * to * 4x and * to ** 1x, tr in next st, join with ss to 3rd ch of stch. {60 sts}

R8: ch4 (stch), dtr in same st as ss, *tr in next 2 sts, htr in next 3 sts, dc in next 4 sts, htr in next 3 sts, tr in next 2 sts**, 3dtr in next st*, rep from * to * 2x and * to ** 1x, dtr in same st as first sts, join with ss to 4th ch of stch. {14 sts on each side; 4 3-st cnrs}

R9: dc in same st as ss, *dc in blo of next 16 sts**, (dc, ch2, dc) in next st*, rep from * to * 2x and * to ** 1x, dc in same st as first st, ch1, join with dc to first st. {18 sts on each side; 4 2-ch cnr sps}

R10: dc over joining dc, *dc in next 18 sts**, (dc, ch2, dc) in 2-ch cnr sp*, rep from * to * 2x and * to ** 1x, dc in same sp as first st, ch2, join with ss to first st. Fasten off. {20 sts on each side; 4 2-ch cnr sps}

Colours by Kim Siebenhausen

Colours by Miranda Howard

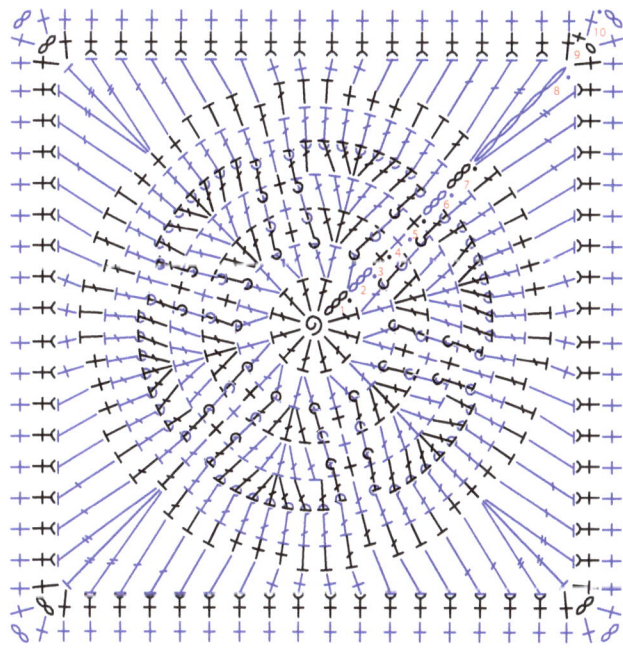

Nosegay

A nosegay is a small, sweet-scented bunch of flowers. This design has aspects of a few different flowers like you'd find in a nosegay.

  42 m / 47 yd

Begin with mc.

R1: ch1, 16dc, join with ss to first st. {16 sts}

R2: ch3 (stch), tr in next 15 sts, join with ss to 3rd ch of stch. {16 sts}

R3: ch3 (stch), tr in same st as ss, *ch2, dc in next st, ch2**, 3tr in next st*, rep from * to * 6x and * to ** 1x, tr in same st as first sts, join with ss to 3rd ch of stch. {32 sts, 16 2-ch sps}

R4: ch3 (stch), tr in same st as ss, *tr in next st, dc in 2-ch sp, skip 1 st, dc in 2-ch sp, tr in next st**, 3tr in next st*, rep from * to * 6x and * to ** 1x, tr in same st as first sts, join with ss to 3rd ch of stch. {56 sts}

R5: ch3 (stch), tr in same st as ss, *2tr in next 2 sts, bpdc around R3 st below, ch2, skip 4 sts, bpdc around next st, ch2, bpdc around R3 st below, skip 4 sts, 2tr in next 2 sts**, 3tr in next st*, rep from * to * 2x and * to ** 1x, tr in same st as first sts, join with ss to 3rd ch of stch. {11 sts, 2 2-ch sps on each side; 4 3-st cnrs}

R6: dc in same st as ss, *spike dc over next st, 2x [dc in next st, spike dc over next st], skip (1 st & 2-ch sp), dc in next st, skip (2-ch sp & 1 st), 2x [spike dc over next st, dc in next st], spike dc over next st**, dc in next st*, rep from * to * 2x and * to ** 1x, join with ss to first st. {11 sts on each side; 4 1-st cnrs}

R7: dc in same st as ss, *ch6, skip 5 sts, 3tr in next st, ch6, skip 5 sts**, (dc, ch2, dc) in next st*, rep from * to * 2x and * to ** 1x, dc in same st as first st, ch1, join with dc to first st. {5 sts, 2 6-ch sps on each side; 4 2-ch cnr sps}

R8: ch3 (stch), tr over joining dc, *tr in next st, 6tr in 6-ch sp, tr in next 3 sts, 6tr in 6-ch sp, tr in next st**, 3tr in 2-ch cnr sp*, rep from * to * 2x and * to ** 1x, tr in same sp as first sts, join with ss to 3rd ch of stch. {17 sts on each side; 4 3-st cnrs}

R9: dc in same st as ss, *dc in next st, fpdtr around R7 st below in front of next R8 st, dc in next 6 sts, fpdtr around next 3 R7 sts below in front of next R8 sts, dc in next 6 sts, fpdtr around R7 st below in front of next R8 st, dc in next st**, (dc, ch2, dc) in next st*, rep from * to * 2x and * to ** 1x, dc in same st as first st, ch1, join with dc to first st. {21 sts on each side; 4 2-ch cnr sps}

R10: dc over joining dc, *dc in next 21 sts**, (dc, ch2, dc) in 2-ch cnr sp*, rep from * to * 2x and * to ** 1x, dc in same sp as first sts, ch2, join with ss to first st. Fasten off. {23 sts on each side; 4 2-ch cnr sps}

Colours by Chelsea Butler

Colours by Yralmy Pereira

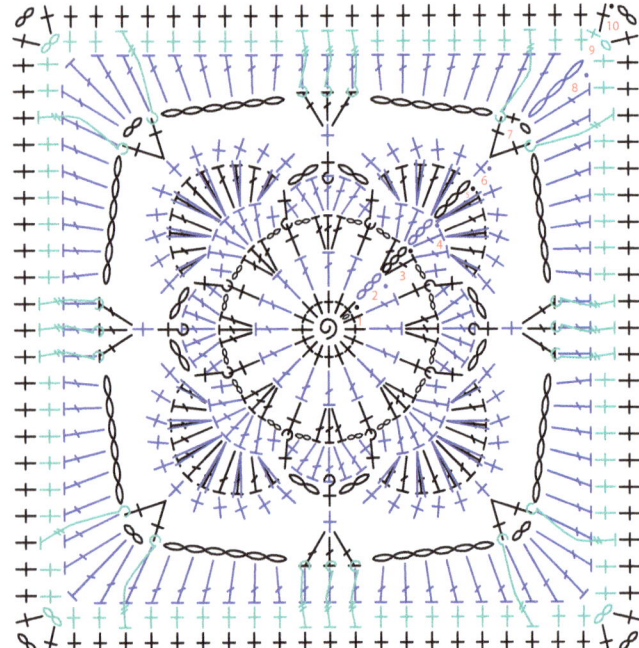

Valance

A valance is a decorative drapery either around a window or the frame of a bed.

  42 m / 47 yd

Begin with mc.

R1: ch3 (stch), 11tr, join with ss to 3rd ch of stch. {12 sts}

R2: ch4 (stch), 2dtrcl in same st as ss, *ch2, dc2tog over next 2 sts, ch2**, (3dtrcl, ch2, 3dtrcl) in next st*, rep from * to * 2x and * to ** 1x, 3dtrcl in same st as first st, ch1, join with dc to top of 2dtrcl.
{3 sts, 2 2-ch sps on each side; 4 2-ch cnr sps}

R3: ch4 (stch), (2dtrcl, ch2, 3dtrcl) over joining dc, *ch2, skip (1 st & 2-ch sp), tr in next st, ch2, skip (2-ch sp & 1 st)**, (2x [3dtrcl, ch2], 3dtrcl) in 2-ch cnr sp*, rep from * to * 2x and * to ** 1x, 3dtrcl in same sp as first sts, ch2, join with ss to top of 2dtrcl.
{3 sts, 4 2-ch sps on each side; 4 1-st cnrs}

R4: ch3 (stch), fptr around same st as ss, *3tr in 2-ch sp, fptr around next st, 2tr in 2-ch sp, tr in next st, 2tr in 2-ch sp, fptr around next st, 3tr in 2-ch sp**, (fptr around, tr in, fptr around) next st*, rep from * to * 2x and * to ** 1x, fptr around same st as ss, join with ss to 3rd ch of stch.
{13 sts on each side; 4 3-st cnrs}

R5: dc in same st as ss, *dc in next 15 sts**, (dc, ch2, dc) in next st*, rep from * to * 2x and * to ** 1x, dc in same st as first st, ch1, join with dc to first st.
{17 sts on each side; 4 2-ch cnr sps}

R6: ch3 (stch), 3tr over joining dc, *2x [skip 2 sts, dc in next st, skip 2 sts, 7tr in next st], skip 2 sts, dc in next st, skip 2 sts**, 7tr in 2-ch cnr sp*, rep from * to * 2x and * to ** 1x, 3tr in same sp as first sts, join with ss to 3rd ch of stch. {17 sts on each side; 4 7-st cnrs}

R7: dc in same st as ss, *dc in lbv of next st, htr in lbv of next st, 2x [tr3tog in lbv of next 3 sts, htr in lbv of next st, dc in lbv of next 3 sts, htr in lbv of next st], tr3tog in lbv of next 3 sts, htr in lbv of next st, dc in lbv of next st**, (dc, ch2, dc) in next st*, rep from * to * 2x and * to ** 1x, dc in same st as first st, ch1, join with dc to first st.
{19 sts on each side; 4 2-ch cnr sps}

R8: dc over joining dc, *dc in next 19 sts**, (dc, ch2, dc) in 2-ch cnr sp*, rep from * to * 2x and * to ** 1x, dc in same sp as first st, ch2, join with ss to first st. Fasten off.
{21 sts on each side; 4 2-ch cnr sps}

Colours by Cheryl Shields

Colours by Kim Siebenhausen

Size 2 Patterns

A little bit bigger, but just as much fun as their smaller buddies. You'll find lots of circles going square in these patterns.

Below are the approximate sizes you will achieve with 3 different yarn weights and hook sizes. The amount of yarn listed on each pattern page is for the middle yarn weight and hook size. The amount of yarn needed for the other yarn weights is on page 177.

hook	3.5 mm hook	4.5 mm hook	5.5 mm hook
yarn	4 ply/sock/fingering	8 ply/DK/light worsted	10 ply/aran/worsted
square	7.5"	9"	10.5"

Aubade
page 26

Caboodle
page 28

Inflorescence
page 30

Persnickety
page 32

The Pretender
page 34

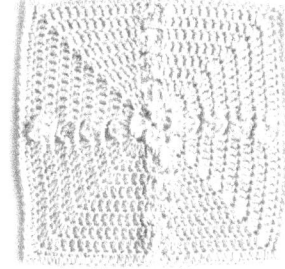

Quarter
page 36

Shine
page 38

Aubade

An aubade is a poem or piece of music about dawn or early morning. The sun-like pattern led me to the name Aubade.

*Colours by
Evangelia V Katsafouros*

*Colours by
Mell Sappho*

  78 m / 86 yd

Begin with mc.

R1: ch1, 12 dc, join with ss to first st. {12 sts}

R2: dc in same st as ss, *ch1, skip 1 st**, dc in next st*, rep from * to * 4x and * to ** 1x, join with ss to first st. {6 sts, 6 1-ch sps}

R3: ch3 (stch), 2tr in same st as ss, *ch2, dc in 1-ch sp, ch2**, 3tr in next st*, rep from * to * 4x and * to ** 1x, join with ss to 3rd ch of stch. {24 sts, 12 2-ch sps}

R4: dc in same st as ss, dc in next 2 sts, *ch3, skip (2-ch sp, 1 st & 2-ch sp)**, dc in next 3 sts*, rep from * to * 4x and * to ** 1x, join with ss to first st. {18 sts, 6 3-ch sps}

R5: dc in same st as ss, dc in next 2 sts, *3dc in 3-ch sp**, dc in next 3 sts*, rep from * to * 4x and * to ** 1x, join with ss to first st. {36 sts}

R6: ch3 (stch), tr2tog over next 2 sts, *ch3**, tr3tog over next 3 sts*, rep from * to * 10x and * to ** 1x, join with ss to top of tr2tog. {12 sts, 12 3-ch sps}

R7: dc in same st as ss, *4dc in 3-ch sp**, dc in next st*, rep from * to * 10x and * to ** 1x, join with ss to first st. {60 sts}

R8: ch3 (stch), tr in next 2 sts, *ch2, dc in next st, ch2**, tr in next 3 sts*, rep from * to * 13x and * to ** 1x, join with ss to 3rd ch of stch. {60 sts, 30 2-ch sps}

R9: dc in same st as ss, dc in next 2 sts, *ch3, skip (2-ch sp, 1 st & 2-ch sp)**, dc in next 3 sts*, rep from * to * 13x and * to ** 1x, join with ss to first st. {45 sts, 15 3-ch sps}

R10: dc in same st as ss, dc in next 2 sts, *3dc in 3-ch sp**, dc in next 3 sts*, rep from * to * 13x and * to ** 1x, join with ss to first st. {90 sts}

R11: 2dc in same st as ss, *dc in next 4 sts**, 2dc in next st*, rep from * to * 16x and * to ** 1x, join with ss to first st. {108 sts}

R12: ch4 (stch), *ch2, 3dtrcl in next st, skip 3 sts, tr in next 2 sts, htr in next 2 sts, dc in next 10 sts, htr in next 2 sts, tr in next 2 sts, skip 3 sts, 3dtrcl in next st, ch2**, (dtr, ch2, dtr) in next st*, rep from * to * 2x and * to ** 1x, dtr in same st as first st, ch1, join with dc to 4th ch of stch. {22 sts, 2 2-ch sps on each side; 4 2-ch cnr sps}

R13: ch3 (stch), *htr in next st, 2dc in 2-ch sp, dc in next 20 sts, 2dc in 2ch sp, htr in next st**, (tr, ch2, tr) in 2-ch cnr sp*, rep from ^ to ^ 2x and ^ to ^^ 1x, tr in same sp as first st, ch1, join with dc to 3rd ch of stch. {28 sts on each side; 4 2-ch cnr sps}

R14: dc over joining dc, *dc in next 28 sts**, (dc, ch2, dc) in 2-ch cnr sp*, rep from * to * 2x and * to ** 1x, dc in same sp as first st, ch1, join with dc to first st. {30 sts on each side; 4 2-ch cnr sps}

R15: ch3 (stch), tr over joining dc, *tr in next 30 sts**, (2tr, ch2, 2tr) in 2-ch cnr sp*, rep from * to * 2x and * to ** 1x, 2tr in same sp as first sts, ch1, join with dc to 3rd ch of stch. {34 sts on each side; 4 2-ch cnr sps}

R16: dc over joining dc, *dc in next 34 sts**, (dc, ch2, dc) in 2-ch cnr sp*, rep from * to * 2x and * to ** 1x, dc in same sp as first st, ch2, join with ss to first st. Fasten off. {36 sts on each side; 4 2-ch cnr sps}

Caboodle

Caboodle means a collection of things in common. This pattern uses common stitches with different techniques and so Caboodle it is.

Colours by Hayley Neubauer

Colours by Jenny Hebbard

  87 m / 96 yd

Begin with mc.

R1: ch3 (stch), 3trcl, *ch2, 3tr, ch2**, 4trcl*, rep from * to * 2x and * to ** 1x, join with ss to top of 3trcl.
{3 sts, 2 2-ch sps on each side; 4 1-st cnrs}

R2: ss to 2-ch sp, ch3 (stch), 3trcl in 2-ch sp, *ch2, skip 1 st, bptr around next st, ch2, skip 1 st, 4trcl in 2-ch sp**, ch2, skip 1 st, 4trcl in 2-ch sp*, rep from * to * 2x and * to ** 1x, ch1, join with dc to top of 3trcl.
{3 sts, 2 ch-sps on each side; 4 2-ch cnr sps}

R3: ch2 (stch), htr over joining dc, *2x [dc in next st, 2dc in 2-ch sp], dc in next st**, (2htr, ch2, 2htr) in 2-ch cnr sp*, rep from * to * 2x and * to ** 1x, 2htr in same sp as first sts, ch1, join with dc to 2nd ch of stch.
{11 sts on each side; 4 2-ch cnr sps}

R4: ch3 (stch), ch1, tr over joining dc, *5x [ch1, skip 1 st, tr in next st], ch1, skip 1 st**, (2x [tr, ch1], tr) in 2-ch cnr sp*, rep from * to * 2x and * to ** 1x, tr in same sp as first sts, ch1, join with ss to 3rd ch of stch.
{7 sts, 8 1-ch sps on each side; 4 1-st cnrs}

R5: dc in same st as ss, *7x [dc in 1-ch sp, dc in next st], dc in 1-ch sp**, (dc, ch2, dc) in next st*, rep from * to * 2x and * to ** 1x, dc in same st as first st, ch1, join with dc to first st. {17 sts on each side; 4 2-ch cnr sps}

R6: ch3 (stch), tr over joining dc, *8x [ch1, skip 1 st, 3trcl in next st], ch1, skip 1 st**, (tr, hdtr, tr) in 2-ch cnr sp*, rep from * to * 2x and * to ** 1x, tr in same sp as first sts, join with ss to 3rd ch of stch. {8 sts, 9 1-ch sps on each side; 4 3-st cnrs}

R7: dc in same st as ss, *9x [dc in next st, dc in 1-ch sp], dc in next st**, (dc, ch2, dc) in next st*, rep from * to * 2x and * to ** 1x, dc in same st as first st, ch1, join with dc to first st. {21 sts on each side; 4 2-ch cnr sps}

R8: ch3 (stch), tr over joining dc, *skip 1 st, 6x [3tr in next st, skip 2 sts], 3tr in next st, skip 1 st**, (tr, hdtr, tr) in 2-ch cnr sp*, rep from * to * 2x and * to ** 1x, tr in same sp as first sts, join with ss to 3rd ch of stch.
{21 sts on each side; 4 3-st cnrs}

R9: dc in same st as ss, *dc in next st, 7x [dc between last and next sts, skip 1 st, dc in next 2 sts], dc between last and next sts, dc in next st**, (dc, ch2, dc) in next st*, rep from * to * 2x and * to ** 1x, dc in same st as first st, ch1, join with dc to first st. {26 sts on each side; 4 2-ch cnr sps}

R10: fpdtr around middle st of 3-st cnr of R8, tr over joining dc, *tr in next 4 sts, 6x [fpdtr around middle st of 3-st group of R8, tr in next 3 sts], fpdtr around middle st of 3-st group of R8, tr in next 4 sts^^, tr in 2-ch cnr sp, fpdtr around middle st of 3-st cnr of R8, tr in same 2-ch cnr sp*, rep from * to * 2x and * to ** 1x, tr in same sp as 2nd st, join with ss to first st. {33 sts on each side; 4 3-st cnrs}

R11: dc in same st as ss, *dc in next 5 sts, 6x [skip 1 st, dc in next 3 sts], skip 1 st, dc in next 5 sts**, (dc, ch2, dc) in next st*, rep from * to * 2x and * to ** 1x, dc in same st as first st, ch1, join with dc to first st. {30 sts on each side; 4 2-ch cnr sps}

R12: ch3 (stch), htr over joining dc, *skip 1 st, htr in next 4 sts, 7x [ch2, tr3tog over next 3 sts], ch2, htr in next 4 sts**, (htr, tr, htr) in 2-ch cnr sp*, rep from * to * 2x and * to ** 1x, htr in same sp as first sts, join with ss to 3rd ch of stch. {15 sts, 8 2-ch sps on each side; 4 3-st cnrs}

R13: dc in same st as ss, *dc in next 5 sts, 7x [2dc in 2-ch sp, dc in next st], 2dc in 2-ch sp, dc in next 5 sts**, (dc, ch2, dc) in next st*, rep from * to * 2x and * to ** 1x, dc in same st as first st, ch2, join with ss to first st. Fasten off. {35 sts on each side; 4-2 ch cnr sps}

Inflorescence

Inflorescence is the complete flower head of a plant, or the process of flowering.

Colours by Cheryl Shields

Colours by Yralmy Pereira

  106 m / 117 yd

Will be very ruffled from Rounds 4 to 6.

Begin with mc.

R1: ch3 (stch), 2tr, *ch1, 3tr*, rep from * to * 4x, join with dc to 3rd ch of stch. {18 sts, 6 1-ch sps}

R2: dc over joining dc, *ch1, skip 1 st, dc in blo of next st, ch1, skip 1 st**, dc in 1-ch sp*, rep from * to * 4x and * to ** 1x, join with ss to first st. {12 sts, 12 1-ch sps}

R3: ch3 (stch), *tr in 1-ch sp**, (tr, ch1, tr) in next st*, rep from * to * 10x and * to ** 1x, tr in same st as first st, join with dc to 3rd ch of stch. {36 sts, 12 1-ch sps}

R4: ch3 (stch), *dc in next 2 sts, dtr in flo of R1 st, dc in next st, (tr, ch1, tr) in 1-ch sp, dc in next st, dtr in same flo of R1, dc in next 2 sts**, (tr, ch1, tr) in 1-ch sp*, rep from * to * 4x and * to ** 1x, tr in same sp as first st, join with dc to 3rd ch of stch. {72 sts, 12 1-ch sps}

R5: ch3 (stch), (2trcl, ch2, 3trcl) over joining dc, *ch1, skip 3 sts, fptr around next st, ch1, skip 2 sts, 5tr in 1-ch sp, ch1, skip 2 sts, fptr around next st, ch1, skip 3 sts**, (2x [3trcl, ch2], 3trcl) in 1-ch sp*, rep from * to * 4x and * to ** 1x, 3trcl in same sp as first sts, ch2, join with ss to top of 2trcl. {60 sts, 24 1-ch sps, 12 2-ch sps}

R6: ch3 (stch), 2trcl in same st as ss, ch2, 3trcl in 2-ch sp, ch2, 3trcl in next st, *ch1, skip 1-ch sp, fpdc around next st, dc in both 1-ch sps either side of next 5 sts at the same time, fpdc around next st, ch1, skip 1-ch sp**, 2x [3trcl in next st, ch2, 3trcl in 2-ch sp, ch2], 3trcl in next st*, rep from * to * 4x and * to ** 1x, 3trcl in next st, ch2, 3trcl in 2-ch sp, ch2, join with ss to top of 2trcl. {48 sts, 24 2-ch sps, 12 1-ch sps}

R7: ch3 (stch), 2trcl in same st as ss, ch2, 3trcl in 2-ch sp, ch2, 3trcl in next st, ch2, 3trcl in 2-ch sp, *ch1, skip (1 st & 1-ch sp), fptr2tog over next 3 sts skipping the middle st, ch1, skip (1-ch sp & 1 st)**, 3x [3trcl in 2-ch sp, ch2, 3trcl in next st, ch2], 3trcl in 2-ch sp*, rep from * to * 4x and * to ** 1x, 3trcl in 2-ch sp, ch2, 3trcl in next st, ch2, 3trcl in 2-ch sp, ch2, join with ss to top of 2trcl. {48 sts, 36 2-ch sps, 12 1-ch sps}

R8: ch1, 3x [2dc in 2-ch sp, dc in next st], *dc3tog over (1-ch sp, next st & 1-ch sp)**, 6x [dc in next st, 2dc in 2-ch sp], dc in next st*, rep from * to * 4x and * to ** 1x, 3x [dc in next st, 2dc in 2-ch sp], join with inv join to first true st. {120 sts}

R9: Attach yarn with stdg bpdc around the middle 3trcl of any 7-cluster petal of R7, *ch2**, bpdc around next 3trcl of R7*, rep from * to * 40x and * to ** 1x, join with ss to first st. {42 sts, 42 2-ch sps}

R10: dc in same st as ss, *dc in 2-ch sp**, dc in next st*, rep from * to * 40x and * to ** 1x, join with ss to first st. {84 sts}

R11: ch3 (stch), tr in next 83 sts, join with ss to 3rd ch of stch. {84 sts}

R12: ch4 (stch), (2dtrcl, ch2, 3dtrcl) in same st as ss, ch2, *skip 3 sts, dc in next 14 sts, ch2, skip 3 sts**, 3x [3dtrcl, ch2] in next st*, rep from * to * 2x and * to ** 1x, 3dtrcl in same st as first sts, ch2, join with ss to top of 2dtrcl. {14 sts, 2 2-ch sps on each side; 4 (3 sts & 2 2-ch sp) cnrs}

R13: ch2 (stch), *2dc in 2-ch sp, 2dc in next st, 2dc in 2-ch sp, dc in next 14 sts, 2dc in 2-ch sp, 2dc in next st, 2dc in 2-ch sp**, (htr, ch2, htr) in next st*, rep from * to * 2x and * to ** 1x, htr in same st as first st, ch1, join with dc to 2nd ch of stch. {28 sts on each side; 4 2-ch cnr sps}

R14: ch3 (stch), *tr in next 28 sts**, (tr, ch2, tr) in 2-ch cnr sp*, rep from * to * 2x and * to ** 1x, tr in same sp as first st, ch1, join with dc to 3rd ch of stch. {30 sts on each side; 4 2-ch cnr sps}

R15: dc over joining dc, *dc in next 30 sts**, (dc, ch2, dc) in 2-ch cnr sp*, rep from * to * 2x and * to ** 1x, dc in same sp as first st, ch2, join with ss to first st. Fasten off. {32 sts on each side; 4 2-ch cnr sps}

Persnickety

When I first designed it, I thought, "Wow that's a very fussy, prissy square". An online thesaurus suggested persnickety as a synonym for fussy.

Colours by
Evangelia V Katsafouros

Colours by
Yralmy Pereira

    105 m / 115 yd

Begin with mc.

R1: ch2 (stch), 23htr, join with ss to top loop of 2nd ch of stch. {24 sts}

R2: ch3 (stch), 3tr in same loop as ss, *skip 2 sts**, 4tr in blo of next st*, rep from * to * 6x and * to ** 1x, join with ss to 3rd ch of stch. {32 sts}

R3: dc in same st as ss, *(htr, tr) in next st, (tr, htr) in next st, dc in next st, dc between last and next sts**, dc in next st*, rep from *to * 6x and * to ** 1x, do not join. {56 sts}

R4: dc in last st of R3, *bptr around next 4 sts of R2, skip 6 sts**, dc in next st*, rep from * to * 6x and * to ** 1x, join with ss to first st. {40 sts}

R5: ch3 (stch), *tr in next 4 sts**, 2tr in next st*, rep from * to * 6x and * to ** 1x, tr in same st as first st, join with ss to 3rd ch of stch. {48 sts}

R6: spike dc over same st as ss into gap between R2 sts below, *dc in next 5 sts**, spike dc over next st into gap between R2 sts below*, rep from * to * 6x and * to ** 1x, join with ss to first st. {48 sts}

R7: ch4 (stch), 2dtrcl in same st as ss, *ch2, 3dtrcl in next st, ch1, tr in next 2 sts, htr in next 2 sts, dc in next st, htr in next 2 sts, tr in next 2 sts, ch1, 3dtrcl in next st, ch2**, 3dtrcl in next st*, rep from * to * 2x and * to ** 1x, join with ss to top of 2dtrcl. {11 sts, 2 2-ch sps, 2 1-ch sps on each side; 4 1-st cnrs}

R8: ch3 (stch), htr in same st as ss, *2dc in 2-ch sp, fpdc around next st, dc in 1-ch sp, dc in next 3 sts, htr in next 3 sts, dc in next 3 sts, dc in 1-ch sp, fpdc around next st, 2dc in 2-ch sp**, (htr, tr, htr) in next st*, rep from * to * 2x and * to ** 1x, htr in same st as first sts, join with ss to 3rd ch of stch. {17 sts on each side; 4 3-st cnrs}

R9: dc in same st as ss, *9x [ch2, skip 1 st, dc in next st], ch2, skip 1 st**, dc in next st*, rep from * to * 2x and * to ** 1x, join with ss to first st. {9 sts, 10 2-ch sps on each side; 4 1-st cnrs}

R10: ch3 (stch), *3trcl into skipped st of R8 in front of 2-ch sp, 9x [ch2, 3trcl in next skipped st of R8 in front of 2-ch sp]**, (tr, ch2, tr) in next st*, rep from * to * 2x and * to ** 1x, tr in same st as first st, ch1, join with dc to 3rd ch of stch. {12 sts, 9 2-ch sps on each side; 4 2-ch cnr sps}

R11: dc over joining dc, *dc in next 2 sts, 9x [spike dc over 2-ch sp into R9 st below, dc in next st], dc in next st**, (dc, ch2, dc) in 2-ch cnr sp*, rep from * to * 2x and * to ** 1x, dc in same sp as first st, ch1, join with dc to first st. {23 sts on each side; 4 2-ch cnr sps}

R12: dc over joining dc, *dc in next 23 sts**, (dc, ch2, dc) in 2-ch cnr sp*, rep from * to * 2x and * to ** 1x, dc in same sp as first st, ch1, join with dc to first st. {25 sts on each side; 4 2-ch cnr sps}

R13: ch3 (stch), tr over joining dc, *ch3, 4x [tr5tog over next 5 sts, ch4], tr5tog over next 5 sts, ch3**, 3tr in 2-ch cnr sp*, rep from * to * 2x and * to ** 1x, tr in same sp as first sts, join with ss to 3rd ch of stch.
{5 sts, 4 4-ch sps, 2 3-ch sps on each side; 4 3-st cnrs}

R14: ch4 (stch), dtr in same st as ss, *hdtr in next st, skip 3-ch sp, 4x [(4tr in, fptr around) next st, skip 4-ch sp], (4tr in, fptr around) next st, skip 3-ch sp, hdtr in next st**, (2dtr, ch2, 2dtr) in next st*, rep from * to * 2x and * to ** 1x, 2dtr in same st as first sts, ch1, join with dc to 4th ch of stch. {31 sts on each side; 4 2-ch cnr sps}

R15: dc over joining dc, *dc in next 3 sts, tight spike dc into 3-ch sp of R13, 4x [bpdc around next 5 sts, tight spike dc into 4-ch sp of R13], bpdc around next 5 sts, tight spike dc into 3-ch sp of R13, dc in next 3 sts**, (dc, ch2, dc) in 2-ch cnr sp*, rep from * to * 2x and * to ** 1x, dc in same sp as first st, ch1, join with dc to first st.
{39 sts on each side; 4 2-ch cnr sps}

R16: dc over joining dc, *dc in next 39 sts**, (dc, ch2, dc) in 2-ch cnr sp*, rep from * to * 2x and * to ** 1x, dc in same sp as first st, ch2, join with ss to first st. Fasten off. {41 sts on each side; 4 2-ch cnr sps}

The Pretender

Designed to demonstrate how to use false stitches instead of starting chains, The Pretender lets you pretend to use real stitches at the start of every round.

Colours by Chelsea Butler

Colours by Jenny Hebbard

  82 m / 90 yd

Begin with mc.

R1: ch4 (stch), 15dtr, join with ss to 4th ch of stch. {16 sts}

R2: ch4 (stch), dtr in same st as ss, 2dtr in next 15 sts, join with ss to 4th ch of stch. {32 sts}

R3: ch4 (stch), *2dtr in next st**, dtr in next st*, rep from * to * 14x and * to ** 1x, join with ss to 4th ch of stch. {48 sts}

R4: ch3 (stch), 2trcl in same st as ss, *ch2, skip 1 st, tr in next st, ch2, skip 1 st**, 3trcl in next st*, rep from * to * 10x and * to ** 1x, join with ss to top of 2trcl. {24 sts, 24 2-ch sps}

R5: ch3 (stch), *3tr in 2-ch sp**, tr in next st*, rep from * to * 22x and * to ** 1x, join with ss to 3rd ch of stch. {96 sts}

R6: ch3 (stch), tr4tog over next 4 sts, *ch3, tr in next st, ch3**, tr5tog over next 5 sts*, rep from * to * 14x and * to ** 1x, join with ss to top of tr4tog. {32 sts, 32 3-ch sps}

R7: dc in same st as ss, *3dc in 3-ch sp**, dc in next st*, rep from * to * 30x and * to ** 1x, join with ss to first st. {128 sts}

R8: ch4 (stch), 4dtrcl in same st as ss, *ch2, 5dtrcl in next st, ch2, skip 3 sts, dc in next 23 sts, ch2, skip 3 sts, 5dtrcl in next st, ch2**, 5dtrcl in next st*, rep from * to * 2x and * to ** 1x, join with ss to top of 4dtrcl. {25 sts, 4 2-ch sps on each side; 4 1-st cnrs}

R9: ch3 (stch), *dc in 2-ch sp, dc in next st, dc in 2-ch sp, dc2tog over next 2 sts, dc in next 19 sts, dc2tog over next 2 sts, dc in 2-ch sp, dc in next st, dc in 2-ch sp**, (tr, ch2, tr) in next st*, rep from * to * 2x and * to ** 1x, tr in same st as first st, ch1, join with dc to 3rd ch of stch. {29 sts on each side; 4 2-ch cnr sps}

R10: ch3 (stch), *tr in next 4 sts, tr2tog over next 2 sts, dc in next 17 sts, tr2tog over next 2 sts, tr in next 4 sts**, (tr, ch2, tr) in 2-ch cnr sp*, rep from * to * 2x and * to ** 1x, tr in same sp as first st, ch1, join with dc to 3rd ch of stch. {29 sts on each side; 4 2-ch cnr sps}

R11: dc over joining dc, *dc in next 29 sts**, (dc, ch2, dc) in 2-ch cnr sp*, rep from * to * 2x and * to ** 1x, dc in same sp as first st, ch2, join with ss to first st. Fasten off. {31 sts on each side; 4 2-ch cnr sps}

Quarter

Named for the four sections you see.

Colours by Chelsea Butler

Colours by Chelsea Butler

  78 m / 86 yd

Quarter can be extended easily by repeating Rounds 9 and 10 as many times as needed, before ending with Rounds 11 and 12.

Begin with mc.

R1: ch1, *dc, 2tr, ch1, 2tr*, rep from * to * 3x, join with ss to first st. {20 sts, 4 1-ch sps}

R2: spike dc over same st as ss, *ch4, skip (2 sts, 1-ch sp & 2 sts)**, spike dc over next st*, rep from * to * 2x and * to ** 1x, join with ss to first st. {4 sts, 4 4-ch sps}

R3: ch3 (stch), 2tr in same st as ss, *(dc, 2dtr, ch1, 2dtr, dc) in 4-ch sp**, 5tr in next st*, rep from * to * 2x and * to ** 1x, 2tr in same st as first sts, join with ss to 3rd ch of stch. {6 sts, 1 1-ch sp on each side; 4 5-st cnrs}

R4: ch3 (stch), tr in same st as ss, *tr in next 3 sts, ch2, skip (2 sts, 1-ch sp & 2 sts), tr in next 3 sts**, 3tr in next st*, rep from * to * 2x and * to ** 1x, tr in same st as first sts, join with ss to 3rd ch of stch.
{6 sts, 1 2-ch sp on each side; 4 3-st cnrs}

R5: ch3 (stch), tr in same st as ss, *tr in next 4 sts, (dc, 2dtr, ch1, 2dtr, dc) in 2-ch sp, tr in next 4 sts**, 3tr in next st*, rep from * to * 2x and * to ** 1x, tr in same st as first sts, join with ss to 3rd ch of stch.
{14 sts, 1 1-ch sp on each side; 4 3-st cnrs}

R6: ch3 (stch), tr in same st as ss, *tr in next 6 sts, ch2, skip (2 sts, 1-ch sp & 2 sts), tr in next 6 sts**, 3tr in next st*, rep from * to * 2x and * to ** 1x, tr in same st as first sts, join with ss to 3rd ch of stch.
{12 sts, 1 2-ch sp on each side; 4 3-st cnrs}

R7: ch3 (stch), tr in same st as ss, *tr in next 7 sts, (dc, 2dtr, ch1, 2dtr, dc) in 2-ch sp, tr in next 7 sts**, 3tr in next st*, rep from * to * 2x and * to ** 1x, tr in same st as first sts, join with ss to 3rd ch of stch.
{20 sts, 1 1-ch sp on each side; 4 3-st cnrs}

R8: ch3 (stch), tr in same st as ss, *tr in next 9 sts, ch2, skip (2 sts, 1-ch sp & 2 sts), tr in next 9 sts**, 3tr in next st*, rep from * to * 2x and * to ** 1x, tr in same st as first sts, join with ss to 3rd ch of stch.
{18 sts, 1 2-ch sp on each side; 4 3-st cnrs}

R9: ch3 (stch), tr in same st as ss, *tr in next 10 sts, (dc, 2dtr, ch1, 2dtr, dc) in 2-ch sp, tr in next 10 sts**, 3tr in next st*, rep from * to * 2x and * to ** 1x, tr in same st as first sts, join with ss to 3rd ch of stch.
{26 sts, 1 1-ch sp on each side; 4 3-st cnrs}

R10: ch3 (stch), tr in same st as ss, *tr in next 12 sts, ch2, skip (2 sts, 1-ch sp & 2 sts), tr in next 12 sts**, 3tr in next st*, rep from * to * 2x and * to ** 1x, tr in same st as first sts, join with ss to 3rd ch of stch. {24 sts, 1 2-ch sp on each side; 4 3-st cnrs}

R11: dc in same st as ss, *dc in next 13 sts, dc in 2-ch sp, dc in next 13 sts**, (dc, ch2, dc) in next st*, rep from * to * 2x and * to ** 1x, dc in same st as first st, ch1, join with dc to first st. {29 sts on each side; 4 2-ch cnr sps}

R12: dc over joining dc, *dc in next 29 sts**, (dc, ch2, dc) in 2-ch cnr sp*, rep from * to * 2x and * to ** 1x, dc in same sp as first st, ch2, join with ss to first st. Fasten off. {31 sts on each side; 4 2-ch cnr sps}

Shine

Shine like the sun. This pattern begins the same as the Hope pattern on page 114.

Colours by Hayley Neubauer

Colours by Jenny Hebbard

  77 m / 85 yd

Begin with mc.

R1: ch2 (stch), 15htr, join with ss to 2nd ch of stch. {16 sts}.

R2: ch4 (stch), dtr in same st as ss, 2dtr in next 15 sts, join with ss to 4th ch of stch. {32 sts}

R3: dc in same st as ss, *ch2, skip 1 st**, dc in next st*, rep from * to * 14x and * to ** 1x, join with ss to first st. {16 sts, 16 2-ch sps}

R4: ch3 (stch), tr in same st as ss, *skip 2-ch sp**, 3tr in next st*, rep from * to * 14x and * to ** 1x, tr in same st as first sts, join with ss to 3rd ch of stch. {48 sts}

R5: dc in same st as ss, *ch3, dc in skipped st of R2 in front of R3 and R4 sts, ch3**, dc in middle st of next 3-st group*, rep from * to * 14x and * to ** 1x, join with ss to first st. {32 sts, 32 3-ch sps}

R6: ch1, bpdc around same st as ss, *dc in next 2 sts of R4**, bpdc around next st*, rep from * to * 14x and * to ** 1x, join with ss to first st. {48 sts}

R7: ch4 (stch), dtr in same st as ss, *tr in next 2 sts, htr in next st, dc in next 5 sts, htr in next st, tr in next 2 sts**, 3dtr in next st*, rep from * to * 2x and * to ** 1x, dtr in same st as first sts, join with ss to 4th ch of stch. {11 sts on each side; 4 3-st cnrs}

R8: dc in same st as ss, *ch2, skip 1 st**, dc in next st*, rep from * to * 26x and * to ** 1x, join with ss to first st. {28 sts, 28 2-ch sps}

R9: ch3 (stch), tr in same st as ss, *skip 2-ch sp**, 3tr in next st*, rep from * to * 26x and * to ** 1x, tr in same st as first sts, join with ss to 3rd ch of stch. {84 sts}

R10: dc in same st as ss, *ch3, dc in skipped st of R7 in front of R8 and R9 sts, ch3**, dc in middle st of next 3-st group*, rep from * to * 26x and * to ** 1x, join with ss to first st. {56 sts, 56 3-ch sps}

R11: ch1, bpdc around same st as ss, *dc in next 2 sts of R9**, bpdc around next st*, rep from * to * 26x and * to ** 1x, join with ss to first st. {84 sts}

R12: ch4 (stch), 2hdtr in same st as ss, *tr in next 20 sts**, (2hdtr, dtr, 2hdtr) in next st*, rep from * to * 2x and * to ** 1x, 2hdtr in same st as first sts, join with ss to 4th ch of stch. {20 sts on each side; 4 5-st cnrs}

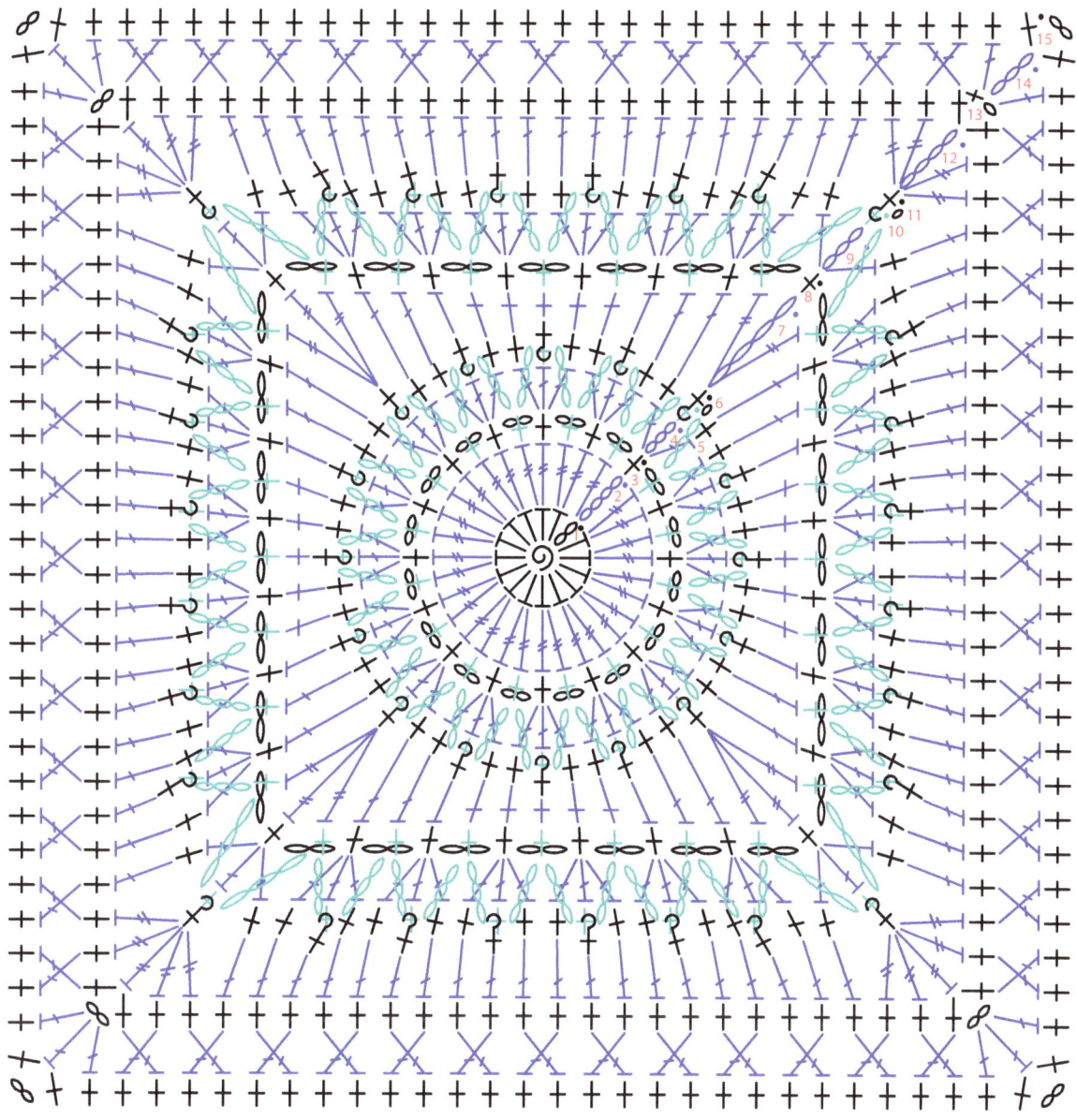

R13: dc in same st as ss, *dc in next 24 sts**, (dc, ch2, dc) in next st*, rep from * to * 2x and * to ** 1x, dc in same st as first st, ch1, join with dc to first st. {26 sts on each side; 4 2-ch cnr sps}

R14: ch3 (stch), tr over joining dc, *13x [skip 1 st, tr in next st, tr in skipped st]**, 3tr in 2-ch cnr sp*, rep from * to * 2x and * to ** 1x, tr in same sp as first sts, join with ss to 3rd ch of stch. {26 sts on each side; 4 3-st cnrs}

R15: dc in same st as ss, *dc in next 28 sts**, (dc, ch2, dc) in next st*, rep from * to * 2x and * to ** 1x, dc in same st as first st, ch2, join with ss to first st. Fasten off. {30 sts on each side; 4 2-ch cnr sps}

Shine - Size 2 Patterns • 39

Size 3 Patterns

The Size 3 (and above) patterns allow for a bit more fun with the designing as there is more room to play with how stitches work together.

Below are the approximate sizes you will achieve with 3 different yarn weights and hook sizes. The amount of yarn listed on each pattern page is for the middle yarn weight and hook size. The amount of yarn needed for the other yarn weights is on page 177.

🪝	3.5 mm hook	4.5 mm hook	5.5 mm hook
🧶	4 ply/sock/fingering	8 ply/DK/light worsted	10 ply/aran/worsted
⬛	10"	12"	14"

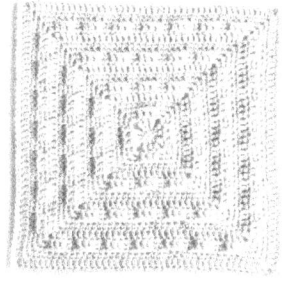

Bushel
page 42

Dendrite
page 45

Diadem
page 47

Flare
page 50

Flourish
page 52

Meander
page 54

Millpond Squared
page 57

Vault
page 60

Size 3 Patterns • 41

Bushel

A bushel is a unit of measurement historically used to measure grain. To me, the raised sections look a little like little bundles of grain.

Colours by Miranda Howard

Colours by Evangelia V Katsafouros

  164 m / 179 yd

Bushel can be extended easily by repeating Rounds 17 to 21 as many times as needed before ending with Round 22.

Your Bushel square may develop a swirl, depending on your crochet style. The swirl can be blocked out or you can turn the square for Rounds 5, 10, 15 and 20.

Begin with mc.

R1: ch4 (stch), 2dtr, *ch2, 3dtr*, rep from * to * 2x, ch1, join with dc to 4th ch of stch. {3 sts on each side; 4 2-ch cnr sps}

R2: dc over joining dc, *bptr around next 3 sts**, (dc, ch2, dc) in 2-ch cnr sp*, rep from * to * 2x and * to ** 1x, dc in same sp as first st, ch1, join with dc to first st. {5 sts on each side; 4 2-ch cnr sps}

R3: dc over joining dc, *dc in next st, tr in next 3 sts of R1 in front of R2 sts, dc in next st**, (dc, ch2, dc) in 2-ch cnr sp*, rep from * to * 2x and * to ** 1x, dc in same sp as first st, ch1, join with dc to first st. {7 sts on each side; 4 2-ch cnr sps}

R4: dc over joining dc, *dc in next 2 sts, tr in next 3 sts of R2 behind R3 sts, dc in next 2 sts**, (dc, ch2, dc) in 2-ch cnr sp*, rep from * to * 2x and * to ** 1x, dc in same sp as first st, ch1, join with dc to first st. {9 sts on each side; 4 2-ch cnr sps}

R5: dc over joining dc, *dc in next 9 sts**, (dc, ch2, dc) in 2-ch cnr sp*, rep from * to * 2x and * to ** 1x, dc in same sp as first st, ch1, join with dc to first st. {11 sts on each side; 4 2-ch cnr sps}

R6: ch3 (stch), *tr in next 11 sts**, (tr, ch2, tr) in 2-ch cnr sp*, rep from * to * 2x and * to ** 1x, tr in same sp as first st, ch1, join with dc to 3rd ch of stch. {13 sts on each side; 4 2-ch cnr sps}

R7: dc over joining dc, *2x [bptr around next 3 sts, dc in next 2 sts], bptr around next 3 sts**, (dc, ch2, dc) in 2-ch cnr sp*, rep from * to * 2x and * to ** 1x, dc in same sp as first st, ch1, join with dc to first st. {15 sts on each side; 4 2-ch cnr sps}

R8: dc over joining dc, *dc in next st, 2x [tr in next 3 sts of R6 in front of R7 sts, dc in next 2 sts], tr in next 3 sts of R6 in front of R7 sts, dc in next st**, (dc, ch2, dc) in 2-ch cnr sp*, rep from * to * 2x and * to ** 1x, dc in same sp as first st, ch1, join with dc to first st. {17 sts on each side; 4 2-ch cnr sps}

R9: dc over joining dc, *dc in next 2 sts, 3x [tr in next 3 sts of R7 behind R8 sts, dc in next 2 sts]**, (dc, ch2, dc) in 2-ch cnr sp*, rep from * to * 2x and * to ** 1x, dc in same sp as first st, ch1, join with dc to first st. {19 sts on each side; 4 2-ch cnr sps}

R10: dc over joining dc, *dc in next 19 sts**, (dc, ch2, dc) in 2-ch cnr sp*, rep from * to * 2x and * to ** 1x, dc in same sp as first st, ch1, join with dc to first st. {21 sts on each side; 4 2-ch cnr sps}

Bushel chart
Rounds 1-15

R11: ch3 (stch), *tr in next 21 sts**, (tr, ch2, tr) in 2-ch cnr sp*, rep from * to * 2x and * to ** 1x, tr in same sp as first st, ch1, join with dc to 3rd ch of stch. {23 sts on each side; 4 2-ch cnr sps}

R12: dc over joining dc, *4x [bptr around next 3 sts, dc in next 2 sts], bptr around next 3 sts**, (dc, ch2, dc) in 2-ch cnr sp*, rep from * to * 2x and * to ** 1x, dc in same sp as first st, ch1, join with dc to first st. {25 sts on each side; 4 2-ch cnr sps}

R13: dc over joining dc, *dc in next st, 4x [tr in next 3 sts of R11 in front of R12 sts, dc in next 2 sts], tr in next 3 sts of R11 in front of R12 sts, dc in next st**, (dc, ch2, dc) in 2-ch cnr sp*, rep from * to * 2x and * to ** 1x, dc in same sp as first st, ch1, join with dc to first st. {27 sts on each side; 4 2-ch cnr sps}

R14: dc over joining dc, *dc in next 2 sts, 5x [tr in next 3 sts of R12 behind R13 sts, dc in next 2 sts]**, (dc, ch2, dc) in 2-ch cnr sp*, rep from * to * 2x and * to ** 1x, dc in same sp as first st, ch1, join with dc to first st. {29 sts on each side; 4 2-ch cnr sps}

R15: dc over joining dc, *dc in next 29 sts**, (dc, ch2, dc) in 2-ch cnr sp*, rep from * to * 2x and * to ** 1x, dc in same sp as first st, ch1, join with dc to first st. {31 sts on each side; 4 2-ch cnr sps}

Bushel chart
Rounds 15-22

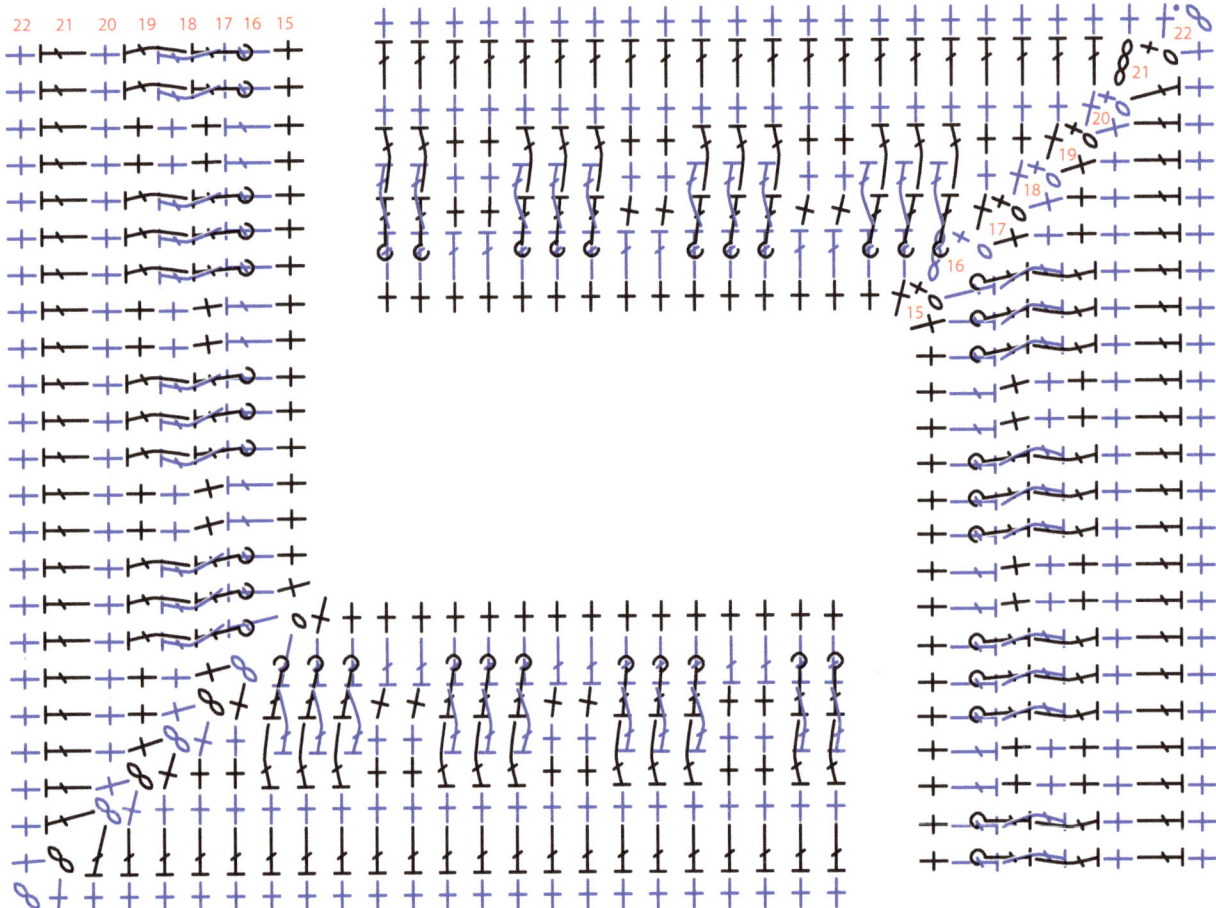

R16: ch3 (stch), *tr in next 31 sts**, (tr, ch2, tr) in 2-ch cnr sp*, rep from * to * 2x and * to ** 1x, tr in same sp as first st, ch1, join with dc to 3rd ch of stch. {33 sts on each side; 4 2-ch cnr sps}

R17: dc over joining dc, *6x [bptr around next 3 sts, dc in next 2 sts], bptr around next 3 sts**, (dc, ch2, dc) in 2-ch cnr sp*, rep from * to * 2x and * to ** 1x, dc in same sp as first st, ch1, join with dc to first st. {35 sts on each side; 4 2-ch cnr sps}

R18: dc over joining dc, *dc in next st, 6x [tr in next 3 sts of R16 in front of R17 sts, dc in next 2 sts], tr in next 3 sts of R16 in front of R17 sts, dc in next st**, (dc, ch2, dc) in 2-ch cnr sp*, rep from * to * 2x and * to ** 1x, dc in same sp as first st, ch1, join with dc to first st. {37 sts on each side; 4 2-ch cnr sps}

R19: dc over joining dc, *dc in next 2 sts, 7x [tr in next 3 sts of R17 behind R18 sts, dc in next 2 sts]**, (dc, ch2, dc) in 2-ch cnr sp*, rep from * to * 2x and * to ** 1x, dc in same sp as first st, ch1, join with dc to first st. {39 sts on each side; 4 2-ch cnr sps}

R20: dc over joining dc, *dc in next 39 sts**, (dc, ch2, dc) in 2-ch cnr sp*, rep from * to * 2x and * to ** 1x, dc in same sp as first st, ch1, join with dc to first st. {41 sts on each side; 4 2-ch cnr sps}

R21: ch3 (stch), *tr in next 41 sts**, (tr, ch2, tr) in 2-ch cnr sp*, rep from * to * 2x and * to ** 1x, tr in same sp as first st, ch1, join with dc to 3rd ch of stch. {43 sts on each side; 4 2-ch cnr sps}

R22: dc over joining dc, *dc in next 43 sts**, (dc, ch2, dc) in 2-ch cnr sp*, rep from * to * 2x and * to ** 1x, dc in same sp as first st, ch2, join with ss to first st. Fasten off. {45 sts on each side; 4 2-ch cnr sps}

Dendrite

Dendrite describes crystalline structures or the nerve branchings impulses travel along. I felt the design was a little crystal-like.

Colours by Evangelia V Katsafouros

Colours by Kim Siebenhausen

  151 m / 166 yd

Begin with mc.

R1: ch3 (stch), 2tr, *ch2, 3tr* rep from * to * 4x, ch1, join with dc to 3rd ch of stch. {18 sts, 6 2-ch sps}

R2: ch3 (stch), 2tr over joining dc, *ch2, fptr3tog over next 3 sts**, ch2, 3tr in 2-ch sp*, rep from * to * 4x and * to ** 1x, ch1, join with dc to 3rd ch of stch. {24 sts, 12 2-ch sps}

R3: ch3 (stch), *ch2, fptr3tog over next 3 sts, ch2, tr in 2-ch sp, ch2, skip 1 st**, tr in 2-ch sp*, rep from * to * 4x and * to ** 1x, join with ss to 3rd ch of stch. {18 sts, 18 2-ch sps}

R4: ch3 (stch), *2tr in 2-ch sp, fptr around next st, 2tr in 2-ch sp, tr in next st, tr in 2-ch sp, fpdtr around R2 st below, tr in same 2-ch sp**, tr in next st*, rep from * to * 4x and * to ** 1x, join with ss to 3rd ch of stch. {60 sts}

R5: dc in same st as ss, dc in next 59 sts, join with ss to first st. {60 sts}

R6: ch3 (stch), 2tr in same st as ss, *ch1, skip 2 sts, 3tr in next st*, rep from * to * 18x, skip 2 sts, join with dc to 3rd ch of stch. {60 sts, 20 1-ch sps}

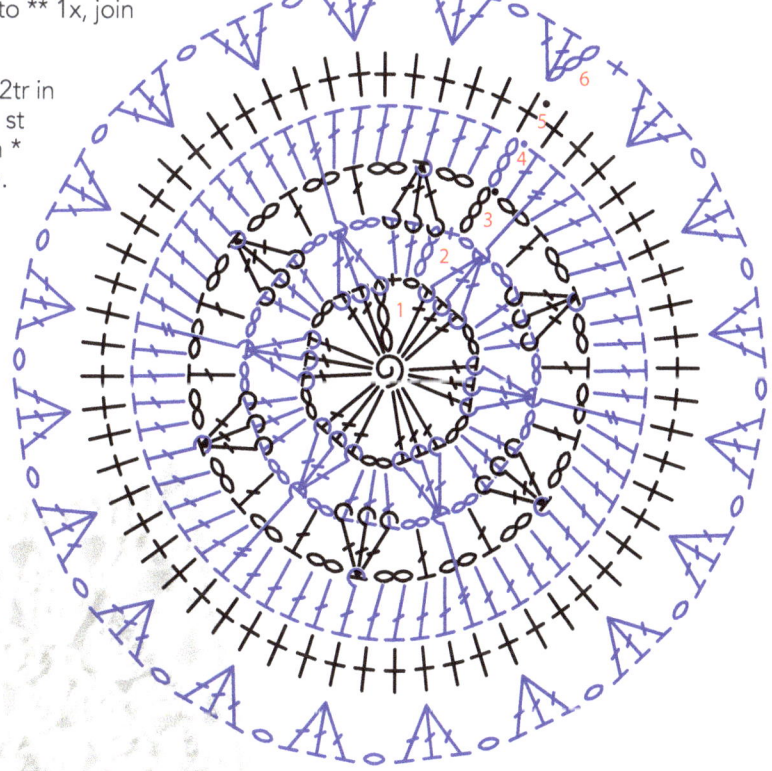

Dendrite - Size 3 Patterns • 45

Dendrite chart
Rounds 6-15

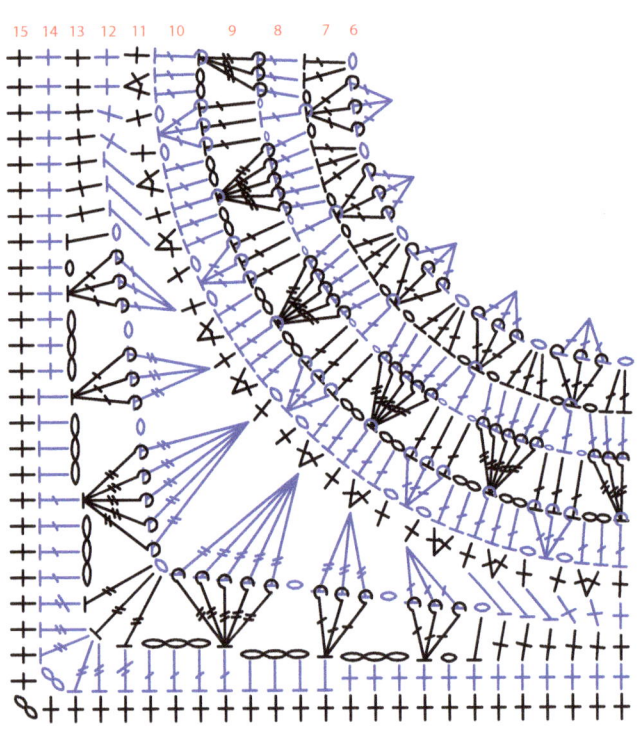
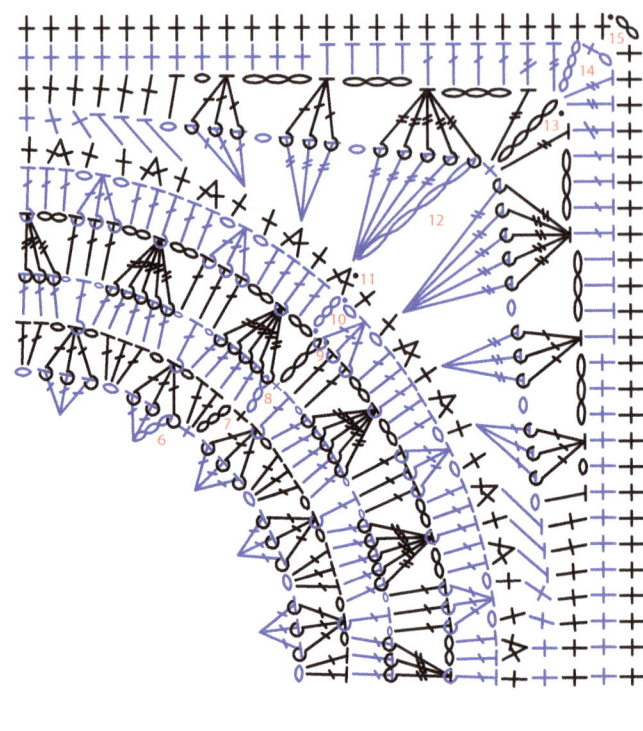

R7: ch3 (stch), 2tr over joining dc, *ch1, fptr3tog over next 3 sts**, ch1, 3tr in 1-ch sp*, rep from * to * 18x and * to ** 1x, join with dc to 3rd ch of stch. {80 sts, 40 1-ch sps}

R8: ch3 (stch), *tr in next 3 sts, tr in 1-ch sp, ch1, fptr around next st**, ch1, tr in 1-ch sp*, rep from * to * 18x and * to ** 1x, join with dc to 3rd ch of stch. {120 sts, 40 1-ch sps}

R9: ch3 (stch), *ch2, fpdtr5tog over next 5 sts, ch2, tr in 1-ch sp, tr in next st**, tr in 1-ch sp*, rep from * to * 18x and * to ** 1x, join with ss to 3rd ch of stch. {80 sts, 40 2-ch sps}

Will be ruffled.

R10: ss in 2-ch sp, ch3 (stch), tr in same 2-ch sp, *fptr around next st, 2tr in 2-ch sp, ch1, fptr3tog over next 3 sts, ch1**, 2tr in 2-ch sp*, rep from * to * 18x and * to ** 1x, join with ss to 3rd ch of stch. {120 sts, 40 1-ch sps}

R11: dc2tog over same st as ss and next st, *dc in next st, dc2tog over next 2 sts, dc in 1-ch sp, skip 1 st, dc in 1-ch sp**, dc2tog over next 2 sts*, rep from * to * 18x and * to ** 1x, join with ss to first st. {100 sts}

R12: ch4 (stch), 4dtr in same st as ss, *ch1, skip 1 st, 3dtr in next st, ch1, skip 1 st, 3tr in next st, ch1, skip 1 st, htr in next 3 sts, dc in next 6 sts, htr in next 3 sts, ch1, skip 1 st, 3tr in next st, ch1, skip 1 st, 3dtr in next st, ch1, skip 1 st, 5dtr in next st**, ch1, skip 1 st, 5dtr in next st*, rep from * to * 2x and * to ** 1x, skip 1 st, join with dc to 4th ch of stch. {34 sts, 6 1-ch sps on each side; 4 1-ch cnr sps}

R13: ch4 (stch), dtr over joining dc, *ch3, fpdtr5tog over next 5 sts, 2x [ch3, skip 1-ch sp, fptr3tog over next 3 sts], ch1, htr in 1-ch sp, dc in next 12 sts, htr in 1-ch sp, ch1, 2x [fptr3tog over next 3 sts, ch3, skip 1-ch sp], fpdtr5tog over next 5 sts, ch3**, 3dtr in 1-ch cnr sp*, rep from * to * 2x and * to ** 1x, dtr in same sp as first sts, join with ss to 4th ch of stch. {20 sts, 6 3-ch sps, 2 1-ch sps on each side; 4 3-st cnrs}

R14: ch4 (stch), dtr in same st as ss, *hdtr in next st, 3tr in 3-ch sp, tr in next st, 3htr in 3-ch sp, htr in next st, 3dc in 3-ch sp, dc in next st, dc in 1-ch sp, dc in next 14 sts, dc in 1-ch sp, dc in next st, 3dc in 3-ch sp, htr in next st, 3htr in 3-ch sp, tr in next st, 3tr in 3-ch sp, hdtr in next st**, (2dtr, ch2, 2dtr) in next st*, rep from * to * 2x and * to ** 1x, 2dtr in same st as first sts, ch1, join with dc to 4th ch of stch. {46 sts on each side; 4 2-ch cnr sps}

R15: dc over joining dc, *dc in next 46 sts**, (dc, ch2, dc) in 2-ch cnr sp*, rep from * to * 2x and * to ** 1x, dc in same sp as first st, ch2, join with ss to first st. Fasten off. {48 sts on each side; 4 2-ch cnr sps}

Diadem

The crown-like shape of the centre of this square led me to the name Diadem.

Colours by Chelsea Butler

Colours by Evangelia V Katsafouros

  153 m / 168 yd

Begin with mc with a long tail.

R1: ch3 (stch), 2tr, *ch2, 3tr*, rep from * to * 6x, ch1, join with dc to 3rd ch of stch.
Pull mc closed to about 1 cm.
{24 sts, 8 2-ch sps}

R2: dc over joining dc, *dc in next 3 sts**, (dc, ch2, dc) in 2-ch sp*, rep from * to * 6x and * to ** 1x, dc in same sp as first st, ch1, join with dc to first st. {40 sts, 8 2-ch sps}

R3: dc over joining dc, *ch5, skip 5 sts**, dc in 2-ch sp*, rep from * to * 6x and * to ** 1x, join with ss to first st.
{8 sts, 8 5-ch sps}

R4: ch3 (stch), *tr in each of next 5 chs**, tr in next st*, rep from * to * 6x and * to ** 1x, join with ss to 3rd ch of stch.
{48 sts}

R5: dc in same st as ss, dc in next 47 sts, join with ss to first st. {48 sts}

R6: ch3 (stch), 6tr in same st as ss, *ch2, skip 5 sts, 7tr in next st*, rep from * to * 6x, ch1, join with dc to 3rd ch of stch.
{56 sts, 8 2-ch sps}

R7: (begpc, ch2, pc) over joining dc, *ch2, skip 3 sts, dc in next st, ch2, skip 3 sts**, (2x [pc, ch2], pc) in 2-ch sp*, rep from * to * 6x and * to ** 1x, pc in same sp as first sts, ch2, join with ss to top of begpc. {32 sts, 32 2-ch sps}

R8: ch3 (stch), *2tr in 2-ch sp, tr in top of pc, skip 2-ch sp, fpdtr5tog over the middle 5 sts of 7-st group of R6, skip (1 st & 2-ch sp), tr in top of pc, 2tr in 2-ch sp**, (tr, ch2, tr) in top of pc*, rep from * to * 6x and * to ** 1x, tr in top of same pc as first st, ch1, join with dc to 3rd ch of stch. {72 sts, 8 2-ch sps}

Diadem chart
Rounds 8–19

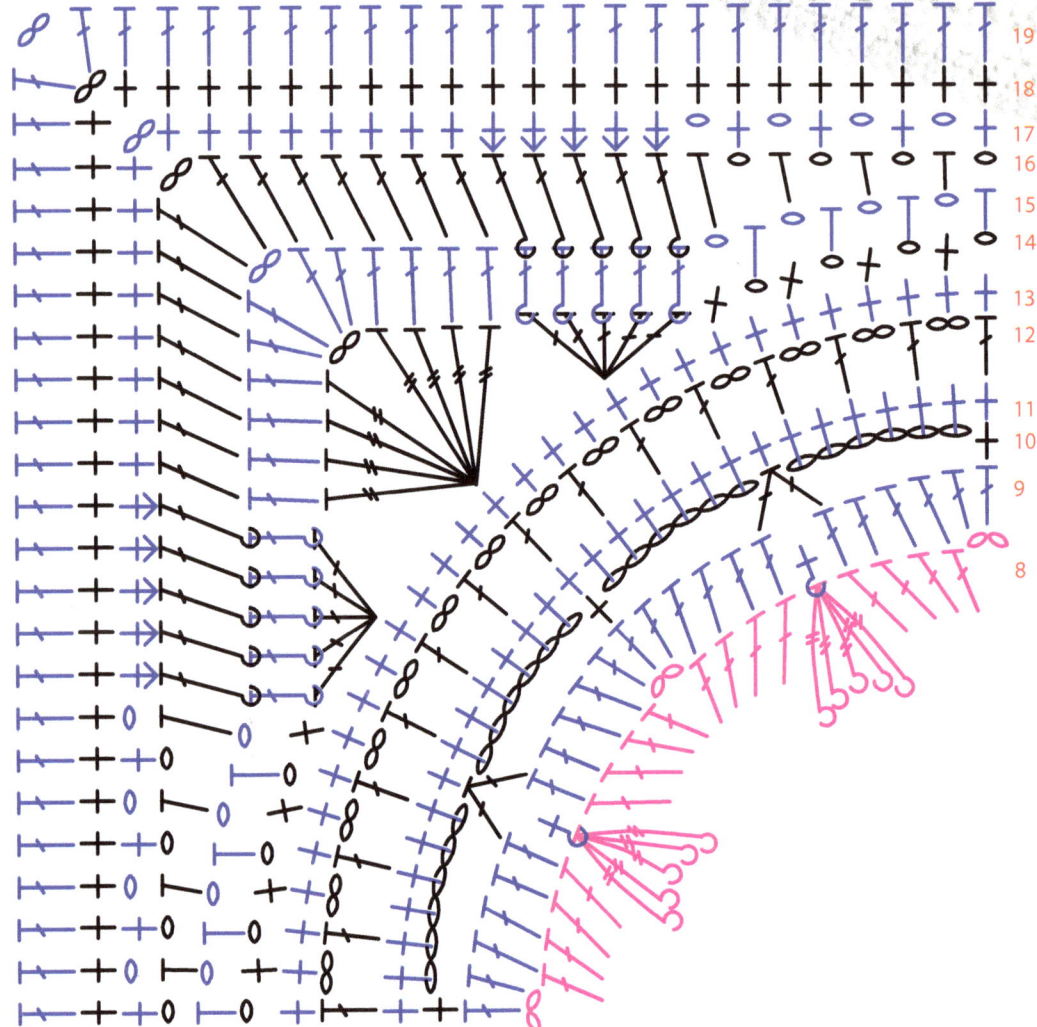

R9: ch3 (stch), tr over joining dc, *tr in next 4 sts, bpdc around next st, tr in next 4 sts**, 3tr in 2-ch sp*, rep from * to * 6x and * to ** 1x, tr in same sp as first sts, join with ss to 3rd ch of stch. {96 sts}

R10: dc in same st as ss, *ch6, skip 4 sts, tr2tog over next 3 sts skipping the middle st, ch6, skip 4 sts**, dc in next st*, rep from * to * 6x and * to ** 1x, join with ss to first st. {16 sts, 16 6-ch sps}

R11: dc in same st as ss, *dc in each of next 6 chs**, dc in next st*, rep from * to * 14x and * to ** 1x, join with ss to first st. {112 sts}

R12: ch3 (stch), *ch2, skip 1 st**, tr in next st*, rep from * to * 54x and * to ** 1x, join with ss to 3rd ch of stch. {56 sts, 56 2-ch sps}

R13: dc in same st as ss, *dc in 2-ch sp**, dc in next st*, rep from * to * 54x and * to ** 1x, join with ss to first st. {112 sts}

R14: ch4 (stch), 3dtr in same st as ss, *skip 3 sts, 5tr in next st, skip 2 sts, 7x [dc in next st, ch1, skip 1 st], dc in next st, skip 2 sts, 5tr in next st, skip 3 sts**, (4dtr, ch2, 4dtr) in next st*, rep from * to * 2x and * to ** 1x, 4dtr in same st as first sts, ch1, join with dc to 4th ch of stch. {26 sts, 7 1-ch sps on each side; 4 2-ch cnr sps}

48 • Size 3 Patterns - Diadem

Diadem chart
Beginning of Rounds 8-19

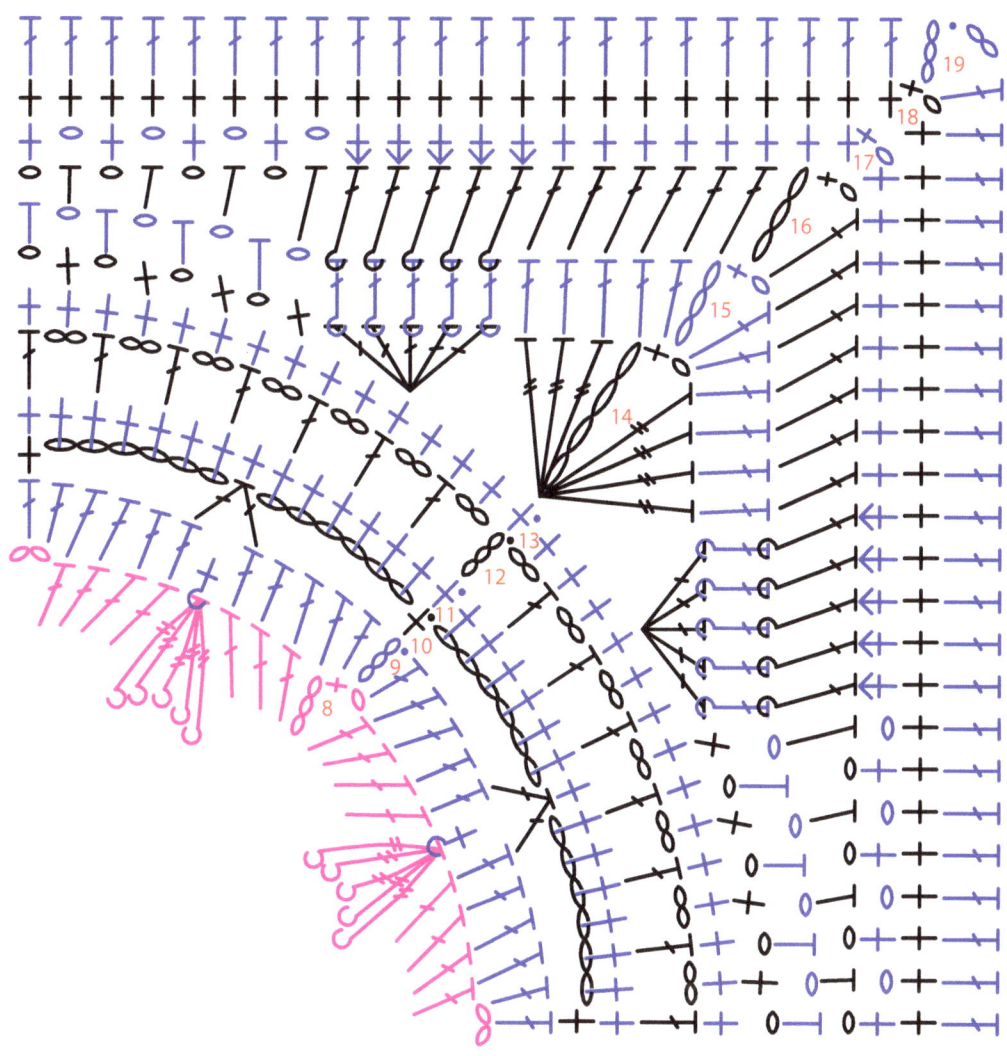

R15: ch3 (stch), tr over joining dc, *tr in next 4 sts, bptr around next 5 sts, 7x [ch1, skip 1 st, htr in 1-ch sp], ch1, skip 1 st, bptr around next 5 sts, tr in next 4 sts**, (2tr, ch2, 2tr) in 2-ch cnr sp*, rep from * to * 2x and * to ** 1x, 2tr in same sp as first sts, ch1, join with dc to 3rd ch of stch. {29 sts, 8 1-ch sps on each side; 4 2-ch cnr sps}

R16: ch3 (stch), *tr in next 6 sts, bptr around next 5 sts, 7x [htr in 1-ch sp, ch1, skip 1 st], htr in 1-ch sp, bptr around next 5 sts, tr in next 6 sts**, (tr, ch2, tr) in 2-ch cnr sp*, rep from * to * 2x and * to ** 1x, tr in same sp as first st, ch1, join with dc to 3rd ch of stch. {32 sts, 7 1-ch sps on each side; 4 2-ch cnr sps}

R17: dc over joining dc, *dc in next 7 sts, dc in lbv of next 5 sts, 7x [ch1, skip 1 st, dc in 1-ch sp], ch1, skip 1 st, dc in lbv of next 5 sts, dc in next 7 sts**, (dc, ch2, dc) in 2-ch cnr sp*, rep from * to * 2x and * to ** 1x, dc in same sp as first st, ch1, join with dc to first st. {33 sts, 8 1-ch sps on each side; 4 2-ch cnr sps}

R18: dc over joining dc, *dc in next 13 sts, 7x [dc in 1-ch sp, dc in next st], dc in 1-ch sp, dc in next 13 sts**, (dc, ch2, dc) in 2-ch cnr sp*, rep from * to * 2x and * to ** 1x, dc in same sp as first st, ch1, join with dc to first st. {43 sts on each side; 4 2-ch cnr sps}

R19: ch3 (stch), *tr in next 43 sts**, (tr,ch2, tr) in 2-ch cnr sp*, rep from * to * 2x and * to ** 1x, tr in same sp as first st, ch2, join with ss to 3rd ch of stch. Fasten off. {45 sts on each side; 4 2-ch cnr sps}

Flare

Another sun-like shape sent me in search of appropriate names. I settled on Flare – a sudden brief burst of light.

Colours by Shelley

Colours by Chelsea Butler

  153 m / 168 yd

Begin with mc.

R1: ch4 (stch), 15dtr, join with ss to 4th ch of stch. {16 sts}

R2: ch3 (stch), tr in same st as ss, 2tr in next 15 sts, join with ss to 3rd ch of stch. {32 sts}

R3: dc in same st as ss, *2dc in next st**, dc in next st*, rep from * to * 14x and * to ** 1x, join with ss to first st. {48 sts}

R4: ch3 (stch), tr in last st of R3, *skip 1 st, tr in next st, tr in skipped st*, rep from * to * 22x, join with ss to 3rd ch of stch. {48 sts}

R5: dc in same st as ss, *dc between last and next sts**, dc in next 2 sts*, rep from * to * 22x and * to ** 1x, dc in next st, join with ss to first st. {72 sts}

R6: ch3 (stch), tr2tog over next 2 sts, *ch3**, tr3tog over next 3 sts*, rep from * to * 22x and * to ** 1x, join with ss to top of tr2tog. {24 sts, 24 3-ch sps}

R7: fpdc around stch and tr2tog at the same time, *3dc in 3-ch sp**, fpdc around next st*, rep from * to * 22x and * to ** 1x, join with ss to first st. {96 sts}

R8: *fpdtr around R6 st below, ch1, tr in next 3 sts, ch1*, rep from * to * 23x, join with ss to first st. {96 sts, 48 1-ch sps}

R9: ch3 (stch), tr in same st as ss, *ch1, skip 1-ch sp, tr3tog over next 3 sts, ch1, skip 1-ch sp**, 3tr in next st*, rep from * to * 22x and * to ** 1x, tr in same st as first sts, join with ss to 3rd ch of stch. {96 sts, 48 1-ch sps}

R10: dc in same st as ss, dc in next st, *dc in 1-ch sp, skip 1 st, dc in 1-ch sp**, dc in next 3 sts*, rep from * to * 22x and * to ** 1x, dc in next st, join with ss to first st. {120 sts}

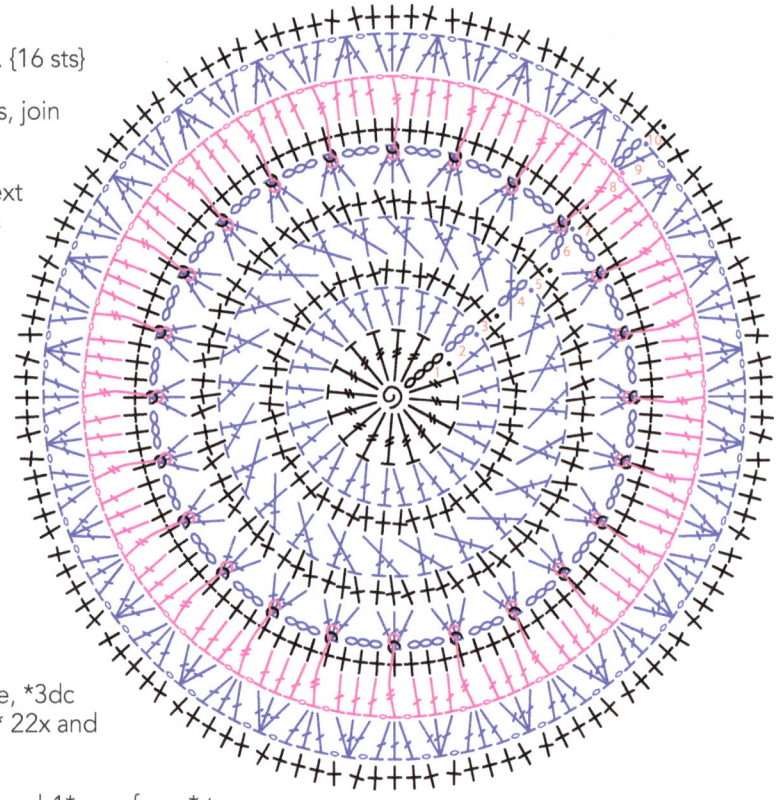

*Flare chart
Rounds 10-19*

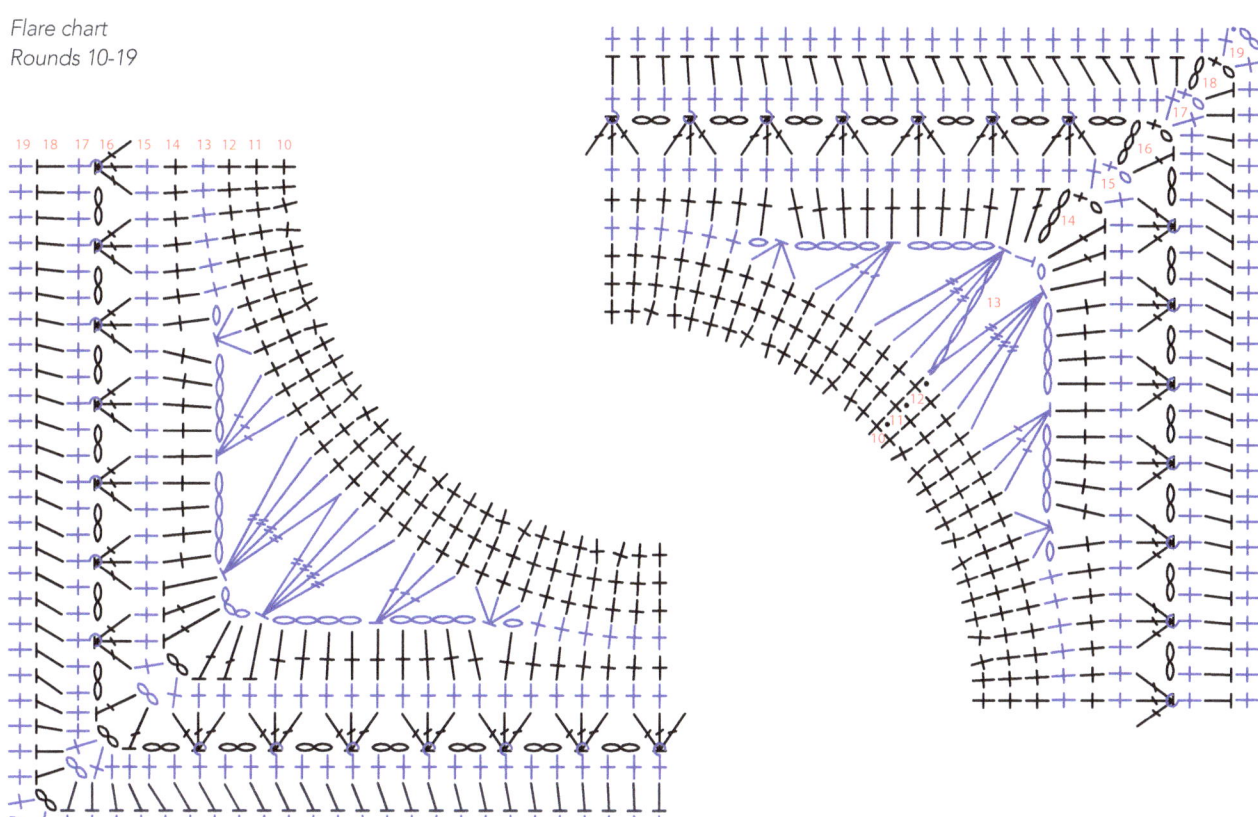

R11: dc in same st as ss, dc in next 119 sts, join with ss to first st. {120 sts}

R12: dc in same st as ss, dc in next 119 sts, join with ss to first st. {120 sts}

R13: *The last leg and first leg of the 2 dtr4togs are worked in the same st.* ch4 (stch), dtr3tog over next 3 sts, *ch4, tr3tog over next 3 sts, ch4, htr3tog over next 3 sts, ch1, dc in next 11 sts, ch1, htr3tog over next 3 sts, ch4, tr3tog over next 3 sts, ch4, dtr4tog over next 4 sts**, ch3, dtr4tog starting in last st of prev dtr4tog and over next 3 sts*, rep from * to * 2x and * to ** 1x, ch1, join with htr to top of dtr3tog.
{17 sts, 4 4-ch sps, 2 1-ch sps on each side; 4 3-ch cnr sps}

R14: ch3 (stch), tr over joining htr, *htr in next st, 4dc in 4-ch sp, dc in next st, 4dc in 4-ch sp, skip 1 st, dc in 1-ch sp, dc in next 11 sts, dc in 1-ch sp, skip 1 st, 4dc in 4-ch sp, dc in next st, 4dc in 4-ch sp, htr in next st**, (2tr, ch2, 2tr) in 3-ch cnr sp*, rep from * to * 2x and * to ** 1x, 2tr in same sp as first sts, ch1, join with dc to 3rd ch of stch.
{37 sts on each side; 4 2-ch cnr sps}

R15: dc over joining dc, *dc in next 37 sts**, (dc, ch2, dc) in 2-ch cnr sp*, rep from * to * 2x and * to ** 1x, dc in same sp as first st, ch1, join with dc to first st. {39 sts on each side; 4 2-ch cnr sps}

R16: ch3 (stch), *13x [ch2, tr3tog over next 3 sts], ch2**, (tr, ch2, tr) in 2-ch cnr sp*, rep from * to * 2x and * to ** 1x, tr in same sp as first st, ch1, join with dc to 3rd ch of stch. {15 sts, 14 2-ch sps on each side; 4 2-ch cnr sps}

R17: 2dc over joining dc, *dc in next st, 13x [2dc in 2-ch sp, fpdc around next st], 2dc in 2-ch sp, dc in next st**, (2dc, ch2, 2dc) in 2-ch cnr sp*, rep from * to * 2x and * to ** 1x, 2dc in same sp as first sts, ch1, join with dc to first st.
{47 sts on each side; 4 2-ch cnr sps}

R18: ch2 (stch), *htr in next 47 sts**, (htr, ch2, htr) in 2-ch cnr sp*, rep from * to * 2x and * to ** 1x, htr in same sp as first st, ch1, join with dc to 2nd ch of stch. {49 sts on each side; 4 2-ch cnr sps}

R19: dc over joining dc, *dc in next 49 sts**, (dc, ch2, dc) in 2-ch cnr sp*, rep from * to * 2x and * to ** 1x, dc in same sp as first st, ch2, join with ss to first st. Fasten off. {51 sts on each side; 4 2-ch cnr sps}

Flourish

I was thinking of the flourishes in calligraphy while naming this pattern. Lots of embellishment to have fun with.

Colours by Joanne Waring

Colours by Jenny Hebbard

  150 m / 164 yd

Begin with mc.

R1: ch3 (stch), *ch2**, 2tr*, rep from * to * 6x and * to ** 1x, tr, join with ss to 3rd ch of stch. {16 sts, 8 2-ch sps}

R2: ss to 2-ch sp, ch3 (stch), 8tr in 2-ch sp, *ch1, skip 2 sts, 9tr in 2-ch sp*, rep from * to * 6x, skip 2 sts, join with dc to 3rd ch of stch. {72 sts, 8 1-ch sps}

Will be very ruffled.

R3: dc over joining dc, *ch2, skip 9 sts**, dc in 1-ch sp*, rep from * to * 6x and * to ** 1x, join with ss to first st. {8 sts, 8 2-ch sps}

R4: ch3 (stch), *3tr in 2-ch sp**, tr in next st*, rep from * to * 6x and * to ** 1x, join with ss to 3rd ch of stch. {32 sts}

R5: ch3 (stch), tr3tog over next 3 sts, *ch5**, tr4tog over next 4 sts*, rep from * to * 6x and * to ** 1x, join with ss to top of tr3tog. {8 sts, 8 5-ch sps}

R6: dc in same st as ss, *5dc in 5-ch sp**, 2dc in next st*, rep from * to * 6x and * to ** 1x, dc in same st as first st, join with ss to first st. {56 sts}

R7: ch3 (stch), *tr in next 6 sts**, 2tr in next st*, rep from * to * 6x and * to ** 1x, tr in same st as first st, join with ss to 3rd ch of stch. {64 sts}

R8: dc in same st as ss, dc in next 63 sts, join with ss to first st. {64 sts}

R9: ch3 (stch), *ch2**, tr in next 4 sts*, rep from * to * 14x and * to ** 1x, tr in next 3 sts, join with ss to 3rd ch of stch. {64 sts, 16 2-ch sps}

R10: dc in 2-ch sp, *ch4, dtr6tog over (same 2-ch sp, next 4 sts & next 2-ch sp), ch4**, dc in same 2-ch sp*, rep from * to * 14x and * to ** 1x, join with ss to first st. {32 sts, 32 4-ch sps}

R11: ch3 (stch), *ch2, skip 4-ch sp, dc in next st, ch2, skip 4-ch sp**, (tr, ch2, tr) in next st*, rep from * to * 14x and * to ** 1x, tr in same st as first st, ch1, join with dc to 3rd ch of stch. {48 sts, 48 2-ch sps}

R12: dc over joining dc, *2x [dc in next st, 2dc in 2-ch sp], dc in next st**, dc in 2-ch sp*, rep from * to * 14x and * to ** 1x, join with ss to first st. {128 sts}

R13: ch4 (stch), dtr in same st as ss, *dtr in next st, ch2, tr in next 2 sts, ch2, htr in next 2 sts, dc in next 21 sts, htr in next 2 sts, ch2, tr in next 2 sts, ch2, dtr in next st**, (2dtr, ch2, 2dtr) in next st*, rep from * to * 2x and * to ** 1x, 2dtr in same st as first sts, ch1, join with dc to 4th ch of stch. {35 sts, 4 2-ch sps on each side; 4 2-ch cnr sps}

R14: ch3, tr over joining dc, *ch2, tr5tog over (same 2-ch cnr sp, next 3 sts & next 2-ch sp), ch2, tr in same 2-ch sp, ch2, tr4tog over (same 2-ch sp, next 2 sts & next 2-ch sp), ch2, tr in same 2-ch sp, skip 4 sts, dc in next 17 sts, skip 4 sts, tr in 2-ch sp, ch2, tr4tog over (same 2-ch sp, next 2 sts, next 2-ch sp), ch2, tr in same 2-ch sp, ch2, tr5tog over (same 2-ch sp, next 3 sts & next 2-ch cnr sp), ch2**, 3tr in same 2-ch cnr sp*, rep from * to * 2x and * to ** 1x, tr in same sp as first sts, join with ss to 3rd ch of stch. {25 sts, 8 2-ch sps on each side; 4 3-st cnrs}

R15: dc in same st as ss, *2x [dc in next st, 2dc in 2-ch sp, skip 1 st, 2dc in 2-ch sp], dc2tog over next 2 sts, dc in next 15 sts, dc2tog over next 2 sts, 2x [2dc in 2-ch sp, skip 1 st, 2dc in 2-ch sp, dc in next st]**, (dc, ch2, dc) in next st*, rep from * to * 2x and * to ** 1x, dc in same st as first st, ch1, join with dc to first st. {39 sts on each side; 4 2-ch cnr sps}

R16: ch3 (stch), *tr in next 39 sts**, (tr, ch2, tr) in 2-ch cnr sp*, rep from * to * 2x and * to ** 1x, tr in same sp as first st, ch1, join with dc to 3rd ch of stch. {41 sts on each side; 4 2-ch cnr sps}

R17: ch3 (stch), *tr in next st, 6x [fpdtr around next 3 sts, bpdtr around next 3 sts], fpdtr around next 3 sts, tr in next st**, (tr, ch2, tr) in 2-ch cnr sp*, rep from * to * 2x and * to ** 1x, tr in same sp as first st, ch1, join with dc to 3rd ch of stch. {43 sts on each side; 4 2-ch cnr sps}

R18: dc over joining dc, *dc in next 43 sts**, (dc, ch2, dc) in 2-ch cnr sp*, rep from * to * 2x and * to ** 1x, dc in same sp as first st, ch2, join with ss to first st. Fasten off. {45 sts on each side; 4 2-ch cnr sps}

Meander

The fun construction of this design led me to the name, as you meander from round to round.

Colours by Shelley

Colours by Evangelia V Katsafouros

  198 m / 217 yd

Rounds 10 to 13 will be ruffled.

Begin with mc.

R1: ch1, 6dc, join with ss to first st. {6 sts}

R2: ch3 (stch), tr in same st as ss, tr around stch and st just made at the same time, *2tr in next st, tr around 2 sts just made at the same time*, rep from * to * 4x, join with ss to 3rd ch of stch. {18 sts}

R3: dc in same st as ss, dc in next 2 sts, *dc between last and next sts**, dc in next 3 sts*, rep from * to * 4x and * to ** 1x, join with ss tofirst st. {24 sts}

R4: ch3 (stch), tr2tog over next 2 sts, *ch1, 3tr in next st**, ch1, tr3tog over next 3 sts*, rep from * to * 4x and * to ** 1x, join with dc to tr2tog. {24 sts, 12 1-ch sps}

R5: ch3 (stch), 2trcl over joining dc, ch2, *skip 1 st, 2x [3trcl, ch2] in 1-ch sp, skip 3 sts**, 2x [3trcl, ch2] in 1-ch sp*, rep from * to * 4x and * to ** 1x, 3trcl in same sp as first sts, ch1, join with dc to 2trcl. {24 sts, 24 2-ch sps}

R6: ch3 (stch), tr over joining dc, *ch2, skip 1 st, dc in 2-ch sp, fptr around R4 st below in front of same 2-ch sp, dc in same 2-ch sp, ch2, skip 1 st, 3tr in 2-ch sp, ch2, skip 1 st, dc in 2-ch sp, fptr3tog over next 3 sts of R4 below in front of same 2-ch sp, dc in same 2-ch sp, ch2, skip 1 st**, 3tr in 2-ch sp*, rep from * to * 4x and * to ** 1x, tr in same sp as first st, join with ss to 3rd ch of stch. {72 sts, 24 2-ch sps}

R7: dc in same st as ss, *ch3, skip (1 st, 2-ch sp & 1 st), fptr around next st, ch3, skip (1 st, 2-ch sp & 1 st)**, dc in next st*, rep from * to * 10x and * to ** 1x, join with ss to first st. {24 sts, 24 3-ch sps}

R8: dc in same st as ss, *3dc in 3-ch sp**, dc in next st*, rep from * to * 22x and * to ** 1x, join with ss to first st. {96 sts}

R9: ch3 (stch), *ch2, tr3tog over next 3 sts, ch2**, tr in next st*, rep from * to * 22x and * to ** 1x, join with ss to 3rd ch of stch. {48 sts, 48 2-ch sps)

R10: ch3 (stch), 2tr in same st as ss, *skip 2-ch sp, (2tr in, fptr around) next st, skip 2-ch sp**, 3tr in next st*, rep from * to * 22x and * to ** 1x, join with ss to 3rd ch of stch. {144 sts}

Will be very ruffled.

Meander chart
Rounds 1-14

R11: fptr3tog over stch and next 2 sts, *ch2**, fptr3tog over next 3 sts*, rep from * to * 46x and * to ** 1x, join with ss to first st. {48 sts, 48 2-ch sps}

R12: ch3 (stch), tr in same st as ss, fptr around st below, *skip 2-ch sp**, (2tr in, fptr around) next st*, rep from * to * 46x and * to ** 1x, join with ss to 3rd ch of stch. {144 sts}

R13: fptr3tog over stch and next 2 sts, *ch2**, fptr3tog over next 3 sts*, rep from * to * 46x and * to ** 1x, join with ss to first st. {48 sts, 48 2-ch sps}

R14: fpdc around same st as ss, *2dc in 2-ch sp**, fpdc around next st*, rep from * to * 46x and * to ** 1x, join with ss to first st. {144 sts}

Meander chart
Rounds 14-20

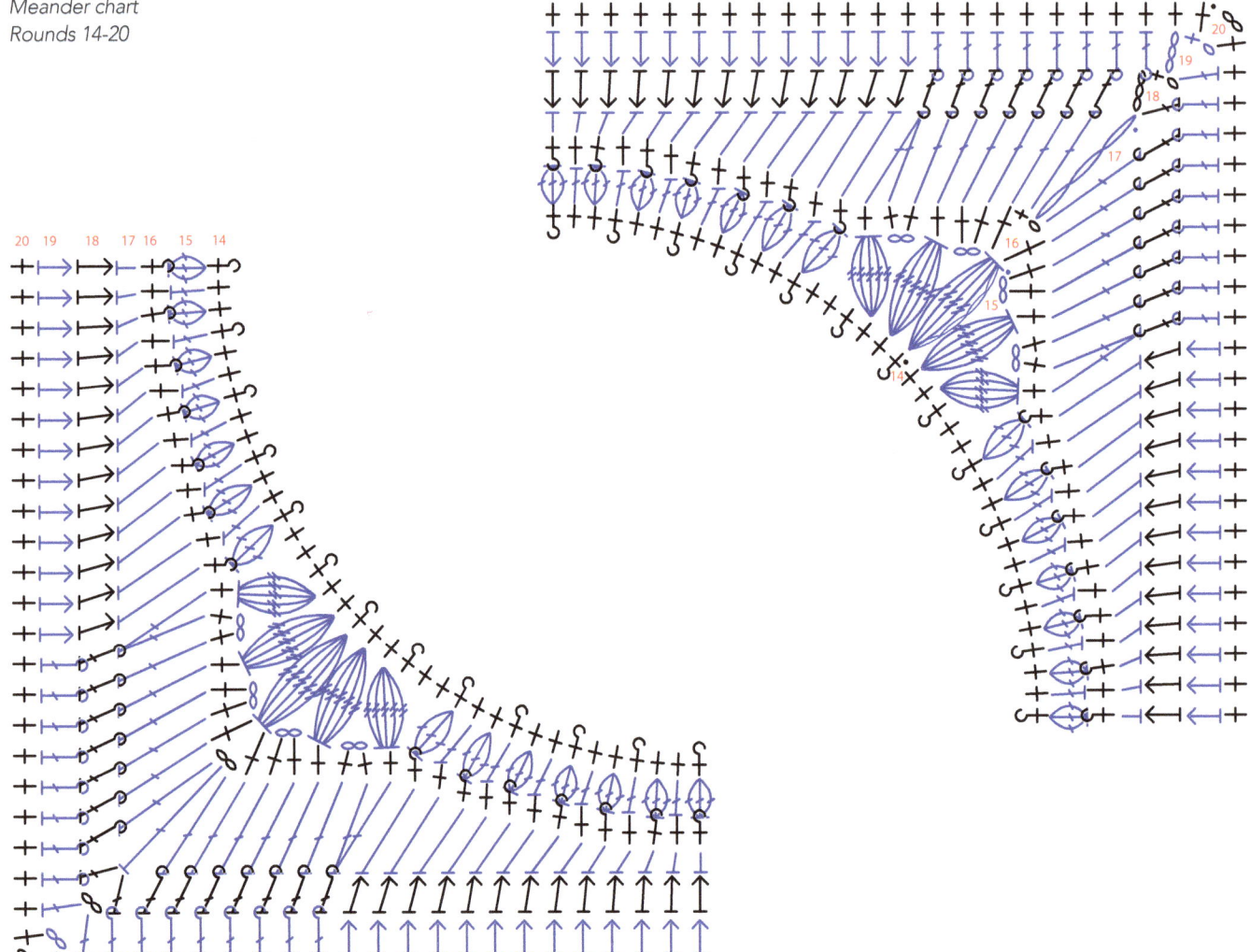

R15: ch4 (stch), 4dtrcl in same st as ss, *2x [ch2, 5dtrcl in next st], skip 3 sts, 12x [3trcl in next st, tr in next st], 3trcl in next st, skip 3 sts, 2x [5dtrcl in next st, ch2]**, 5dtrcl in next st*, rep from * to * 2x and * to ** 1x, join with ss to top of 4dtrcl. {29 sts, 4 2-ch sps on each side; 4 1-st cnrs}

R16: dc in same st as ss, *2x [2dc in 2-ch sp, dc in next st], 12x [fpdc around next st, dc in next st], fpdc around next st, 2x [dc in next st, 2dc in 2-ch sp]**, (dc, ch2, dc) in next st*, rep from * to * 2x and * to ** 1x, dc in same st as first st, ch1, join with dc to first st. {39 sts on each side; 4 2-ch cnr sps}

R17: ch3 (stch), tr over joining dc, *tr in next 5 sts, tr2tog over next 2 sts, htr in next 25 sts, tr2tog over next 2 sts, tr in next 5 sts**, 3tr in 2-ch cnr sp*, rep from * to * 2x and * to ** 1x, tr in same sp as first sts, join with ss to 3rd ch of stch. {37 sts on each side; 4 3-st cnrs}

R18: ch3 (stch), *fptr around next 7 sts, htr in lbv of next 25 sts, fptr around next 7 sts**, (tr, ch2, tr) in next st*, rep from * to * 2x and * to ** 1x, tr in same st as first st, ch1, join with dc to 3rd ch of stch. {41 sts on each side; 4 2-ch cnr sps}

R19: ch3 (stch), *fptr around next 8 sts, htr in lbv of next 25 sts, fptr around next 8 sts**, (tr, ch2, tr) in 2-ch cnr sp*, rep from * to * 2x and * to ** 1x, tr in same sp as first st, ch1, join with dc to 3rd ch of stch. {43 sts on each side; 4 2-ch cnr sps}

R20: dc over joining dc, *dc in next 43 sts**, (dc, ch2, dc) in 2-ch cnr sp*, rep from * to * 2x and * to ** 1x, dc in same sp as first st, ch2, join with ss to first st. Fasten off. {45 sts on each side; 4 2-ch cnr sps}

Millpond Squared

The centre of this square and the smaller Millpond Mini on page 21 are from a large circular baby blanket I designed a couple of years ago.

Colours by Kim Siebenhausen

Colours by Miranda Howard

  170 m / 186 yd

Begin with mc.

R1: ch3 (stch), 11tr, join with ss to 3rd ch of stch. {12 sts}

R2: ch3 (stch), tr in same st as ss, 2tr in next 11 sts, join with ss to 3rd ch of stch. {24 sts}

R3: dc in same st as ss, *fptr around next st, 3tr in next st, fptr around next st**, dc in next st*, rep from * to * 4x & * to ** 1x, join with ss to first st. {36 sts}

R4: dc in same st as ss, *fptr around next st, tr in next st, 3tr in next st, tr in next st, fptr around next st**, dc in next st*, rep from * to * 4x & * to ** 1x, join with ss to first st. {48 sts}

R5: dc in same st as ss, *fptr around next st, tr in next 2 sts, 3tr in next st, tr in next 2 sts, fptr around next st**, dc in next st*, rep from * to * 4x & * to ** 1x, join with ss to first st. {60 sts}

R6: ch3 (stch), *fptr around next st, bptr around next 7 sts, fptr around next st**, tr in next st*, rep from * to * 4x & * to ** 1x, join with ss to 3rd ch of stch. {60 sts}

R7: *fptr around next st, tr2tog over next 2 sts, fptr around next st, tr in next st, fptr around next st, tr2tog over next 2 sts, fptr around next st, 5tr in next st*, rep from * to * 5x, join with ss to first st. {72 sts}

R8: fptr around st below, *3x [tr in next st, fptr around next st], tr in next 2 sts, 3tr in next st, tr in next 2 sts**, fptr around next st*, rep from * to * 4x & *to ** 1x, join with ss to first st. {84 sts}

R9: fptr around st below, *tr in next st, fptr around next st, 5tr in next st, fptr around next st, tr in next st, fptr around next st, bptr around next 7 sts**, fptr around next st*, rep from * to * 4x & * to ** 1x, join with ss to first st. {108 sts}

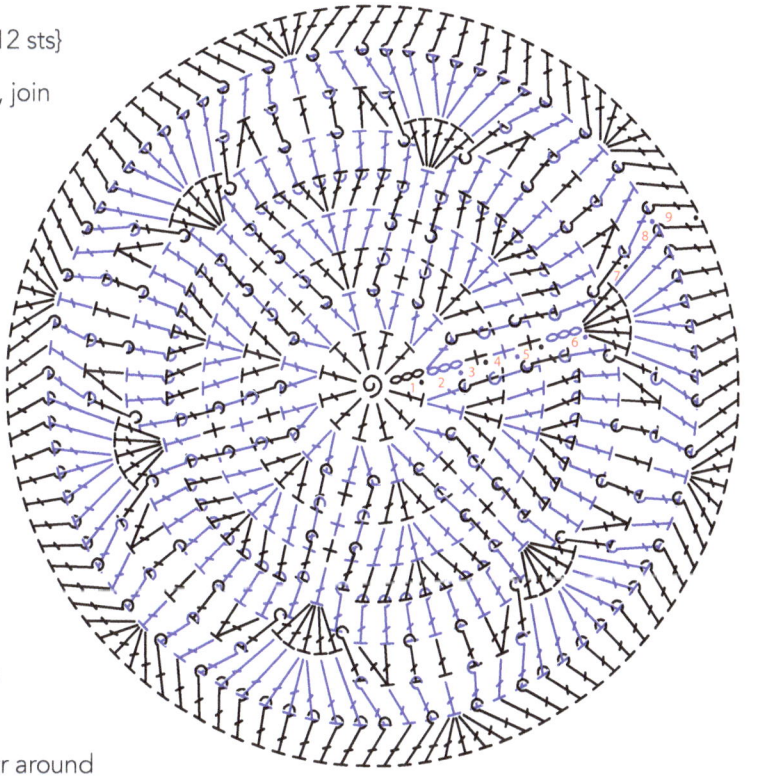

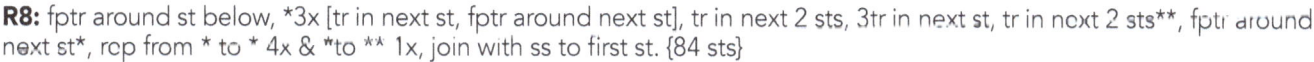

Millpond Squared chart
Rounds 9-20

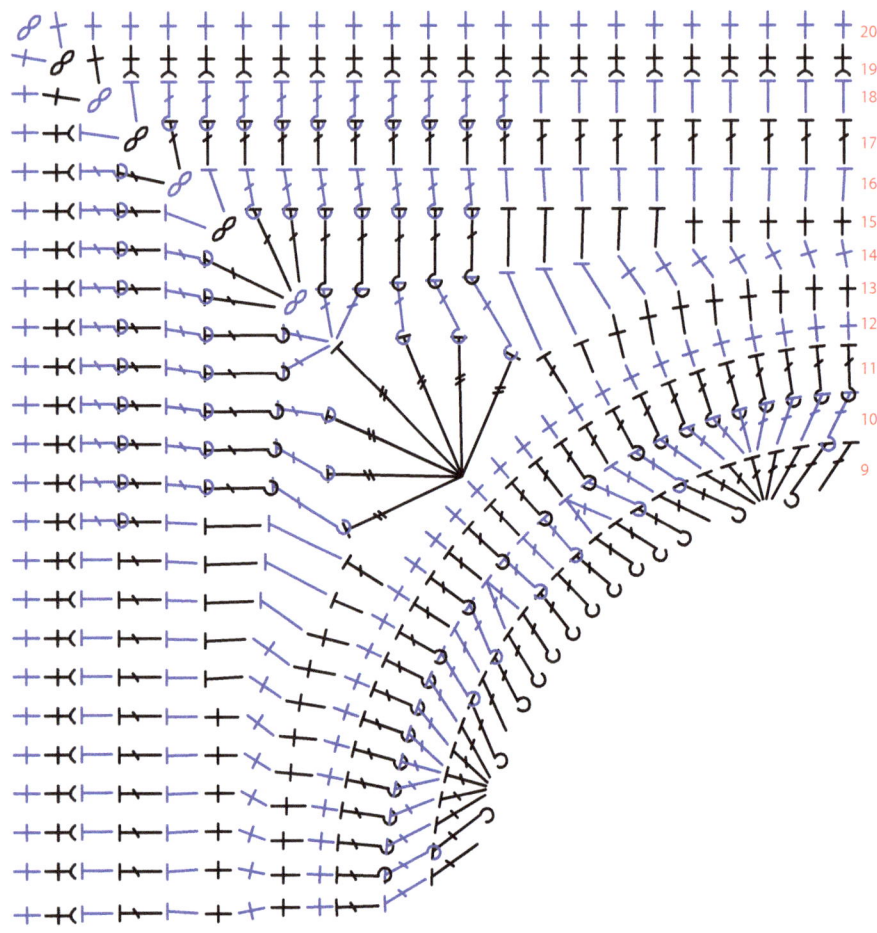

R10: fptr around st below, *tr in next st, fptr around next st, tr in next 2 sts, 3tr in next st, tr in next 2 sts, fptr around next st, tr in next st, fptr around next st, tr2tog over next 2 sts, fptr around next st, tr in next st, fptr around next st, tr2tog over next 2 sts **, fptr around next st*, rep from * to * 4x & * to ** 1x, join with ss to first st. {108 sts}

R11: fptr around st below, *tr in next st, fptr around next st, bptr around next 7 sts, 4x [fptr around next st, tr in next st]**, fptr around next st*, rep from * to * 4x & * to ** 1x, join with ss to first st. {108 sts}

R12: dc in same st as ss, dc in next 107 sts, join with ss to first st. Cut yarn. {108 sts}

R13: Attach with a stdg dtr to st above middle st of any group of 7 bp sts of R11, 3dtr in same st, *skip 3 sts, tr in next st, htr in next st, dc in next 16 sts, htr in next st, tr in next st, skip 3 sts**, 7dtr in next st*, rep from * to * 2x and * to ** 1x, 3dtr in same st as first sts, join with ss to first st. {20 sts on each side; 4 7-st cnrs}

R14: ch3 (stch), tr in same st as ss, *bptr around next 3 sts, htr in next 3 sts, dc in next 14 sts, htr in next 3 sts, bptr around next 3 sts**, (2tr, ch2, 2tr) in next st*, rep from * to * 2x and * to ** 1x, 2tr in same st as first sts, ch1, join with dc to 3rd ch of stch. {30 sts on each side; 4 2-ch cnr sps}

Millpond Squared chart
Beginning of Rounds 9-20

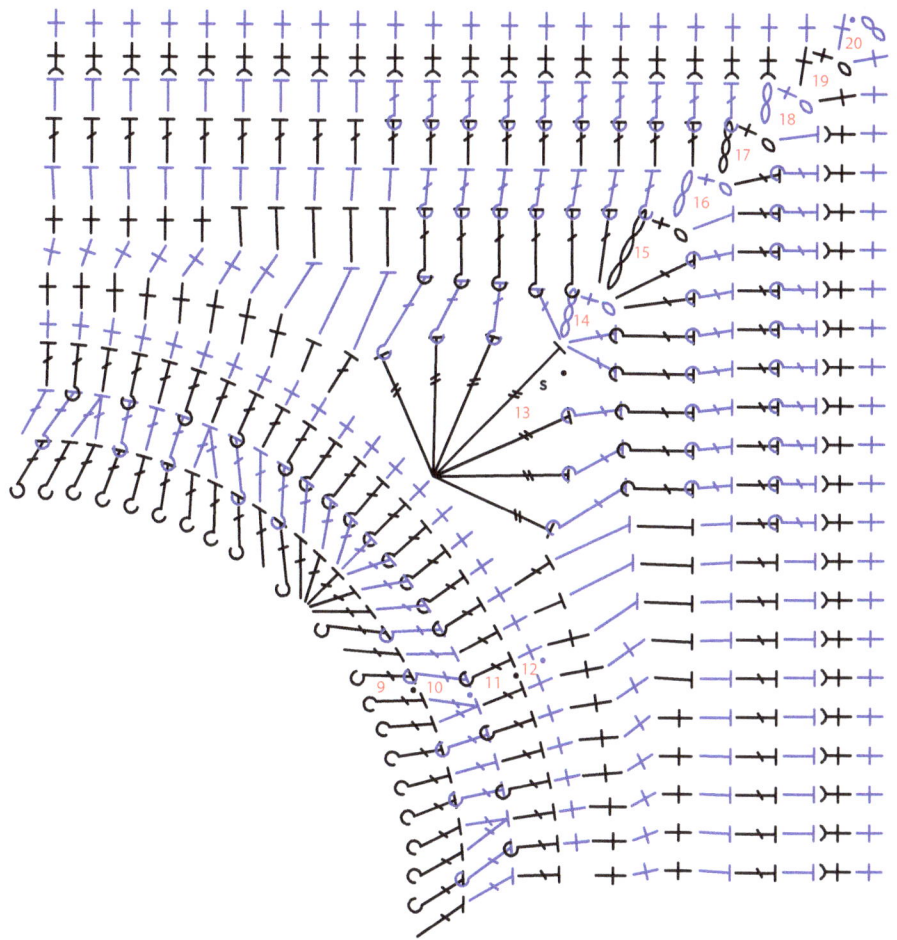

R15: ch3 (stch), tr over joining dc, *bptr around next 5 sts, htr in next 5 sts, dc in next 10 sts, htr in next 5 sts, bptr around next 5 sts**, (2tr, ch2, 2tr) in 2-ch cnr sp*, rep from * to * 2x and * to ** 1x, 2tr in same sp as first sts, ch1, join with dc to 3rd ch of stch. {34 sts on each side; 4 2-ch cnr sps}

R16: ch2 (stch), *bptr around next 7 sts, htr in next 20 sts, bptr around next 7 sts**, (htr, ch2, htr) in 2-ch cnr sp*, rep from * to * 2x and * to ** 1x, htr in same sp as first st, ch1, join with dc to 2nd ch of stch. {36 sts on each side; 4 2-ch cnr sps}

R17: ch3 (stch), *tr in next 36 sts**, (tr, ch2, tr) in 2-ch cnr sp*, rep from * to * 2x and * to ** 1x, tr in same sp as first st, ch1, join with dc to 3rd ch of stch. {38 sts on each side; 4 2-ch cnr sps}

R18: ch2 (stch),*bptr around next 10 sts, htr in next 18 sts, bptr around next 10 sts**, (htr, ch2, htr) in 2-ch cnr sp*, rep from * to * 2x and * to ** 1x, htr in same sp as first st, ch1, join with dc to 2nd ch of stch. {40 sts on each side; 4 2-ch cnr sps}

R19: dc over joining dc, *dc in blo of next 40 sts**, (dc, ch2, dc) in 2-ch cnr sp*, rep from * to * 2x and * to ** 1x, dc in same sp as first st, ch1, join with dc to first st. {42 sts on each side; 4 2-ch cnr sps}

R20: dc over joining dc, *dc in next 42 sts**, (dc, ch2, dc) in 2-ch cnr sp*, rep from * to * 2x and * to ** 1x, dc in same sp as first st, ch2, join with ss to first st. Fasten off. {44 sts on each side; 4 2-ch cnr sps}

Vault

The arches are reminiscent of the vaulted ceilings and arches seen in architecture.

Colours by Shelley

Colours by Kim Siebenhausen

  141 m / 155 yd

Due to the stitches used and construction, this pattern will require blocking. At times it will be ruffled and buckled but a block at the end will sort all that out. If you are a tight chainer, do an extra chain from R9 to R15 along the sides for each ch space.

Begin with mc.

R1: ch4 (stch), 15dtr, join with ss to 4th ch of stch. {16 sts}

R2: ch3 (stch), tr in same st as ss, 2tr in next 15 sts, join with ss to 3rd ch of stch. {32 sts}

R3: 2dc in same st as ss, 2dc in next 31 sts, join with ss to first st. {64 sts}

R4: ch3 (stch), tr in next 63 sts, join with ss to 3rd ch of stch. {64 sts}

R5: ch4 (stch), dtr in next 63 sts, join with ss to 4th ch of stch. (64 sts)

R6: dc in same st as ss, dc in next 63 sts, join with ss to first st. {64 sts}

R7: ch4 (stch), 2dtrcl in same st as ss, *ch2, 3dtrcl in next st, ch4, dc in next 6 sts, ch2, skip 1 st, dc in next 6 sts, ch4, 3dtrcl in next st, ch2**, 3dtrcl in next st*, rep from * to * 2x and * to ** 1x, join with ss to top of 2dtrcl. {14 sts, 3 2-ch sps, 2 4-ch sps on each side; 4 1-st cnrs}

R8: ch4 (stch), 3dtr in same st as ss, *skip (2-ch sp & 1 st), dc in 4-ch sp, ch3, dc in next 4 sts, skip 2 sts, 7dtr in 2-ch sp, skip 2 sts, dc in next 4 sts, ch3, dc in 4-ch sp, skip (1 st & 2-ch sp)**, 7dtr in next st*, rep from * to * 2x and * to ** 1x, 3dtr in same st as first sts, join with ss to 4th ch of stch. {17 sts, 2 3-ch sps on each side; 4 7-st cnrs}

R9: dc in same st as ss, *2dc in next 3 sts, dc in next st, ch3, skip (3-ch sp & 1 st), dc2tog over next 2 sts, skip 1 st, 2dc in next 7 sts, skip 1 st, dc2tog over next 2 sts, ch3, skip (1 st & 3-ch sp), dc in next st, 2dc in next 3 sts**, (dc, ch2, dc) in next st*, rep from * to * 2x and * to ** 1x, dc in same st as first st, ch1, join with dc to first st. {32 sts, 2 3-ch sps on each side; 4 2-ch cnr sps}

R10: dc over joining dc, *dc in next 8 sts, ch3, skip 3-ch sp, dc in next st, skip 1 st, dc in next 12 sts, skip 1 st, dc in next st, ch3, skip 3-ch sp, dc in next 8 sts**, (dc, ch2, dc) in 2-ch cnr sp*, rep from * to * 2x and * to ** 1x, dc in same sp as first st, ch1, join with dc to first st. {32 sts, 2 3-ch sps on each side; 4 2-ch cnr sps}

Vault chart
Rounds 1-10

Vault - Size 3 Patterns • 61

Vault chart
Rounds 10-19

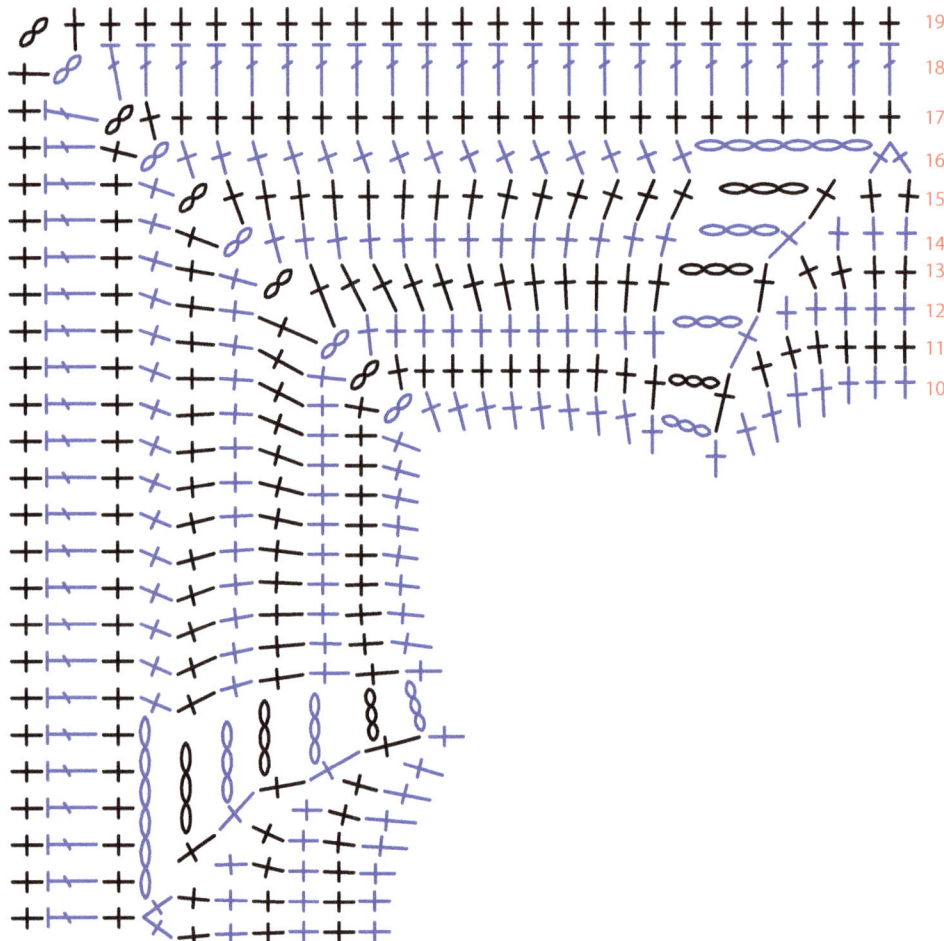

R11: dc over joining dc, *dc in next 9 sts, ch3, skip 3-ch sp, dc in next st, skip 1 st, dc in next 10 sts, skip 1 st, dc in next st, ch3, skip 3-ch sp, dc in next 9 sts**, (dc, ch2, dc) in 2-ch cnr sp*, rep from * to * 2x and * to ** 1x, dc in same sp as first st, ch1, join with dc to first st. {32 sts, 2 3-ch sps on each side; 4 2-ch cnr sps}

R12: dc over joining dc, *dc in next 10 sts, ch3, skip 3-ch sp, dc in next st, skip 1 st, dc in next 8 sts, skip 1 st, dc in next st, ch3, skip 3-ch sp, dc in next 10 sts**, (dc, ch2, dc) in 2-ch cnr sp*, rep from * to * 2x and * to ** 1x, dc in same sp as first st, ch1, join with dc to first st. {32 sts, 2 3-ch sps on each side; 4 2-ch cnr sps}

R13: dc over joining dc, *dc in next 11 sts, ch3, skip 3-ch sp, dc in next st, skip 1 st, dc in next 6 sts, skip 1 st, dc in next st, ch3, skip 3-ch sp, dc in next 11 sts**, (dc, ch2, dc) in 2-ch cnr sp*, rep from * to * 2x and * to ** 1x, dc in same sp as first st, ch1, join with dc to first st. {32 sts, 2 3-ch sps on each side; 4 2-ch cnr sps}

R14: dc over joining dc, *dc in next 12 sts, ch3, skip 3-ch sp, dc in next st, skip 1 st, dc in next 4 sts, skip 1 st, dc in next st, ch3, skip 3-ch sp, dc in next 12 sts**, (dc, ch2, dc) in 2-ch cnr sp*, rep from * to * 2x and * to ** 1x, dc in same sp as first st, ch1, join with dc to first st. {32 sts, 2 3-ch sps on each side; 4 2-ch cnr sps}

Vault chart
Beginning of Rounds 10-19

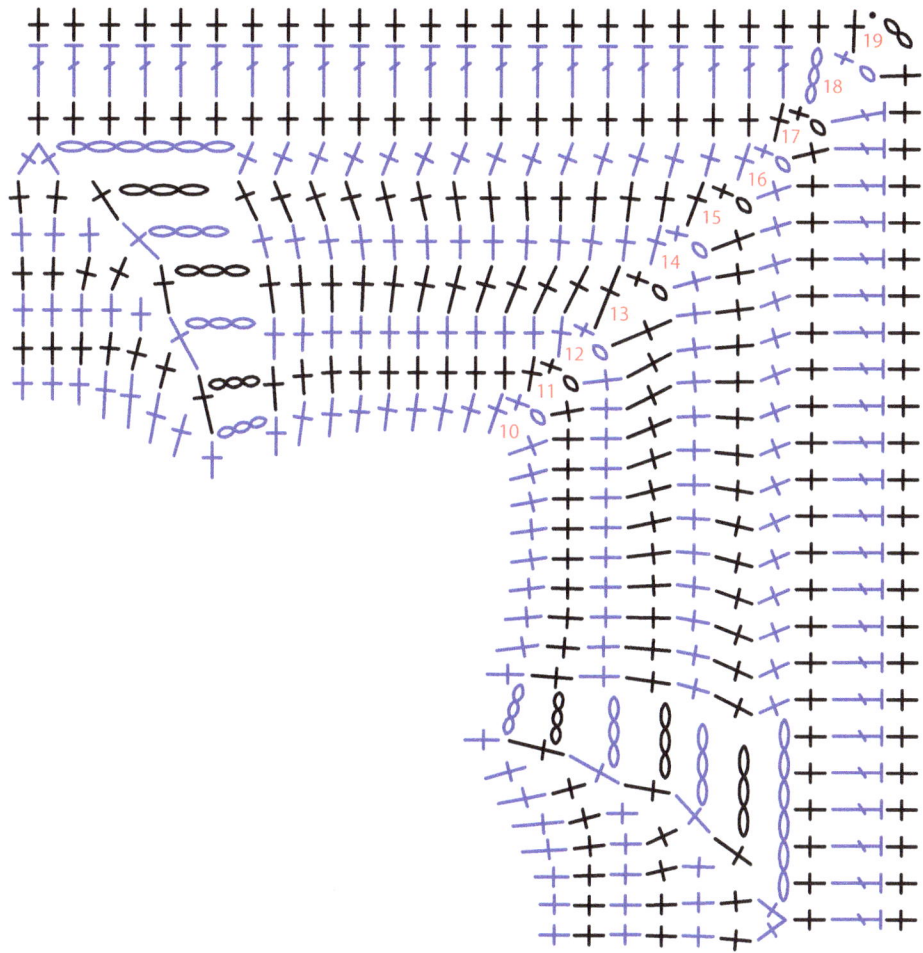

R15: dc over joining dc, *dc in next 13 sts, ch3, skip 3-ch sp, dc in next st, skip 1 st, dc in next 2 sts, skip 1 st, dc in next st, ch3, skip 3-ch sp, dc in next 13 sts**, (dc, ch2, dc) in 2-ch cnr sp*, rep from * to * 2x and * to ** 1x, dc in same sp as first st, ch1, join with dc to first st. {32 sts, 2 3-ch sps on each side; 4 2-ch cnr sps}

R16: dc over joining dc, *dc in next 14 sts, ch6, skip (3-ch sp & 1 st), dc2tog over next 2 sts, ch6, skip 1 st & 3-ch sp), dc in next 14 sts**, (dc, ch2, dc) in 2-ch cnr sp*, rep from * to * 2x and * to ** 1x, dc in same sp as first st, ch1, join with dc to first st. {31 sts, 2 6-ch sps on each side; 4 2-ch cnr sps}

R17: dc over joining dc, *dc in next 15 sts, 5dc in 6-ch sp, dc in next st, 5dc in 6-ch sp, dc in next 15 sts**, (dc, ch2, dc) in 2-ch cnr sp*, rep from * to * 2x and * to ** 1x, dc in same sp as first st, ch1, join with dc to first st. {43 sts on each side; 4 2-ch cnr sps}

R18: ch3 (stch), *tr in next 43 sts**, (tr, ch2, tr) in 2-ch cnr sp*, rep from * to * 2x and * to ** 1x, tr in same sp as first st, ch1, join with dc to 3rd ch of stch. {45 sts on each side; 4 2-ch cnr sps}

R19: dc over joining dc, *dc in next 45 sts**, (dc, ch2, dc) in 2-ch cnr sp*, rep from * to * 2x and * to ** 1x, dc in same sp as first st, ch2, join with ss to first st. Fasten off. {47 sts on each side; 4 2-ch cnr sps}

Size 4 Patterns

From here on in, you will need to commit more time to completing the squares, but don't let that put you off! They are fun to make, no matter the size.

Below are the approximate sizes you will achieve with 3 different yarn weights and hook sizes. The amount of yarn listed on each pattern page is for the middle yarn weight and hook size. The amount of yarn needed for the other yarn weights is on page 177.

🪝	3.5 mm hook	4.5 mm hook	5.5 mm hook
🧶	4 ply/sock/fingering	8 ply/DK/light worsted	10 ply/aran/worsted
⬜	12.5"	15"	17.5"

Bob
page 66

Giantess
page 69

Maxim
page 73

Melbourne
page 76

Nymph
page 78

Pagoda
page 82

Paradigm
page 85

Size 4 Patterns • 65

Bob

Bob stands for Bodacious, Outlandish and Beguiling and is the largest square from my GREG blanket (Grand and Resplendent Endeavour in Gaiety). A bit of acronym fun.

*Colours by
Kim Siebenhausen*

*Colours by
Miranda Howard*

  250 m / 273 yd

Begin with mc.

R1: ch3 (stch), 11tr, join with ss to 3rd ch of stch. {12 sts}

R2: ch3 (stch), *ch2, tr in next st*, rep from * to * 10x, ch2, join with ss to 3rd ch of stch. {12 sts, 12 2-ch sps}

R3: dc in same st as ss, *2dc in 2-ch sp**, dc in next st*, rep from * to * 10x and * to ** 1x, join with ss to first st. {36 sts}

R4: ch3 (stch), *ch1, tr2tog over next 2 sts, ch1**, tr in next st*, rep from * to * 10x and * to ** 1x, join with ss to 3rd ch of stch. {24 sts, 24 1-ch sps}

R5: dc in same st as ss, *dc in 1-ch sp**, dc in next st*, rep from * to * 22x and * to ** 1x, join with ss to first st. {48 sts}

R6: ch4 (stch), *4hdtr in next st, skip 2 sts, dc in next st, skip 2 sts, 4hdtr in next st**, (dtr, ch2, dtr) in next st*, rep from * to * 4x and * to ** 1x, dtr in same st as first st, ch1, join with dc to 4th ch of stch. {66 sts, 6 2-ch sps}

R7: dc over joining dc, *dc in next 5 sts, ch3, skip 1 st, dc in next 5 sts**, (dc, ch2, dc) in 2-ch sp*, rep from * to * 4x and * to ** 1x, dc in same sp as first st, ch1, join with dc to first st. {72 sts, 6 3-ch sps, 6 2-ch sps}

R8: dc over joining dc, *ch7, skip 6 sts, tr in 3-ch sp, ch7, skip 6 sts**, dc in 2-ch sp*, rep from * to * 4x and * to ** 1x, join with ss to first st. {12 sts, 12 7-ch sps}

R9: Don't work a false st. ch3 (stch), *tr in each of next 7 chs**, tr in next st*, rep from * to * 10x and * to ** 1x, join with inv join to first true st. {96 sts}

R10: Attach with a stdg dc to blo of any st above a star point, dc in blo of next 95 sts, join with ss to first st. {96 sts}

Bob chart
Rounds 1-14

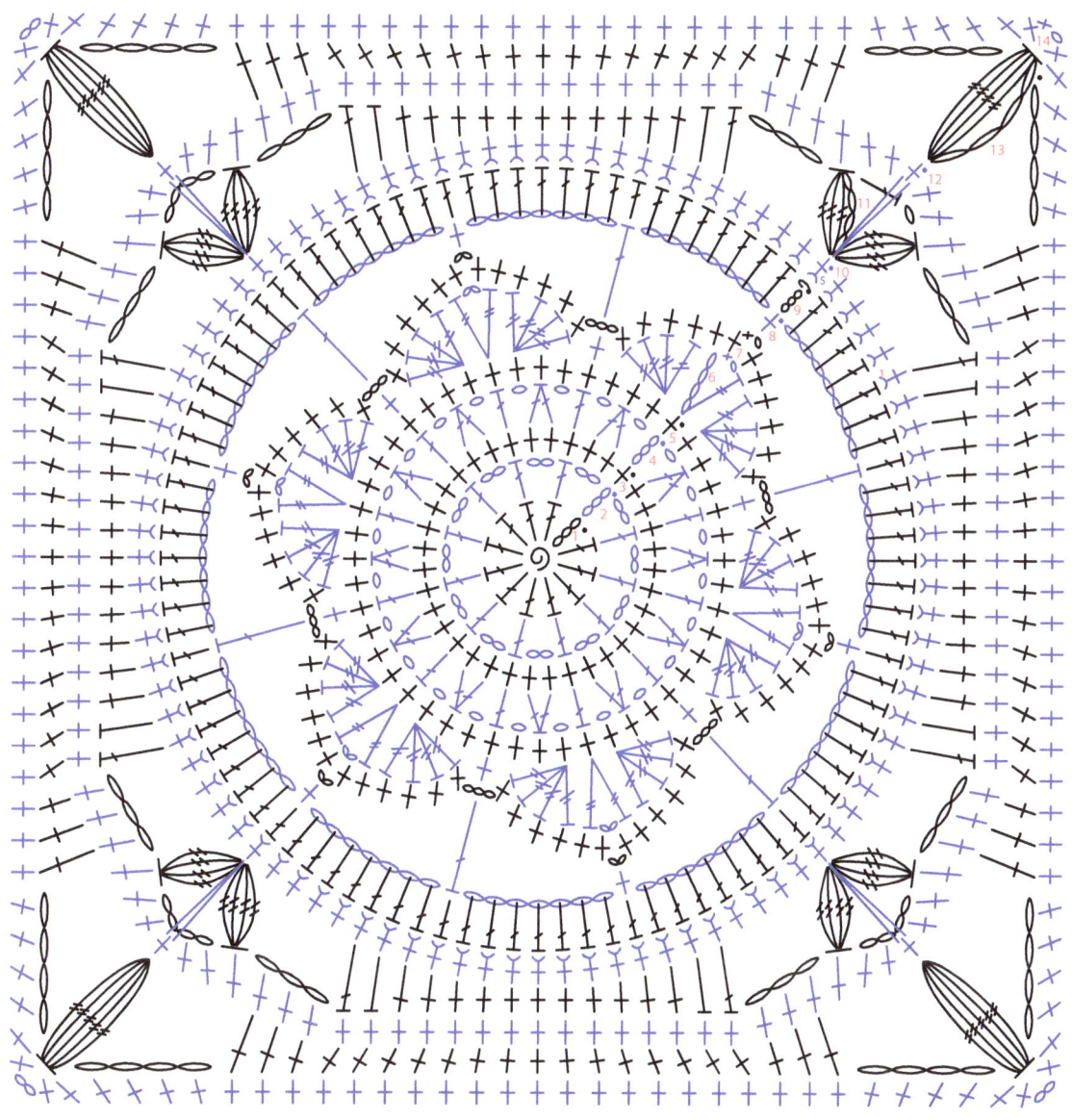

R11: ch4 (stch), 3dtrcl in same st as ss, *ch3, skip 4 sts, tr in next st, htr in next st, dc in next 11 sts, htr in next st, tr in next st, ch3, skip 4 sts**, (4dtrcl, ch4, 4dtrcl) in next st*, rep from * to * 2x and * to ** 1x, 4dtrcl in same st as first st, ch1, join with tr to top of 3dtrcl. {17 sts, 2 3-ch sps on each side; 4 4-ch cnr sps}

R12: spike dc in same st clusters are worked into, 2dc over joining tr, *dc in next st, 3dc in 3-ch sp, dc in next 15 sts, 3dc in 3-ch sp, dc in next st**, 2dc in 4-ch cnr sp, spike dc into same st clusters are worked into, 2dc in same 4-ch cnr sp*, rep from * to * 2x and * to ** 1x, 2dc in same sp as first sts, join with ss to first st. {27 sts on each side; 4 1-st cnrs}

R13: ch3 (stch), 4dtrcl in same st as ss, *ch4, skip 3 sts, dc in next 21 sts, ch4, skip 3 sts**, 5dtrcl in next st*, rep from * to * 2x and * to ** 1x, join with ss to top of 4dtrcl. {21 sts, 2 4-ch sps on each side; 4 1-st cnrs}

R14: 2dc in same st as ss, *4dc in 4-ch sp, dc in next 21 sts, 4dc in 4-ch sp**, (2dc, ch2, 2dc) in next st*, rep from * to * 2x and * to ** 1x, 2dc in same st as first sts, ch1, join with dc to first st. {33 sts on each side; 4 2-ch cnr sps}

Bob chart
Rounds 14-22

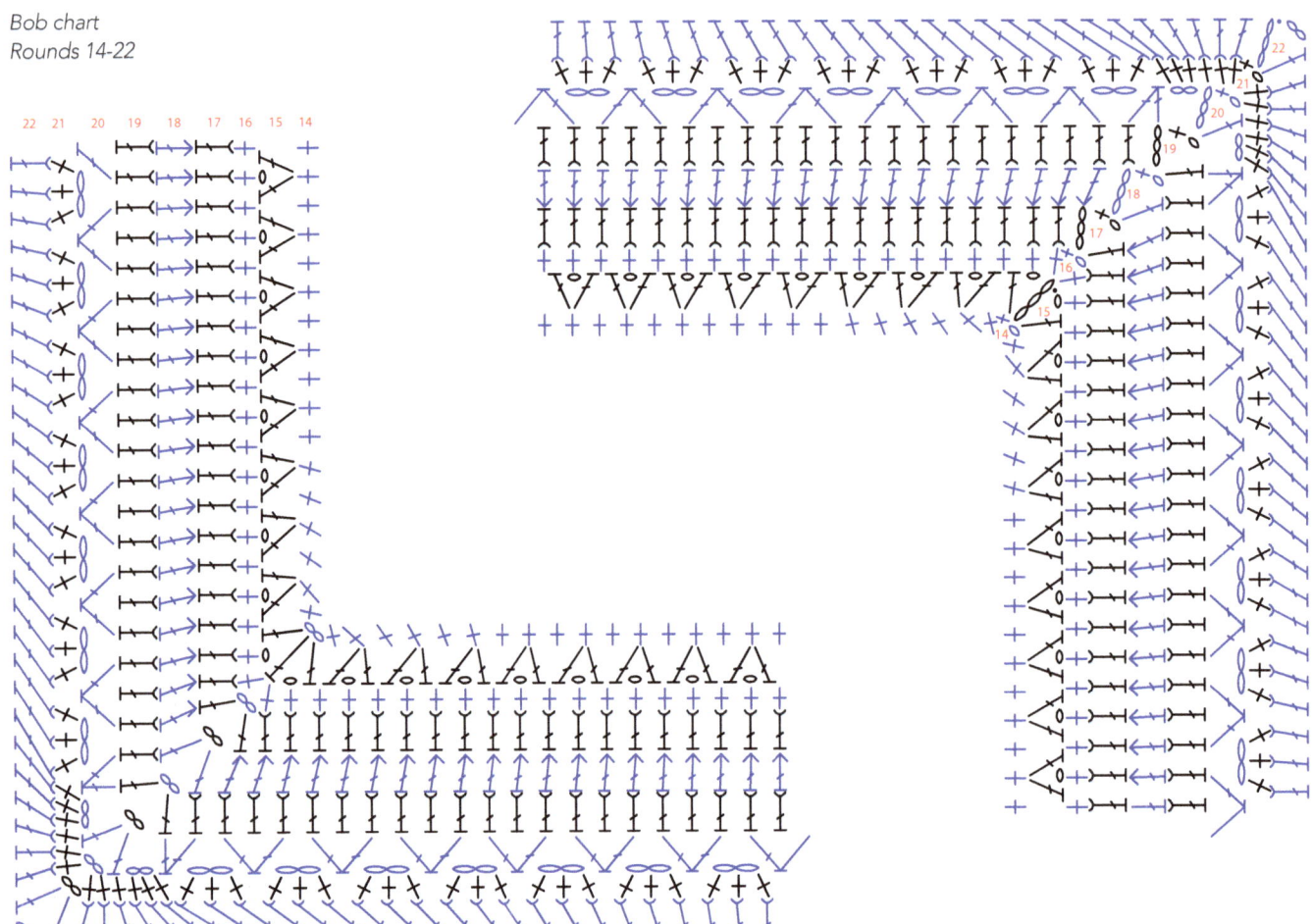

R15: ch3 (stch), ch1, tr over joining dc, *16x [skip 1 st, (tr, ch1, tr) in next st], skip 1 st**, (2x [tr, ch1], tr) in 2-ch cnr sp*, rep from * to * 2x and * to ** 1x, tr in same sp as first sts, ch1, join with ss to 3rd ch of stch. {34 sts, 18 1-ch sps on each side; 4 1-st cnrs}

R16: dc in same st as ss, *17x [dc in 1-ch sp, dc between next 2 sts], dc in 1-ch sp**, (dc, ch2, dc) in next st*, rep from * to * 2x and * to ** 1x, dc in same st as first st, ch1, join with dc to first st. {37 sts on each side; 4 2-ch cnr sps}

R17: ch3 (stch), *tr in blo of next 37 sts**, (tr, ch2, tr) in 2-ch cnr sp*, rep from * to * 2x and * to ** 1x, tr in same sp as first st, ch1, join with dc to 3rd ch of stch. {39 sts on each side; 4 2-ch cnr sps}

R18: ch3 (stch), *tr in lbv of next 39 sts**, (tr, ch2, tr) in 2-ch cnr sp*, rep from * to * 2x and * to ** 1x, tr in same sp as first st, ch1, join with dc to 3rd ch of stch. {41 sts on each side; 4 2-ch cnr sps}

R19: ch3 (stch), *tr in blo of next 41 sts**, (tr, ch2, tr) in 2-ch cnr sp*, rep from * to * 2x and * to ** 1x, tr in same sp as first st, ch1, join with dc to 3rd ch of stch. {43 sts on each side; 4 2-ch cnr sps}

R20: ch3 (stch), *ch2, tr2tog over next 2 sts, 13x [ch2, tr2tog over next 3 sts skipping the middle st], ch2, tr2tog over next 2 sts, ch2**, (tr, ch2, tr) in 2-ch cnr sp*, rep from * to * 2x and * to ** 1x, tr in same sp as first st, ch1, join with dc to 3rd ch of stch. {17 sts, 16 2-ch sps on each side; 4 2-ch cnr sps}

R21: 2dc over joining dc, *dc in next st, 15x [3dc in 2-ch sp, skip 1 st], 3dc in 2-ch sp, dc in next st**, (2dc, ch2, 2dc) in 2-ch cnr sp*, rep from * to * 2x and * to ** 1x, 2dc in same sp as first sts, ch1, join with dc to first st. {54 sts on each side; 4 2-ch cnr sps}

R22: ch3 (stch), *tr in blo of next 54 sts**, (tr, ch2, tr) in 2-ch cnr sp*, rep from * to * 2x and * to ** 1x, tr in same sp as first st, ch2, join with ss to 3rd ch of stch. Fasten off. {56 sts on each side; 4 2-ch cnr sps}

Giantess

Named for the first time I designed large granny squares. This one has had a bit more added to the original design.

Colours by Evangelia V Katsafouros

Colours by Jenny Hebbard

  248 m / 272 yd

Begin with mc.

R1: ch3 (stch), *ch2, tr*, rep from * to * 6x, ch1, join with dc to 3rd ch of stch. {8 sts, 8 2-ch sps}

R2: begpc over joining dc, *ch2, skip 1 st**, pc in 2-ch sp*, rep from * to * 6x and from * to ** 1x, join with ss to top of first st. {8 sts, 8 2-ch sps}

R3: ch3 (stch), tr in same st as ss, *ch2, dc in 2-ch sp, ch2**, 3tr in pc*, rep from * to * 6x and from * to ** 1x, tr in same st as first sts, join with ss to 3rd ch of stch. {32 sts, 16 2-ch sps}

R4: ch3 (stch), tr in same st as ss, 2tr in next st, *skip 2-ch sp, fpdtr around next st, skip 2-ch sp**, 2tr in next st, (2tr, ch2, 2tr) in next st, 2tr in next st*, rep from * to * 6x and from * to ** 1x, 2tr in next st, 2tr in same st as first sts, ch1, join with dc to 3rd ch of stch. {72 sts, 8 2-ch sps}

R5: ch3 (stch), ch2, fptr4tog over next 4 sts, *ch2, fptr around next st, ch2**, fptr4tog over next 4 sts, ch2, tr in 2-ch sp, ch2, fptr4tog over next 4 sts*, rep from * to * 6x and from * to ** 1x, fptr4tog over next 4 sts, ch2, join with ss to 3rd ch of stch. {32 sts, 32 2-ch sps}

R6: begpc in same st as ss, *ch5, skip (2-ch sp, 1 st & 2-ch sp)**, pc in next st*, rep from * to * 14x and from * to ** 1x, join with ss to top of first st. {16 sts, 16 5-ch sps}

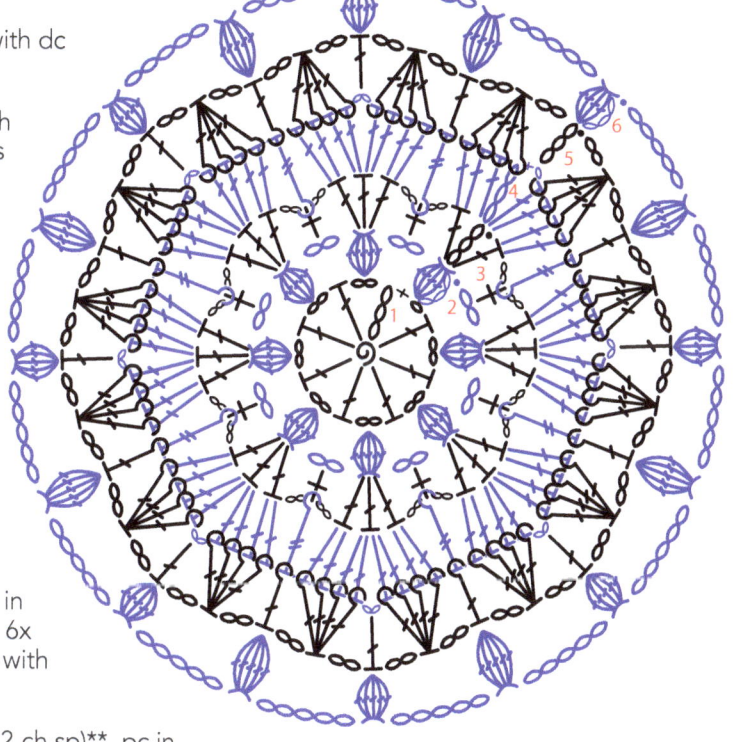

Giantess chart
Rounds 6-13

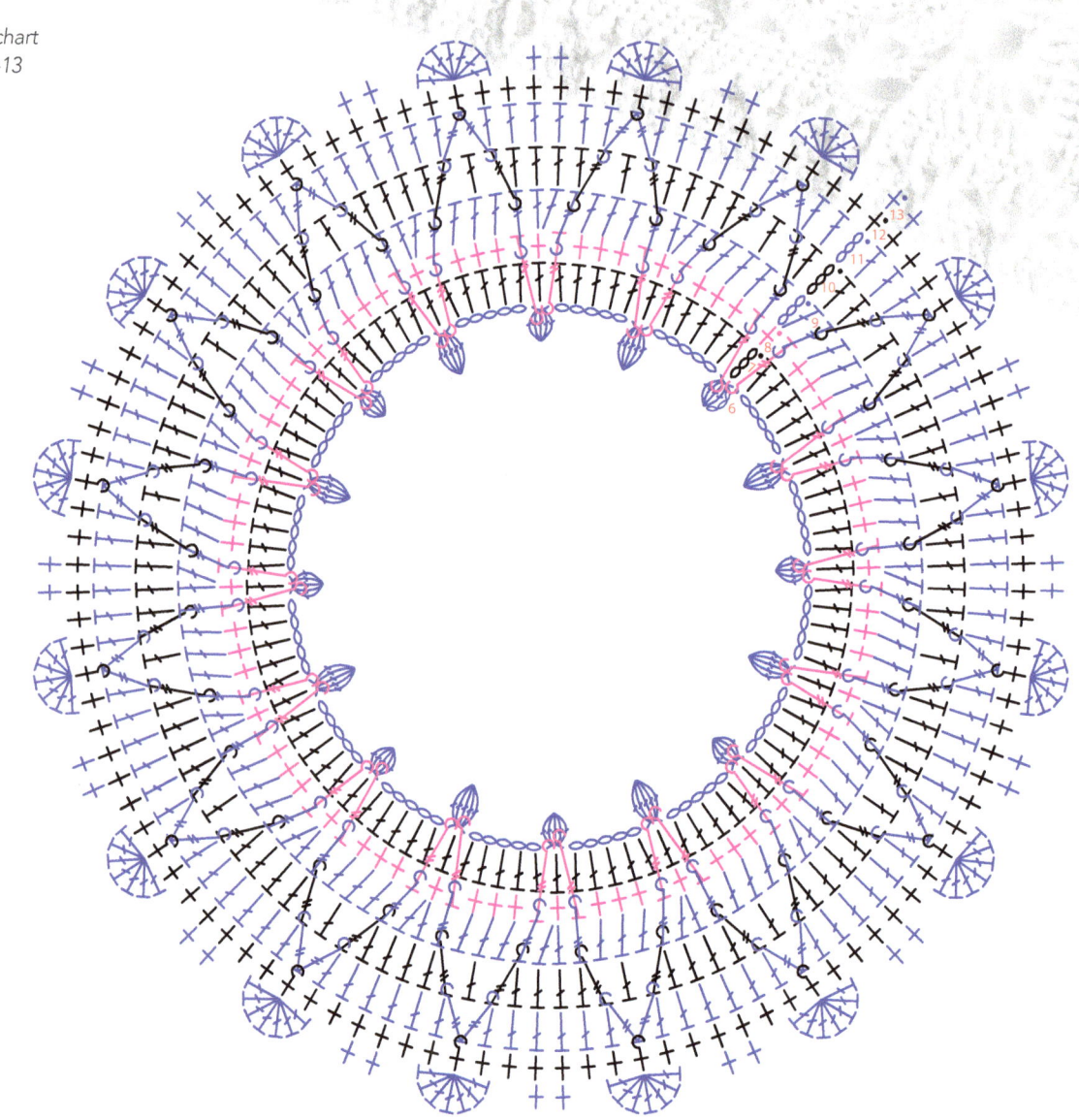

R7: ch3 (stch), *5tr in 5-ch sp** , tr in top of pc*, rep from * to * 14x and from * to ** 1x, join with ss to 3rd ch of stch. {96 sts}

R8: dc in same st as ss, fpdtr around pc of R6, *skip 1 st, dc in next 3 sts, fpdtr around next pc of R6, skip 1 st** , dc in next st, fpdtr around same pc of R6*, rep from * to * 14x and from * to ** 1x, join with ss to first st. {96 sts}

R9: ch3 (stch), *fpdtr around next st, tr in next 3 sts, fpdtr around next st** , 2tr in next st*, rep from * to * 14x and from * to ** 1x, tr in same st as first st, join with ss to 3rd ch of stch. {112 sts}

R10: ch3 (stch), *(tr in, fpdtr around) next st, skip 1 st, tr in next st, skip 1 st, (fpdtr around, tr in next st** , tr in next 2 sts*, rep from * to * 14x and from * to ** 1x, tr in next st, join with ss to 3rd ch of stch. {112 sts}

R11: ch3 (stch), tr in next 2 sts, * fpdtr2tog over same fp st as last st worked into and next fp st skipping st between, tr in same st just worked around** , tr in next 5 sts*, rep from * to * 14x and from * to ** 1x, tr in next 2 sts, join with ss to 3rd ch of stch. {112 sts}

R12: dc in same st as ss, dc in next 2 sts, *fpdc around next st** , dc in next 6 sts*, rep from * to * 14x and from * to ** 1x, dc in next 3 sts, join with ss to first st. {112 sts}

R13: dc in same st as ss, *skip 2 sts, 7tr in next st, skip 2 sts** , dc in next 2 sts*, rep from * to * 14x and from * to ** 1x, dc in next st, join with ss to first st. {144 sts}

Giantess chart
Rounds 13-17

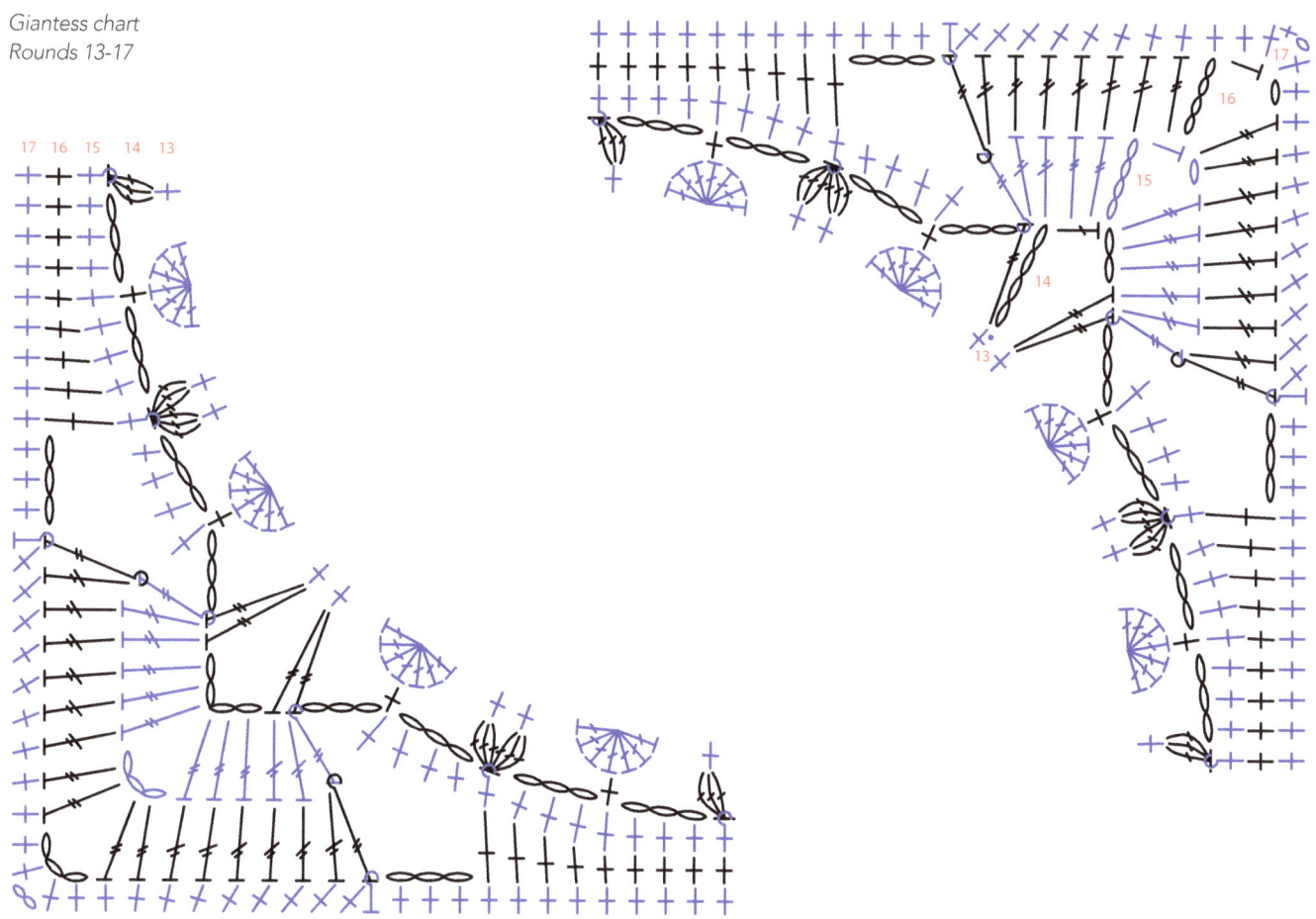

R14: ch4 (stch), dtr in same st as ss, *3x [ch3, skip 3 sts, dc in next st, ch3, skip 3 sts, 6trcl over next 2 sts with 3 sts begun in each st], ch3, skip 3 sts, dc in next st, ch3, skip 3 sts, 2dtr in next st**, ch4, 2dtr in next st*, rep from * to * 2x and from * to ** 1x, ch2, join with tr to 4th ch of stch. {11 sts, 8 3-ch sps on each side; 4 4-ch cnr sps}

R15: ch4 (stch), 2dtr over joining tr, *hdtr in next st, (hdtr in, fpdtr around) next st, skip 3 ch sp, 3x [dc in next st, 3dc in 3-ch sp, fpdc around next st, 3dc in 3-ch sp], dc in next st, skip 3-ch sp, (fpdtr around, hdtr in) next st, hdtr in next st**, (3dtr, ch3, 3dtr) in 4-ch cnr sp*, rep from * to * 2x and from * to ** 1x, 3dtr in same sp as first sts, ch1, join with htr to 4th ch of stch. {37 sts on each side; 4 3-ch cnr sps}

R16: ch4 (stch), dtr over joining htr, *hdtr in next 5 sts, (hdtr in, fpdtr around) next st, ch3, skip 4 sts, dc in next 17 sts, ch3, skip 4 sts, (fpdtr around, hdtr in) next st, hdtr in next 5 sts**, (2dtr, ch3, 2dtr) in 3-ch cnr sp*, rep from * to * 2x and from * to ** 1x, 2dtr in same sp as first sts, ch1, join with htr to 4th ch of stch. {35 sts, 2 3-ch sps on each side; 4 3-ch cnr sps}

R17: 2dc over joining htr, *dc in next 8 sts, (dc in, fphtr around) next st, 3dc in 3-ch sp, dc in next 17 sts, 3dc in 3-ch sp, (fphtr around, dc) in next st, dc in next 8 sts**, (2dc, ch2, 2dc) in 3-ch cnr sp*, rep from * to * 2x and from * to ** 1x, 2dc in same sp as first sts, ch1, join with dc to first st. {47 sts on each side, 4 2-ch cnr sps}

R18: ch3 (stch), *tr in next 11 sts, fpdtr around next st, tr in next 23 sts, fpdtr around next st, tr in next 11 sts**, (tr, ch2, tr) in 2-ch cnr sp*, rep from * to * 2x and * to ** 1x, tr in same sp as first st, ch1, join with dc to 3rd ch of stch.
{49 sts on each side; 4 2-ch cnr sps}

R19: ch3 (stch), *4x [ch2, fptr2tog over next 3 sts skipping middle st], (tr in, fptr around) next st, 3x [ch2, fptr2tog over next 3 sts skipping middle st], ch4, fptr3tog over next 5 sts skipping 2nd and 4th sts, ch4, 3x [fptr2tog over next 3 sts skipping middle st, ch2], (fptr around, tr in) next st, 4x [fptr2tog over next 3 sts skipping middle st, ch2]**, (tr, ch2, tr) in 2-ch cnr sp*, rep from * to * 2x and * to ** 1x, tr in same sp as first st, ch1, join with dc to 3rd ch of stch.
{21 sts, 14 2-ch sps, 2 4-ch sps on each side; 4 2-ch cnr sps}

R20: ch3 (stch), *tr in next st, 2x [2tr in 2-ch sp, tr in next st, fpdtr2tog around same st as last st and next st skipping 2-ch sp, tr in same st as last st], tr in next st, (tr in, fptr around) next st, tr in 2-ch sp, fptr around next st, 2tr in 2-ch sp, tr in next st, fpdtr2tog around same st as last st and next st skipping 2-ch sp, tr in same st as last st, 4tr in 4-ch sp, fptr around next st, 4tr in 4-ch sp, tr in next st, fpdtr2tog around same st as last st and next st skipping 2-ch sp, tr in same st as last st, 2tr in 2-ch sp, fptr around next st, tr in 2-ch sp, (fptr around, tr in) next st, tr in next st, 2x [tr in next st, fpdtr2tog around same st as last st and next st skipping 2-ch sp, tr in same st as last st, 2tr in 2-ch sp], tr in next st**, (tr, ch2, tr) in 2-ch cnr sp*, rep from * to * 2x and * to ** 1x, tr in same sp as first st, ch1, join with dc to 3rd ch of stch.
{53 sts on each side; 4 2-ch cnr sps}

R21: ch3 (stch), *tr in next 5 sts, 2x [fptr around next st, tr in next 4 sts], fptr2tog around same st as last st and next fp st skipping st between, tr in same st as last st, tr in next 3 sts, 2x [fptr around next st, tr in next 5 sts], fptr around next st, tr in next 4 sts, fptr2tog around same st as last st and next fp st skipping st between, tr in same st as last st, tr in next 3 sts, fptr around next st, tr in next 4 sts, fptr around next st, tr in next 5 sts**, (tr, ch2, tr) in 2-ch cnr sp*, rep from * to * 2x and * to ** 1x, tr in same sp as first st, ch1, join with dc to 3rd ch of stch. {55 sts on each side; 4 2-ch cnr sps}

R22: dc over joining dc, *dc in next 55 sts**, (dc, ch2, dc) in 2-ch cnr sp*, rep from * to * 2x and * to ** 1x, dc in same sp as first st, ch2, join with ss to first st. Fasten off. {57 sts on each side; 4 2-ch cnr sps}

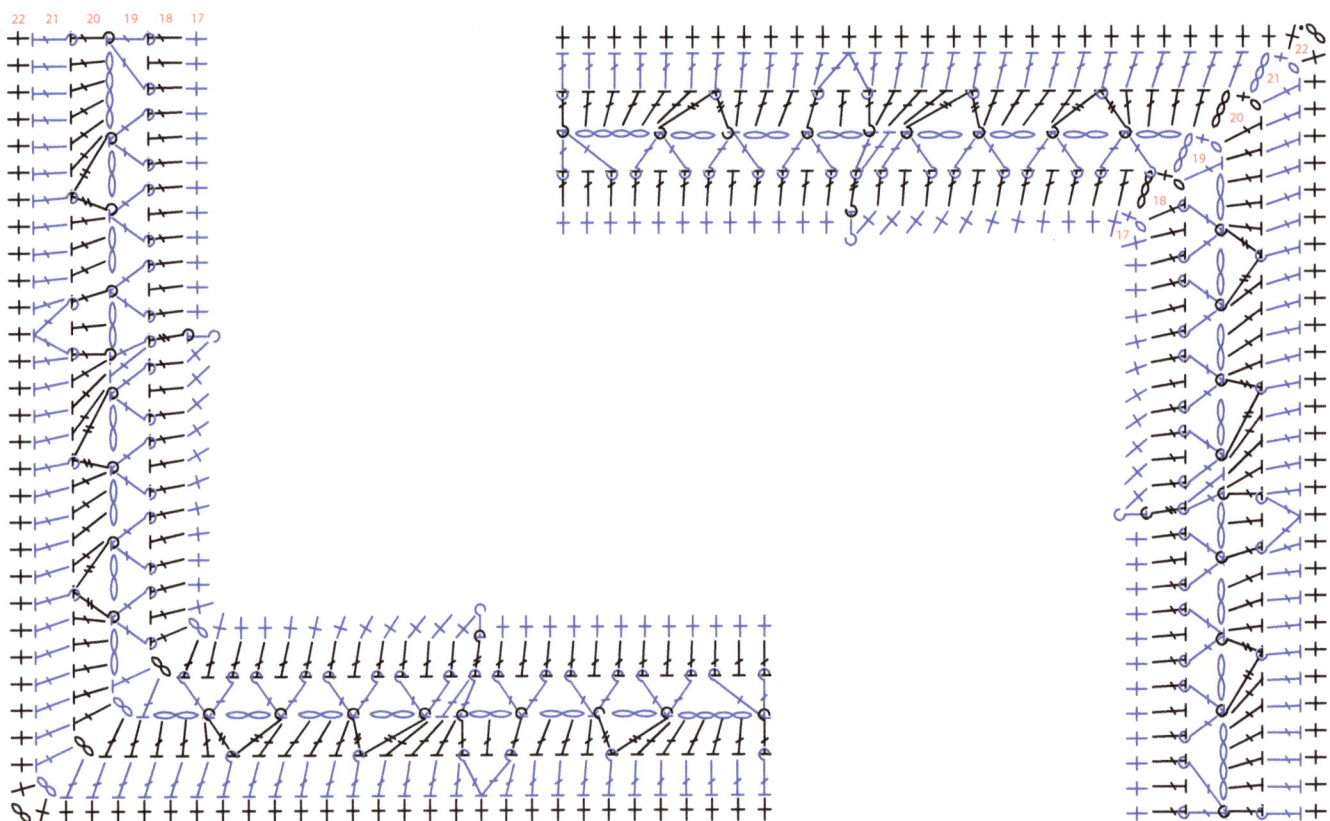

Giantess chart
Rounds 17-22

Maxim

Maxim is one of the 3 patterns named after characters in the book Rebecca by Daphne du Maurier that make up the Manderley Blanket.

Colours by Kim Siebenhausen

Colours by Mell Sappho

  248 m / 272 yd

Begin with mc with a long tail.

R1: ch3 (stch), 23tr, join with ss to 3rd ch of stch. {24 sts}

R2: ch3 (stch), *ch1, 3trcl in next st, ch1**, tr in next st*, rep from * to * 10x and from * to ** 1x, join with ss to 3rd ch of stch. {24 sts, 24 1-ch sps}

R3: fpdc around same st as ss, *dc in 1-ch sp**, fpdc around next st*, rep from * to * 22x and from * to ** 1x, join with ss to first st. {48 sts}

R4: *Don't work a false st.* ch3 (stch), 6tr in same st as ss, *skip 2 sts, dc in next st, skip 2 sts**, 7tr in next st*, rep from * to * 6x and from * to ** 1x, join with inv join to first true st. {64 sts}

R5: Attach with stdg dc to lbv of the 4th st of any 7-st group, dc in lbv of next st, *htr in lbv of next 2 sts, tr in lbv of next st, htr in lbv of next 2 sts**, dc in lbv of next 3 sts*, rep from * to * 6x and from * to ** 1x, dc in lbv of next st, join with ss to first st. {64 sts}

R6: dc in same st as ss, dc in next 63 sts, join with ss to first st. {64 sts}

R7: ch3 (stch), *ch1, 3trcl in next st, ch1**, tr in next st*, rep from * to * 30x and from * to ** 1x, join with ss to 3rd ch of stch. {64 sts, 64 1-ch sps}

R8: fpdc around same st as ss, *dc in 1-ch sp, skip 1 st, dc in 1-ch sp**, fpdc around next st*, rep from * to * 30x and from * to ** 1x, join with ss to first st. {96 sts}

R9: *Don't work a false st.* ch3 (stch), 6tr in same st as ss, *skip 2 sts, dc in next st, skip 2 sts**, 7tr in next st*, rep from * to * 14x and from * to ** 1x, join with inv join to first true st. {128 sts}

R10: Attach with stdg dc to lbv of the 4th st of any 7-st group, dc in lbv of next st, *htr in lbv of next 2 sts, tr in lbv of next st, htr in lbv of next 2 sts**, dc in lbv of next 3 sts*, rep from * to * 14x and from * to ** 1x, dc in lbv of next st, join with ss to first st. {128 sts}

R11: dc in same st as ss, dc in next 127 sts, join with ss to first st. {128 sts}

R12: ch3 (stch), tr in next st, *3trcl in next st, tr in next st, 2tr in next st, tr in next st, 3trcl in next st**, tr in next 3 sts*, rep from * to * 14x and from * to ** 1x, tr in next st, join with ss to 3rd ch of stch. {144 sts}

R13: fpdc around same st as ss, fpdc around next 143 sts, join with ss to first st. {144 sts}

Maxim chart
Rounds 1-17

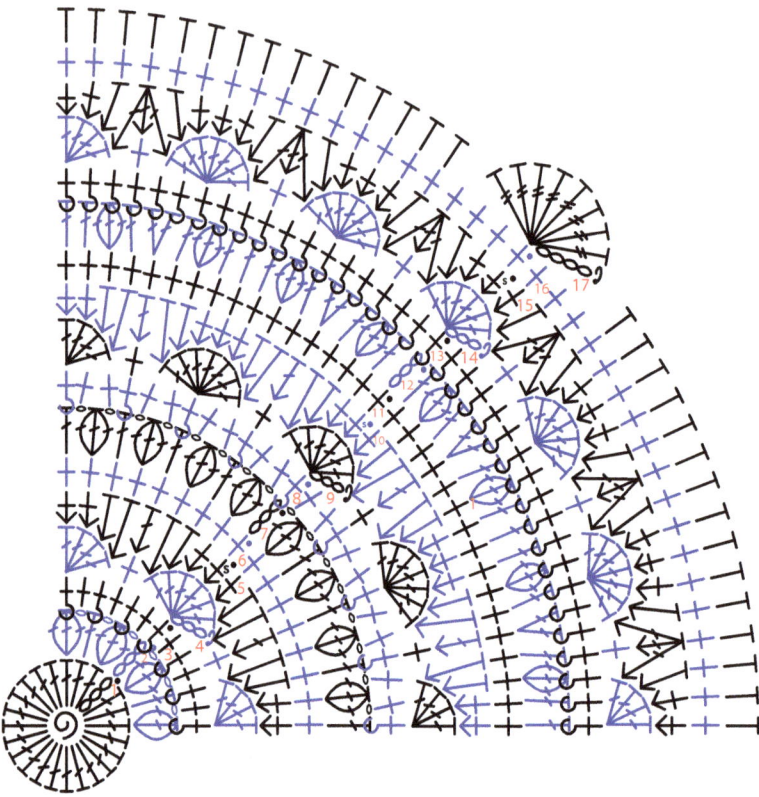

R14: Don't work a false st. ch3 (stch), 6tr in same st as ss, *skip 2 sts, dc in next st, skip 2 sts**, 7tr in next st*, rep from * to * 22x and from * to ** 1x, join with inv join to first true st. {192 sts}

R15: Attach with stdg dc to lbv of the 4th st of any 7-st group, dc in lbv of next st, *htr in lbv of next st, tr3tog in lbv of next 3 sts, htr in lbv of next st**, dc in lbv of next 3 sts*, rep from * to *22x and from * to ** 1x, dc in lbv of next st, join with ss to first st. {144 sts}

R16: dc in same st as ss, dc in next 143 sts, join with ss to first st. {144 sts}

R17: Don't work a false st. ch4 (stch), 8dtr in same st as ss, *skip 3 sts, htr in next 29 sts, skip 3 sts**, 9dtr in next st*, rep from * to * 2x and from * to ** 1x, join with inv join to first true st. {29 sts on each side; 4 9-st cnrs}

R18: Don't work a false st. Attach with ss to lbv of the first st of any 9-st cnr, ch4 (stch), dtr in same lbv, 2dtr in lbv of next 8 sts, *skip 3 sts, tr in lbv of next 3 sts, htr in lbv of next 3 sts, dc in lbv of next 11 sts, htr in lbv of next 3 sts, tr in lbv of next 3 sts, skip 3 sts**, 2dtr in lbv of next 9 sts*, rep from * to * 2x and from * to ** 1x, join with inv join to first true st. {23 sts on each side; 4 18-st cnrs}

R19: Attach with stdg tr to lbv of the 10th st of any 18-st cnr, tr in same lbv, 2tr in lbv of next st, *htr in lbv of next 2 sts, dc in lbv of next 3 sts, htr in lbv of next st, tr in lbv of next st, tr in next st, dc in next 21 sts, tr in next st, tr in lbv of next st, htr in lbv of next st, dc in lbv of next 3 sts, htr in lbv in next 2 sts, 2tr in lbv of next 2 sts**, ch2, 2tr in lbv of next 2 sts*, rep from * to * 2x and from * to ** 1x, ch1, join with dc to first st. {45 sts on each side; 4 2-ch cnr sps}

R20: dc over joining dc, *dc in next 45 sts**, (dc, ch2, dc) in 2-ch cnr sp*, rep from * to * 2x and * to ** 1x, dc in same sp as first st, ch1, join with dc to first st. {47 sts on each side; 4 2-ch cnr sps}

R21: ch2 (stch), *htr in next 47 sts**, (htr, ch2, htr) in 2-ch cnr sp*, rep from * to * 2x and * to ** 1x, htr in same sp as first st, ch1, join with dc to 2nd ch of stch. {49 sts on each side; 4 2-ch cnr sps}

R22: ch3 (stch), *tr in lbv of next 49 sts**, (tr, ch2, tr) in 2-ch cnr sp*, rep from * to * 2x and * to ** 1x, tr in same sp as first st, ch1, join with dc to 3rd ch of stch. {51 sts on each side; 4 2-ch cnr sps}

R23: dc over joining dc, *dc in next 51 sts**, (dc, ch2, dc) in 2-ch sp*, rep from * to * 2x and * to ** 1x, dc in same sp as first st, ch1, join with dc to first st. {53 sts on each side; 4 2-ch cnr sps}

R24: ch2 (stch), *htr in next 53 sts**, (htr, ch2, htr) in 2-ch cnr sp*, rep from * to * 2x and * to ** 1x, htr in same sp as first st, ch1, join with dc to 2nd ch of stch. {55 sts on each side; 4 2-ch cnr sps}

R25: dc over joining dc, *dc in next 55 sts**, (dc, ch2, dc) in 2-ch sp*, rep from * to * 2x and * to ** 1x, dc in same sp as first st, ch2, join with ss to first st. Fasten off. {57 sts on each side; 4 2-ch cnr sps}

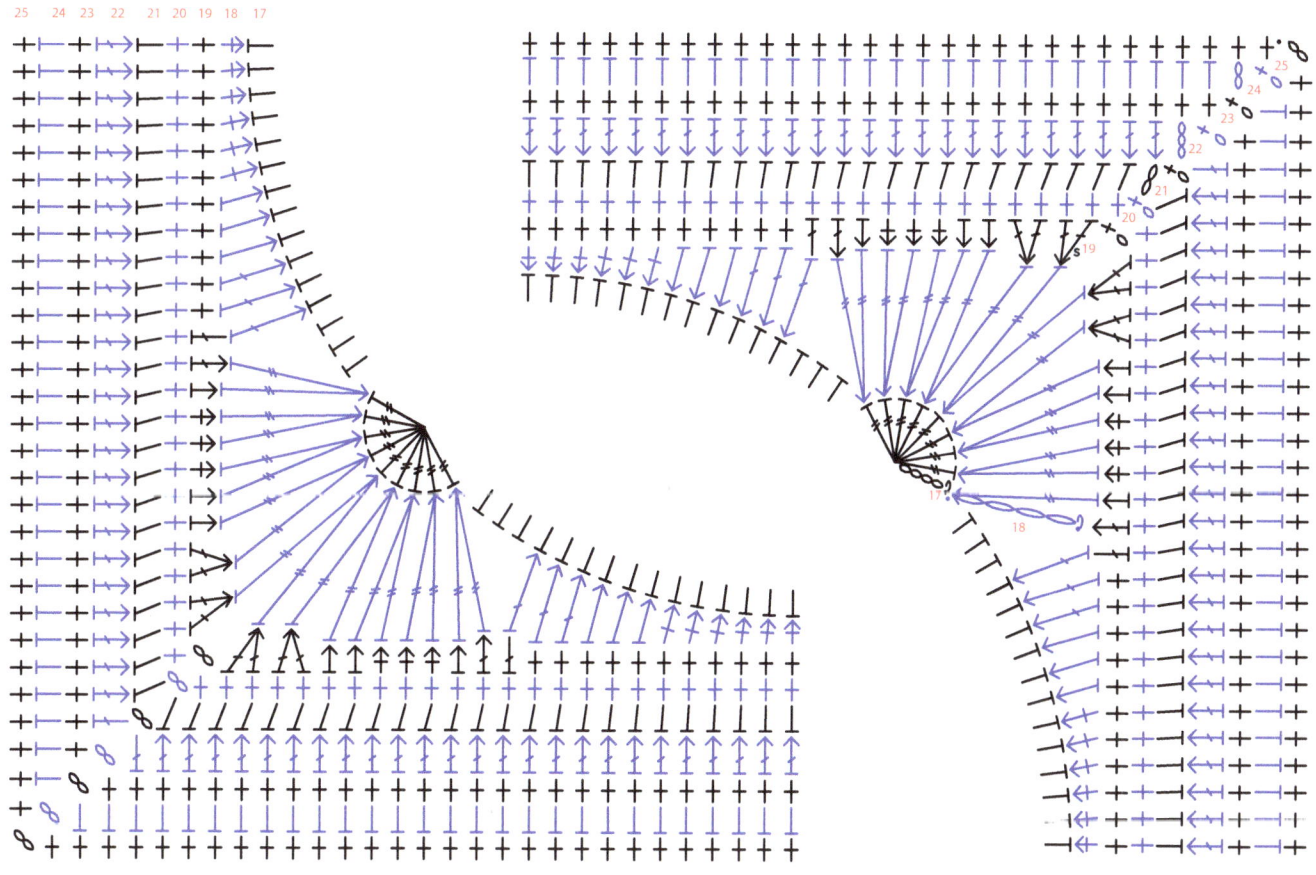

Maxim chart
Rounds 17-25

Melbourne

Named for the city I grew up in. It's versatile, classic and timeless. Just like Melbourne.

Colours by Chelsea Butler

Colours by Mell Sappho

  154 m / 169 yd

Melbourne can be extended easily by repeating Rounds 16 to 19 as many times as needed. This pattern will need blocking, particularly if you find a swirl develops.

Begin with mc.

R1: ch4 (stch), *ch1, dtr, ch1**, dtr, ch3, dtr*, rep from * to * 2x and * to ** 1x, dtr, ch1, join with htr to 4th ch of stch. {3 sts, 2 1-ch sps on each side; 4 3-ch cnr sps}

R2: 2dc over joining htr, *2x [dc in next st, dc in 1-ch sp], dc in next st**, (2dc, ch2, 2dc) in 3-ch sp*, rep from * to * 2x and * to ** 1x, 2dc in same sp as first sts, ch1, join with dc to first st. {9 sts on each side; 4 2-ch cnr sps}

R3: ch3 (stch), *tr in next 9 sts**, (tr, ch2, tr) in 2-ch sp*, rep from * to * 2x and * to ** 1x, tr in same sp as first st, ch1, join with dc to 3rd ch of stch. {11 sts on each side; 4 2-ch cnr sps}

R4: dc over joining dc, *dc in next 11 sts**, (dc, ch2, dc) in 2-ch sp*, rep from * to * 2x and * to ** 1x, dc in same sp as first st, ch1, join with dc to first st. {13 sts on each side; 4 2-ch cnr sps}

R5: ch4 (stch), *6x [ch1, skip 1 st, dtr in next st], ch1, skip 1 st**, (dtr, ch3, dtr) in 2-ch sp*, rep from * to * 2x and * to ** 1x, dtr in same sp as first st, ch1, join with htr to 4th ch of stch. {8 sts, 7 1-ch sps on each side; 4 3-ch cnr sps}

R6: 2dc over joining htr, *7x [dc in next st, dc in 1-ch sp], dc in next st**, (2dc, ch2, 2dc) in 3-ch sp*, rep from * to * 2x and * to ** 1x, 2dc in same sp as first sts, ch1, join with dc to first st. {19 sts on each side; 4 2-ch cnr sps}

R7: ch3 (stch), *tr in next 19 sts**, (tr, ch2, tr) in 2-ch sp*, rep from * to * 2x and * to ** 1x, tr in same sp as first st, ch1, join with dc to 3rd ch of stch. {21 sts on each side; 4 2-ch cnr sps}

R8: dc over joining dc, *dc in next 21 sts**, (dc, ch2, dc) in 2-ch sp*, rep from * to * 2x and * to ** 1x, dc in same sp as first st, ch1, join with dc to first st. {23 sts on each side; 4 2-ch cnr sps}

R9: ch4 (stch), *11x [ch1, skip 1 st, dtr in next st], ch1, skip 1 st**, (dtr, ch3, dtr) in 2-ch sp*, rep from * to * 2x and * to ** 1x, dtr in same sp as first st, ch1, join with htr to 4th ch of stch. {13 sts, 12 1-ch sps on each side; 4 3-ch cnr sps}

R10: 2dc over joining htr, *12x [dc in next st, dc in 1-ch sp], dc in next st**, (2dc, ch2, 2dc) in 3-ch sp*, rep from * to * 2x and * to ** 1x, 2dc in same sp as first sts, ch1, join with dc to first st. {29 sts on each side; 4 2-ch cnr sps}

R11: ch3 (stch), *tr in next 29 sts**, (tr, ch2, tr) in 2-ch sp*, rep from * to * 2x and * to ** 1x, tr in same sp as first st, ch1, join with dc to 3rd ch of stch. {31 sts on each side; 4 2-ch cnr sps}

R12: dc over joining dc, *dc in next 31 sts**, (dc, ch2, dc) in 2-ch sp*, rep from * to * 2x and * to ** 1x, dc in same sp as first st, ch1, join with dc to first st. {33 sts on each side; 4 2-ch cnr sps}

R13: ch4 (stch), *16x [ch1, skip 1 st, dtr in next st], ch1, skip 1 st** (dtr, ch3, dtr) in 2-ch sp*, rep from * to * 2x and * to ** 1x, dtr in same sp as first st, ch1, join with htr to 4th ch of stch. {18 sts, 17 1-ch sps on each side; 4 3-ch cnr sps}

R14: 2dc over joining htr, *17x [dc in next st, dc in 1-ch sp], dc in next st** (2dc, ch2, 2dc) in 3-ch sp*, rep from * to * 2x and * to ** 1x, 2dc in same sp as first sts, ch1, join with dc to first st. {39 sts on each side; 4 2-ch cnr sps}

R15: ch3 (stch), *tr in next 39 sts** (tr, ch2, tr) in 2-ch sp*, rep from * to * 2x and * to ** 1x, tr in same sp as first st, ch1, join with dc to 3rd ch of stch. {41 sts on each side; 4 2-ch cnr sps}

R16: dc over joining dc, *dc in next 41 sts** (dc, ch2, dc) in 2-ch sp*, rep from * to * 2x and * to ** 1x, dc in same sp as first st, ch1, join with dc to first st. {43 sts on each side; 4 2-ch cnr sps}

R17: ch4 (stch), *21x [ch1, skip 1 st, dtr in next st], ch1, skip 1 st** (dtr, ch3, dtr) in 2-ch sp*, rep from * to * 2x and * to ** 1x, dtr in same sp as first st, ch1, join with htr to 4th ch of stch. {23 sts, 22 1-ch sps on each side; 4 3-ch cnr sps}

R18: 2dc over joining htr, *22x [dc in next st, dc in 1-ch sp], dc in next st** (2dc, ch2, 2dc) in 3-ch sp*, rep from * to * 2x and * to ** 1x, 2dc in same sp as first sts, ch1, join with dc to first st. {49 sts on each side; 4 2-ch cnr sps}

R19: ch3 (stch), *tr in next 49 sts** (tr, ch2, tr) in 2-ch sp*, rep from * to * 2x and * to ** 1x, tr in same sp as first st, ch2, join with ss to 3rd ch of stch. Fasten off. {51 sts on each side; 4 2-ch cnr sps}

Nymph

I started with the thought of a lotus or water lily flower but wanted something a little more exotic. So the water based deity it is.

Colours by Chris Wilkins

Colours by Joanne Waring

  293 m / 321 yd

If making more than one of these squares, make sure you join R20 at the same point to keep the centre orientation the same.

Begin with mc.

R1: ch1, *dc, 5tr*, rep from * to * 3x, join with ss to first st. {24 sts}

R2: ch3 (stch), *ch2, skip 2 sts, dc in next st, ch2, skip 2 sts**, tr in next st*, rep from * to *2x and * to ** 1x, join with ss to 3rd ch of stch. {8 sts, 8 2-ch sps}

R3: dc in same st as ss, *3dc in 2-ch sp**, dc in next st*, rep from * to * 6x and * to ** 1x, join with ss to first st. {32 sts}

R4: ch3 (stch), tr in same st as ss, *tr in next 3 sts**, 2tr in next st*, rep from * to * 6x and * to ** 1x, join with ss to 3rd ch of stch. {40 sts}

R5: dc in same st as ss, dc in next 39 sts, join with ss to first st. {40 sts}

R6: dc in same st as ss, *ch1, fphdtr around R4 st below next st, ch1, skip 1 st**, dc in next st*, rep from * to * 18x and * to ** 1x, join with ss to first st. {40 sts, 40 1-ch sps}

R7: ch3 (stch), *tr in 1-ch sp, fphdtr around next st, tr in 1-ch sp**, tr in next st*, rep from * to * 18x and * to ** 1x, join with ss to 3rd ch of stch. {80 sts}

R8: dc in same st as ss, *skip 1 st, (fphdtr around, tr in, fphdtr around) next st, skip 1 st**, dc in next st*, rep from * to * 18x and * to ** 1x, join with ss to first st. {80 sts}

R9: *This round will be very ruffled.* ch3 (stch), *(fptr around, tr in) next st, ch1, 5tr in next st, ch1, (tr in, fptr around) next st**, tr in next st*, rep from * to * 18x and * to ** 1x, join with ss to 3rd ch of stch. {200 sts, 40 1-ch sps}

R10: ch1, fpdc around 2 fp sts below at the same time skipping st ss'd into, *dc in next st, dc in both 1-ch sps either side of next 5 sts at the same time, dc in next st**, fpdc around next 2 fp sts at the same time skipping st between*, rep from * to * 18x and * to ** 1x, join with ss to first st. {80 sts}

R11: dc in same st as ss, dc in next 79 sts. {80 sts}

R12: dc in same st as ss, *ch2, skip 1 st**, dc in next st*, rep from * to * 38x and * to ** 1x, join with ss to first st. {40 sts, 40 2-ch sps}

Nymph chart
Rounds 1-12

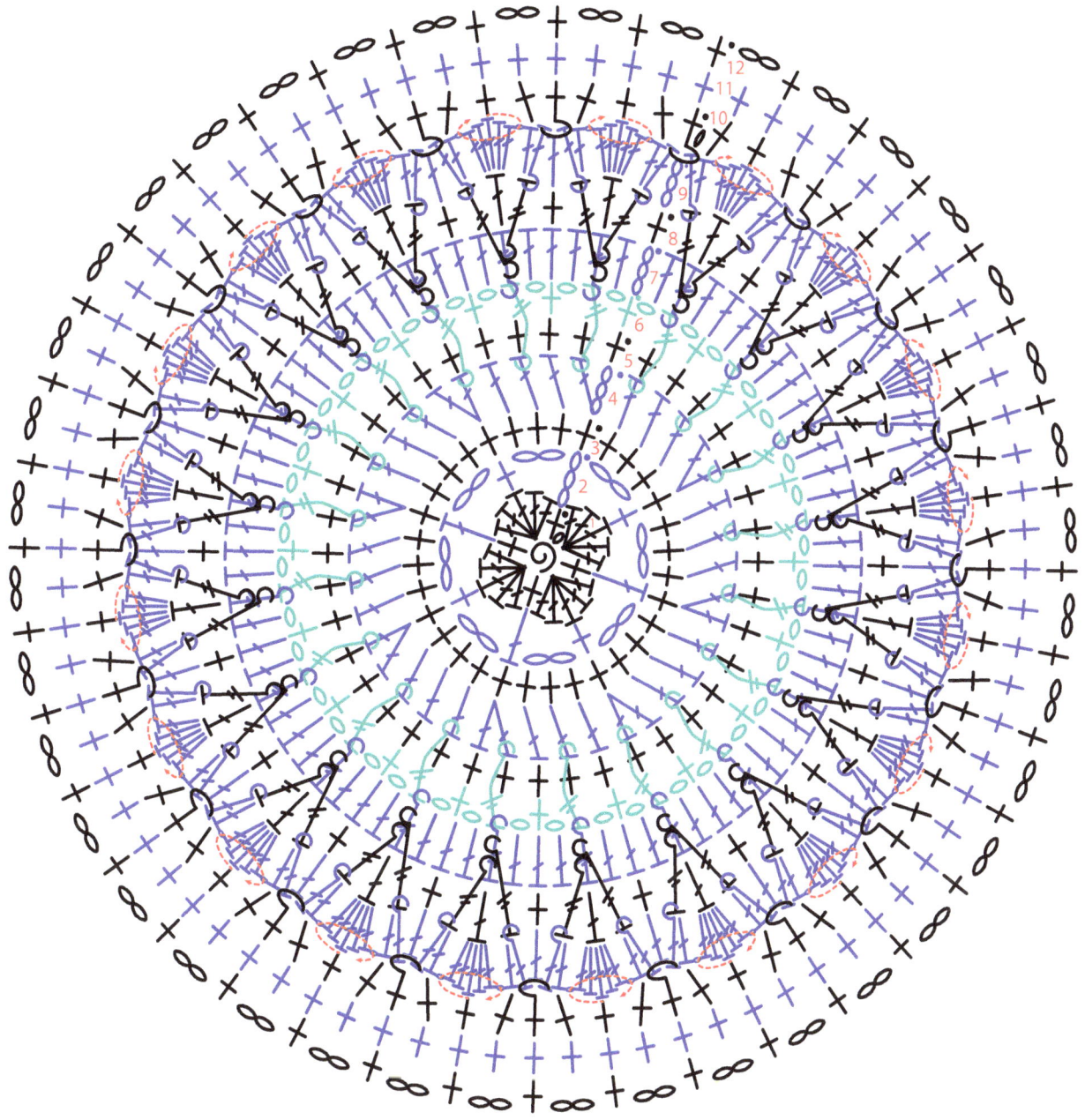

Nymph - Size 4 Patterns • 79

Nymph chart
Rounds 12-21

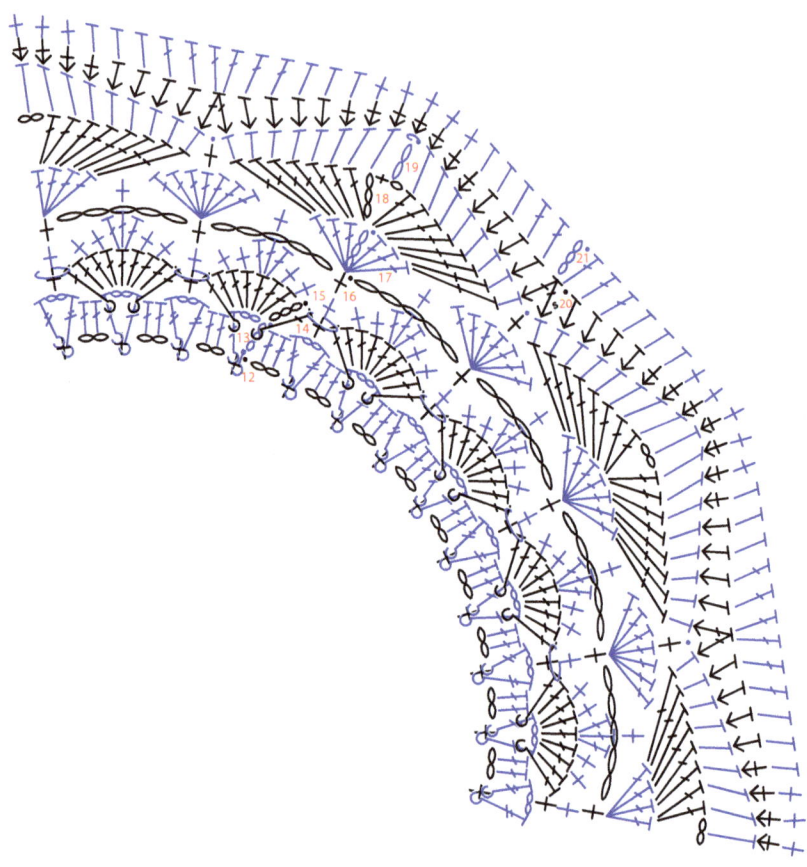

R13: fpss around st ss'd into, ch3 (stch), ch2, fphdtr around same st as ss, *2tr in 2-ch sp**, (fphdtr around, ch2, fphdtr around) next st*, rep from * to * 38x and * to ** 1x, join with ss to 3rd ch of stch. {160 sts, 40 2-ch sps}

R14: ch3 (stch), *5tr in 2-ch sp, (tr in, fptr around) next st, skip 3 sts, dc in 2-ch sp, skip 3 sts**, (fptr around, tr in) next st*, rep from * to * 18x and * to ** 1x, fptr around next st, join with ss to 3rd ch of stch. {200 sts}

R15: *dc next 2 sts, 3tr in next st, dc in next 2 sts, skip 1 st, fpdc around next 2 fp sts at the same time skipping st between**, skip 1 st*, rep from * to * 18x and * to ** 1x, do not join. {160 sts}

R16: dc in last st of R15, *ch5, skip 7 sts**, dc in next st*, rep from * to * 18x and * to ** 1x, join with ss to first st. {20 sts, 20 5-ch sps}

R17: ch3 (stch), 3tr in same st as ss, *dc in 5-ch sp**, 7tr in next st*, rep from * to * 18x and * to ** 1x, 3tr in same st as first sts, join with ss to 3rd ch of stch. {160 sts}

R18: ch3 (stch), tr in same st as ss, *2tr in next 3 sts, skip 4 sts, dc in next st, skip 4 sts, 2tr in next 3 sts**, (2tr, ch2, 2tr) in next st*, rep from * to * 8x and * to ** 1x, 2tr in same st as first sts, ch1, join with dc to 3rd ch of stch. {170 sts, 10 2-ch sps}

R19: ch2 (stch), *htr in next 8 sts, ss in next st, htr in next 8 sts**, htr in 2-ch sp*, rep from * to * 8x and * to ** 1x, join with inv join to first true st. {180 sts}

R20: Attach with a stdg tr2tog in lbv of the sts either side of any ss, *htr in lbv of next 4 sts, dc in lbv of next 7 sts, htr in lbv of next 4 sts**, tr2tog in lbv of next 3 sts skipping the middle st*, rep from * to * 8x and * to ** 1x, join with ss to first st. {160 sts}

R21: ch3 (stch), *tr in next 2 sts, htr in next 3 sts, dc in next 5 sts, htr in next 3 sts, tr in next 2 sts**, 2tr in next st*, rep from * to * 8x and * to ** 1x, tr in same st as first st, join with ss to 3rd ch of stch. {170 sts}

Nymph chart
Rounds 21-28

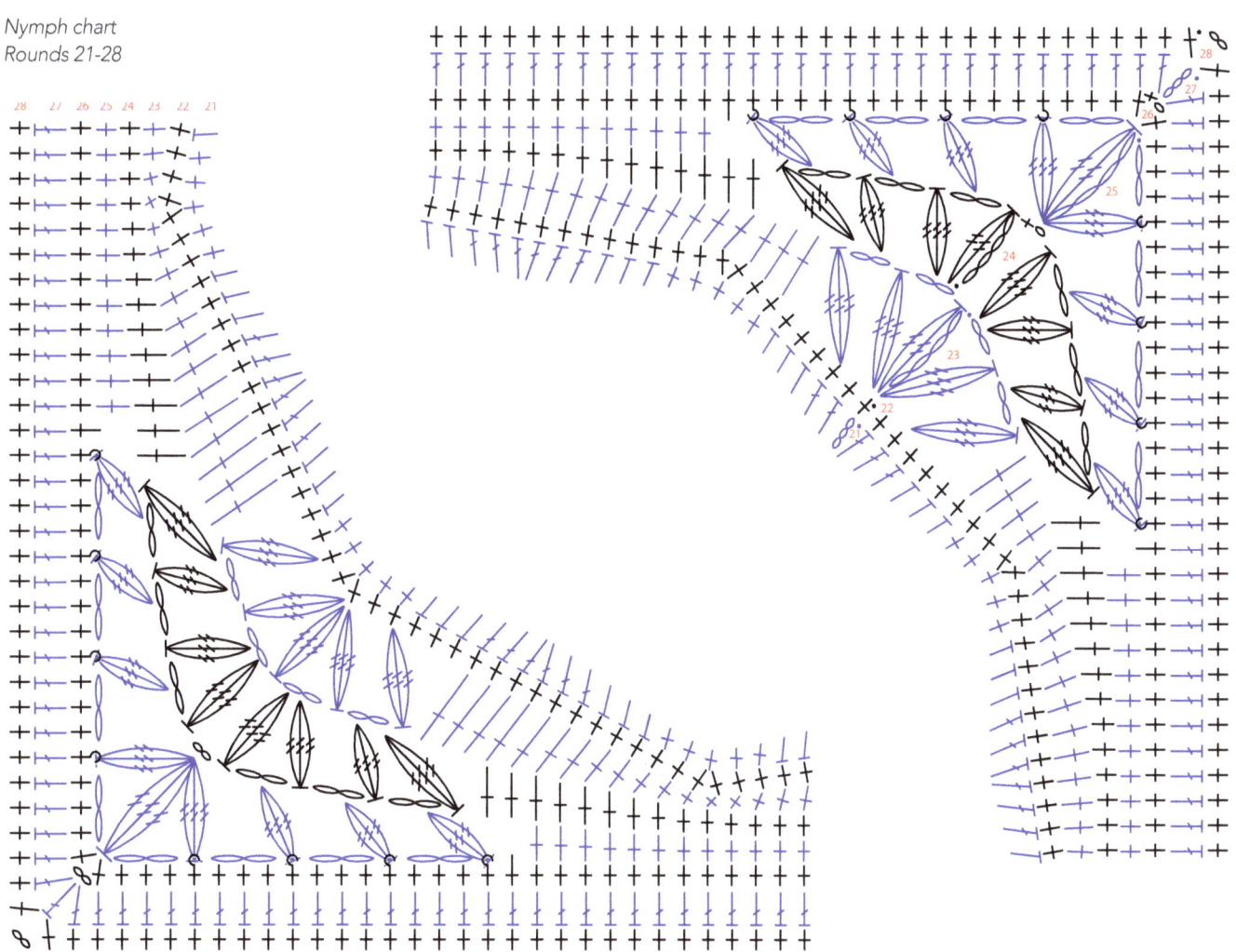

R22: dc in same st as ss, dc in next 7 sts, *2dc in next st**, dc in next 16 sts*, rep from * to * 8x and * to ** 1x, dc in next 8 sts, join with ss to first st. {180 sts}

R23: ch4, (2dtrcl, ch2, 3dtrcl) in same st as ss, *ch2, skip 1 st, 3dtrcl in next st, skip 3 sts, dc in next 34 sts, skip 3 sts, 3dtrcl in next st, ch2, skip 1 st**, (2x [3dtrcl, ch2], 3dtrcl) in next st*, rep from * to * 2x and * to ** 1x, 3dtrcl in same sp as first sts, ch2, join with ss to top of 2dtrcl. {34 sts on each side; 4 (5-st & 4 2-ch sp) cnrs}

R24: ss to 2-ch sp, ch4 (stch), (2dtrcl, ch2, 3dtrcl) in same sp, skip 1 st, 2x [ch2, 3dtrcl] in 2-ch sp, *skip 4 sts, dc in next 28 sts, skip 4 sts**, 3x [(3dtrcl, ch2, 3dtrcl, ch2) in 2-ch sp, skip 1 st], (3dtrcl, ch2, 3dtrcl) in 2-ch sp*, rep from * to * 2x and * to ** 1x, 2x [(3dtrcl, ch2) in 2-ch sp, skip 1 st], (3dtrcl, ch2, 3dtrcl) in 2-ch sp, ch1, join with dc to top of 2dtrcl. {28 sts on each side; 4 (8-st & 7 2-ch sp) cnrs}

R25: ch4 (stch), (2dtrcl, ch2, 3dtrcl) over joining dc, *3x [ch2, skip 1 st, 3dtrcl in 2-ch sp], skip 3 sts, dc in next 24 sts, skip 3 sts, 3x [3dtrcl in 2-ch sp, ch2, skip 1 st]**, (2x [3dtrcl, ch2], 3dtrcl) in 2-ch cnr sp*, rep from * to * 2x and * to ** 1x, 3dtrcl in same sp as first sts, ch2, join with ss to top of 2dtrcl. {24 sts on each side; 4 (9-st & 8 2-ch sp) cnrs}

R26: dc in same st as ss, *4x [3dc in 2-ch sp, fpdc around next st], dc between last and next sts, dc in next 24 sts, dc between last and next sts, 4x [fpdc around next st, 3dc in 2-ch sp]**, (dc, ch2, dc) in next st*, rep from * to * 2x and * to ** 1x, dc in same st as first st, ch1, join with dc to first st. {60 sts on each side; 4 2-ch cnr sps}

R27: ch3 (stch), tr over joining dc, *tr in next 60 sts**, 3tr in 2-ch cnr sp*, rep from * to * 2x and * to ** 1x, tr in same sp as first sts, join with ss to 3rd ch of stch. {60 sts on each side; 4 3-st cnrs}

R28: dc in same st as ss, *dc in next 62 sts**, (dc, ch2, dc) in next st*, rep from * to * 2x and * to ** 1x, dc in same st as first st, ch2, join with ss to first st. Fasten off. {64 sts on each side; 4 2-ch cnr sps}

Pagoda

Named Pagoda for the stacked pagoda-like shapes throughout the square.

Colours by Chelsea Butler

Colours by Kim Siebenhausen

  219 m / 240 yd

When instructed to work into chains, work over the top 2 strands.

Begin with mc.

R1: ch3 (stch), 15tr, join with ss to 3rd ch of stch. {16 sts}

R2: dc in same st as ss, *ch2, skip 1 st, dc in next st, ch2, skip 1 st**, (dc, ch2, dc) in next st*, rep from * to * 2x and * to ** 1x, dc in same st as first st, ch1, join with dc to first st. {3 sts, 2 2-ch sps on each side; 4 2-ch cnr sps}

R3: ch3 (stch), tr over joining dc, *tr in next st, 2trcl in 2-ch sp, ch1, skip 1 st, 2trcl in 2-ch sp, tr in next st**, (2tr, ch2, 2tr) in 2-ch cnr sp*, rep from * to * 2x and * to ** 1x, 2tr in same sp as first sts, ch1, join with dc to 3rd ch of stch. {8 sts on each side; 4 2-ch cnr sps}

R4: ch3 (stch), ch2, dc over joining dc, *dc in next 3 sts, fpdc around next st, ch2, tr in 1-ch sp, ch2, fpdc around next st, dc in next 3 sts**, (dc, ch2, tr, ch2, dc) in 2-ch cnr sp*, rep from * to * 2x and * to ** 1x, dc in same sp as first sts, ch2, join with ss to 3rd ch of stch. {11 sts, 4 2-ch sps on each side; 4 1-st cnrs}

R5: dc in same st as ss, *ch3, skip (2-ch sp & 1 st), tr in blo of next 3 sts, ch1, skip (1 st & 2-ch sp), dc in next st, ch1, skip (2-ch sp & 1 st), tr in blo of next 3 sts, ch3, skip (1 st & 2-ch sp)**, dc in next st*, rep from * to * 2x and * to ** 1x, join with ss to first st. {7 sts, 2 3-ch sps, 2 1-ch sps on each side; 4 1-st cnrs}

R6: ch3 (stch), tr in same st as ss, *tr in each of next 3 chs, tr in blo of next 3 sts, tr in next ch, tr in blo of next st, tr in next ch, tr in blo of next 3 sts, tr in each of next 3 chs**, (2tr, ch2, 2tr) in next sts*, rep from * to * 2x and * to ** 1x, 2tr in same st as first sts, ch1, join with dc to 3rd ch of stch. {19 sts on each side; 4 2-ch cnr sps}

R7: dc over joining dc, *dc in blo of next 19 sts**, (dc, ch2, dc) in 2-ch cnr sp*, rep from * to * 2x and * to ** 1x, dc in same sp as first st, ch1, join with dc to first st. {21 sts on each side; 4 2-ch cnr sps}

R8: dc over joining dc, *ch2, skip 2 sts, dc in next st, 4x [ch3, skip 3 sts, dc in next st], ch2, skip 2 sts**, (dc, ch2, dc) in 2-ch cnr sp*, rep from * to * 2x and * to ** 1x, dc in same sp as first st, ch1, join with dc to first st. {7 sts, 2 2-ch sps, 4 3-ch sps on each side; 4 2-ch cnr sps}

R9: ch3 (stch), *tr in blo of next st, tr in each of next 2 chs, tr in blo of next st, 4x [ch1, 2trcl in 3-ch sp, ch1, tr in blo of next st], tr in each of next 2 chs, tr in blo of next st**, (tr, ch2, tr) in 2-ch cnr sp*, rep from * to * 2x and * to ** 1x, tr in same sp as first st, ch1, join with dc to 3rd ch of stch. {17 sts, 8 1-ch sps on each side; 4 2-ch cnr sps}

Pagoda chart
Rounds 1-16

R10: ch3 (stch), ch2, dc over joining dc, *dc in next 5 sts, dc in 1-ch sp, 3x [fpdc around next st, dc in 1-ch sp, ch2, tr in next st, ch2, dc in 1-ch sp], fpdc around next st, dc in 1-ch sp, dc in next 5 sts**, (dc, ch2, tr, ch2, dc) in 2-ch cnr sp*, rep from * to * 2x and * to ** 1x, dc in same sp as first sts, ch2, join with ss to 3rd ch of stch.
{27 sts, 8 2-ch sps on each side; 4 1-st cnrs}

R11: dc in same st as ss, *ch3, skip (2-ch sp & 1 st), tr in blo of next 6 sts, ch1, skip (2 sts & 2-ch sp), 2x [dc in next st, ch3, skip (2-ch sp, 3 sts & 2-ch sp)], dc in next st, ch1, skip (2-ch sp & 2 sts), tr in blo of next 6 sts, ch3, skip (1 st & 2-ch sp)**, dc in next st*, rep from * to * 2x and * to ** 1x, join with ss to first st.
{15 sts, 4 3-ch sps & 2 1-ch sps on each side; 4 1-st cnrs}

R12: ch3 (stch), tr in same st as ss, *tr in each of next 3 chs, tr in blo of next 6 sts, tr in next ch, 2x [tr in blo of next st, tr in each of next 3 chs], tr in blo of next st, tr in next ch, tr in blo of next 6 sts, tr in each of next 3 chs**, (2tr, ch2, 2tr) in next st*, rep from * to * 2x and * to ** 1x, 2tr in same st as first sts, ch1, join with dc to 3rd ch of stch.
{33 sts on each side; 4 2-ch cnr sps}

R13: dc over joining dc, *dc in blo of next 33 sts**, (dc, ch2, dc) in 2-ch cnr sp*, rep from * to * 2x and * to ** 1x, dc in same sp as first st, ch1, join with dc to first st. {35 sts on each side; 4 2-ch cnr sps}

R14: dc over joining dc, *2x [ch2, skip 2 sts, dc in next st], 6x [ch3, skip 3 sts, dc in next st], ch2, skip 2 sts, dc in next st, ch2, skip 2 sts**, (dc, ch2, dc) in 2-ch cnr sp*, rep from * to * 2x and * to ** 1x, dc in same sp as first st, ch1, join with dc to 3rd ch of stch. {11 sts, 4 2-ch sps, 6 3-ch sps on each side; 4 2-ch cnr sps}

R15: ch3 (stch), *2x [tr in blo of next st, tr in each of next 2 chs], tr in blo of next st, 6x [ch1, 2trcl in 3-ch sp, ch1, tr in blo of next st], 2x [tr in each of next 2 chs, tr in blo of next st]**, (tr, ch2, tr) in 2-ch cnr sp*, rep from * to * 2x and * to ** 1x, tr in same sp as first sts, ch1, join with dc to 3rd ch of stch. {27 sts, 12 1-ch sps on each side; 4 2-ch cnr sps}

R16: ch3 (stch), ch2, dc over joining dc, *dc in next 8 sts, dc in 1-ch sp, 5x [fpdc around next st, dc in 1-ch sp, ch2, tr in next st, ch2, dc in 1-ch sp], fpdc around next st, dc in 1-ch sp, dc in next 8 sts**, (dc, ch2, tr, ch2, dc) in 2-ch cnr sp*, rep from * to * 2x and * to ** 1x, dc in same sp as first sts, ch2, join with ss to 3rd ch of stch.
{41 sts, 12 2-ch sps on each side; 4 1-st cnrs}

Pagoda chart
Rounds 16-24

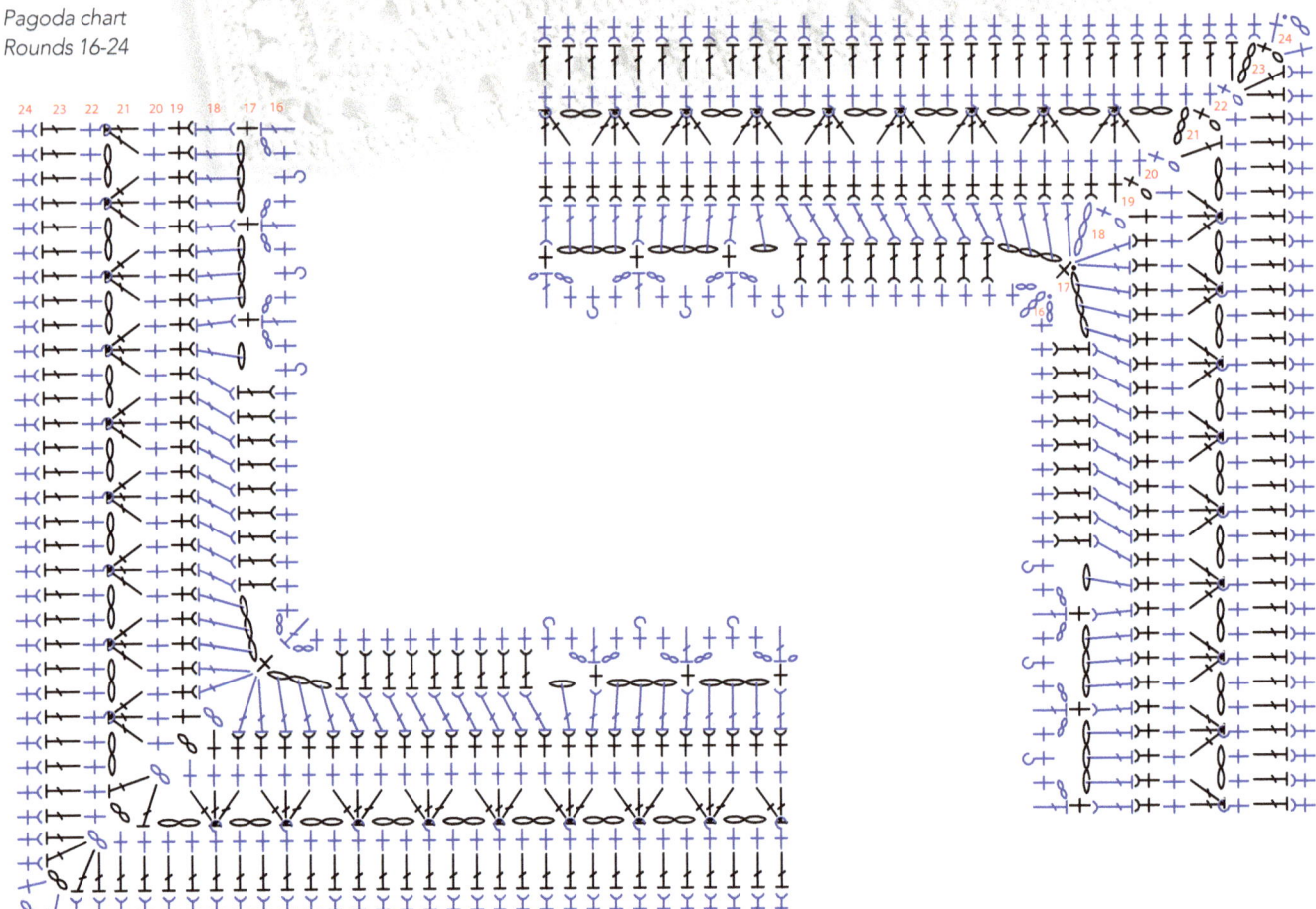

R17: dc in same st as ss, *ch3, skip (2-ch sp & 1 st), tr in blo of next 9 sts, ch1, skip (2 sts & 2-ch sp), 4x [dc in next st, ch3, skip (2-ch sp, 3 sts & 2-ch sp)], dc in next st, ch1, skip (2-ch sp & 2 sts), tr in blo of next 9 sts, ch3, skip (1 st & 2-ch sp)**, dc in next st*, rep from * to * 2x and * to ** 1x, join with ss to first st.
{23 sts, 6 3-ch sps & 2 1-ch sps on each side; 4 1-st cnrs}

R18: ch3 (stch), tr in same st as ss, *tr in each of next 3 chs, tr in blo of next 9 sts, tr in next ch, 4x [tr in blo of next st, tr in each of next 3 chs], tr in blo of next st, tr in next ch, tr in blo of next 9 sts, tr in each of next 3 chs**, (2tr, ch2, 2tr) in next st*, rep from * to * 2x and * to ** 1x, 2tr in same st as first sts, ch1, join with dc to 3rd ch of stch.
{47 sts on each side; 4 2-ch cnr sps}

R19: dc over joining dc, *dc in blo of next 47 sts**, (dc, ch2, dc) in 2-ch cnr sp*, rep from * to * 2x and * to ** 1x, dc in same sp as first st, ch1, join with dc to first st. {49 sts on each side; 4 2-ch cnr sps}

R20: dc over joining dc, *dc in next 49 sts**, (dc, ch2, dc) in 2-ch cnr sp*, rep from * to * 2x and * to ** 1x, dc in same sp as first st, ch2, join with ss to first st. {51 sts on each side; 4 2-ch cnr sps}

R21: ch3 (stch), *17x [ch2, tr3tog over next 3 sts], ch2**, (tr, ch2, tr) in 2-ch cnr sp*, rep from * to * 2x and * to ** 1x, tr in same sp as first st, ch1, join with dc to 3rd ch of stch. {19 sts, 18 2-ch sps on each side; 4 2-ch cnr sps}

R22: dc over joining dc, *dc in next st, 17x [2dc in 2-ch sp, fpdc around next st], 2dc in 2-ch sp, dc in next st**, (dc, ch2, dc) in 2-ch cnr sp*, rep from * to * 2x and * to ** 1x, dc in same sp as first st, ch1, join with dc to first st.
{57 sts on each side; 4 2-ch cnr sps}

R23: ch3 (stch), tr over joining dc, *tr in next 57 sts**, (2tr, ch2, 2tr) in 2-ch cnr sp*, rep from * to * 2x and * to ** 1x, 2tr in same sp as first sts, ch1, join with dc to 3rd ch of stch. {61 sts on each side; 4 2-ch cnr sps}

R24: dc over joining dc, *dc in blo of next 61 sts**, (dc, ch2, dc) in 2-ch cnr sp*, rep from * to * 2x and * to ** 1x, dc in same sp as first st, ch2, join with ss to first st. Fasten off. {63 sts on each side; 4 2-ch cnr sps}

Paradigm

This one is a typical example of the patterns that can be made using the most simple stitches. Paradigm means a typical example of something.

Colours by Shelley

Colours by Joanne Waring

  232 m / 254 yd

Check the written pattern if using the chart as Rounds 11, 14, 19 and 23 have stitches worked in front of and/or behind chain spaces. This pattern will be ruffled at certain points.

Begin with mc.

R1: ch3 (stch), 15tr, join with ss to 3rd ch of stch. {16 sts}

R2: dc in same st as ss, dc in next 15 sts, join with ss to first st. {16 sts}

R3: ch3 (stch), 4trcl in same st as ss, *(tr, ch2, tr) in next st** 5trcl in next st*, rep from * to * 6x and * to ** 1x, join with ss to top of 4trcl. {24 sts, 8 2-ch sps}

R4: fpdc around (stch & 4trcl), *dc in next st, 2dc in 2-ch sp, dc in next st** fpdc around next st*, rep from * to * 6x and * to ** 1x, join with ss to first st. {40 sts}

R5: ch3 (stch), 4trcl in same st as ss, *tr in next st** 5trcl in next st*, rep from * to * 18x and * to ** 1x, join with ss to top of 4trcl. {40 sts}

R6: fpdc around (stch & 4trcl), *dc between last and next sts, dc in next st, dc between last and next sts** fpdc around next st*, rep from * to * 18x and * to ** 1x, join with ss to first st. {80 sts}

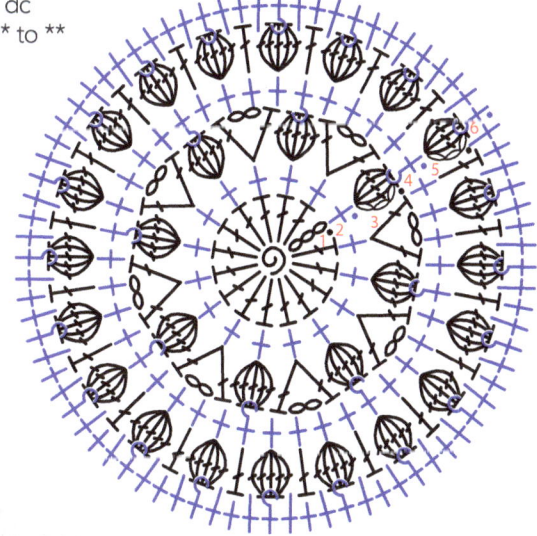

Paradigm chart
Rounds 6-18

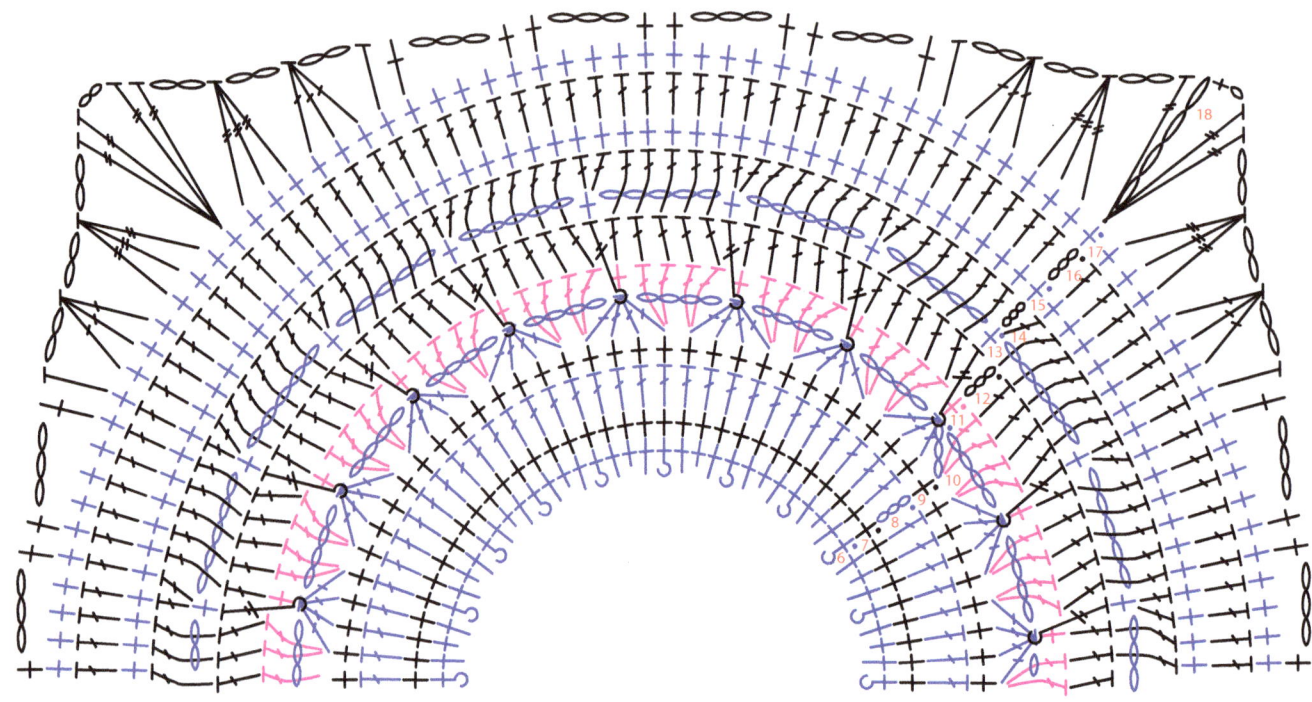

R7: dc in same st as ss, dc in next 79 sts, join with ss to first st. {80 sts}

R8: ch3 (stch), tr in next 79 sts, join with ss to 3rd ch of stch. {80 sts}

R9: dc in same st as ss, dc in next 79 sts, join with ss to first st. {80 sts}

R10: ch3 (stch), tr3tog over next 3 sts, *ch4**, tr4tog over next 4 sts*, rep from * to * 18x and * to ** 1x, join with ss to top of tr3tog. {20 sts, 20 4-ch sps}

R11: dc in same st as ss, *(2tr in same R9 st as last leg of tr4tog, 2tr in same R9 st as first leg of next tr4tog) behind the 4-ch sp, dc in next st, (2tr in same R9 st as last leg of tr4tog, 2tr in same R9 st as first leg of next tr4tog) in front of 4-ch sp**, dc in next st*, rep from * to * 8x and * to ** 1x, join with ss to first st. {100 sts}

R12: ch3 (stch), fphdtr around (stch & tr4tog), *tr in next 5 sts, fphdtr around R10 tr4tog below*, rep from * to * 18x, tr in next 4 sts, join with ss to 3rd ch of stch. {120 sts}

R13: *dc in next st, ch5, skip 5 sts*, rep from * to * 19x, join with ss to first st. {20 sts, 20 5-ch sps}

R14: ch3 (stch), *tr in next 5 sts of R12 in front of 5-ch sp, 2tr in next st, tr in next 5 sts of R12 behind 5-ch sp**, 2tr in next st*, rep from * to * 8x and * to ** 1x, tr in same st as first st, join with ss to 3rd ch of stch. {140 sts}

R15: dc in same st as ss, dc in next 139 sts, join with ss to first st. {140 sts}

R16: ch3 (stch), tr in next 139 sts, join with ss to 3rd ch of stch. {140 sts}

R17: dc in same st as ss, dc in next 139 sts, join with ss to first st. {140 sts}

R18: ch4 (stch), dtr in same st as ss, *ch2, dtr3tog over next 3 sts, ch2, tr3tog over next 3 sts, ch2, htr in next st, dc in next st, 3x [ch3, skip 3 sts, dc in next 2 sts], ch3, skip 3 sts, dc in next st, htr in next st, ch2, tr3tog over next 3 sts, ch2, dtr3tog over next 3 sts, ch2**, (2dtr, ch2, 2dtr) in next st*, rep from * to * 2x and * to ** 1x, 2dtr in same st as first sts, ch1, join with dc to 4th ch of stch. {18 sts, 6 2-ch sps, 4 3-ch sps on each side; 4 2-ch cnr sps}

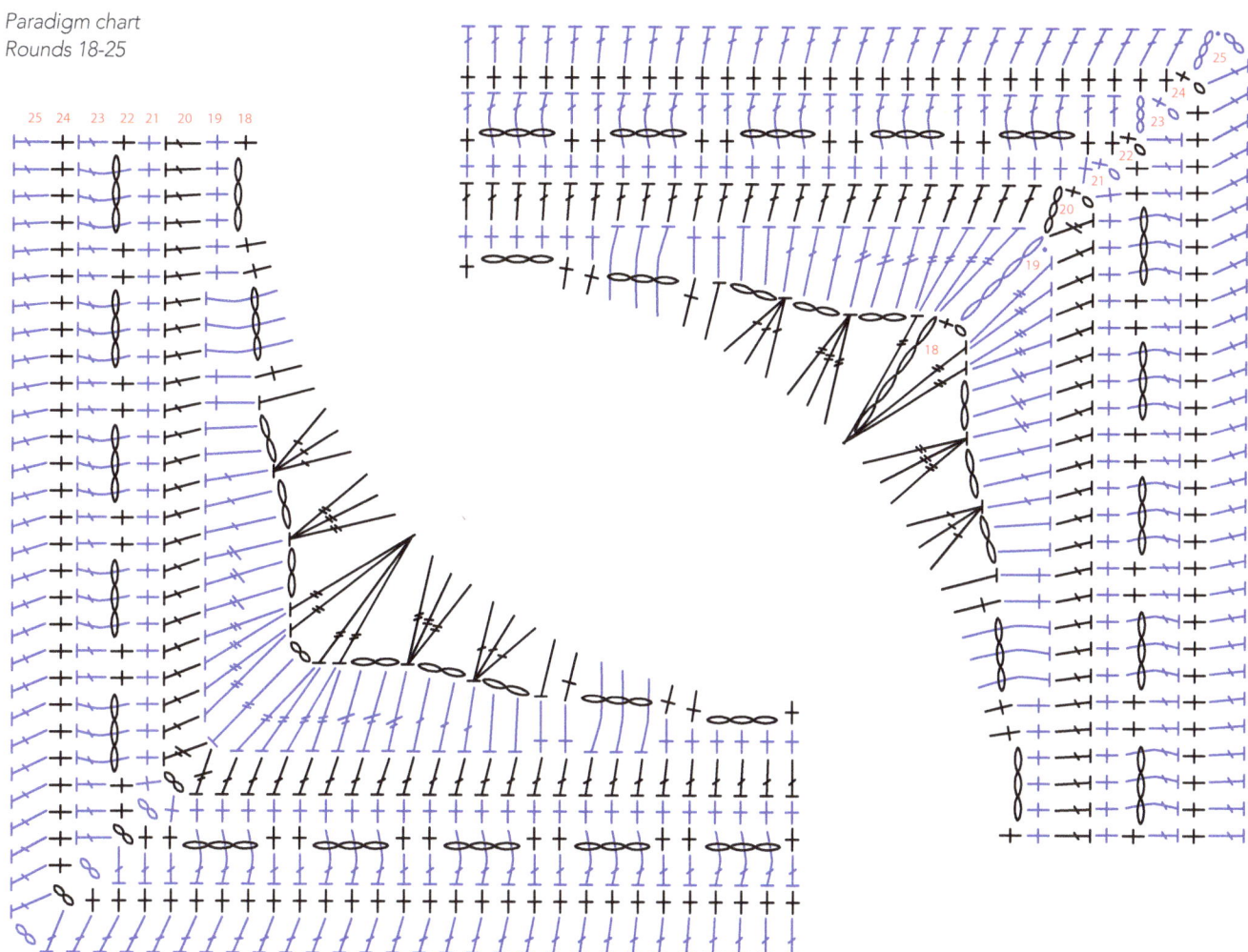

Paradigm chart
Rounds 18-25

R19: ch4 (stch), *2dtr in next 2 sts, 2hdtr in 2-ch sp, hdtr in next st, 2tr in 2-ch sp, tr in next st, 2htr in 2-ch sp, dc in next 2 sts, htr in next 3 sts of R17 behind 3-ch sp, 2x [dc in next 2 sts, dc in next 3 sts of R17 behind 3-ch cp], dc in next 2 sts, htr in next 3 sts of R17 behind 3-ch sp, dc in next 2 sts, 2htr in 2-ch sp, tr in next st, 2tr in 2-ch sp, hdtr in next st, 2hdtr in 2-ch sp, 2dtr in next 2 sts**, dtr in 2-ch cnr sp*, rep from * to * 2x and * to ** 1x, join with ss to 4th ch of stch. {46 sts on each side; 4 1-st cnrs}

R20: ch3 (stch), * tr in next 46 sts**, (hdtr, ch2, hdtr) in next st*, rep from * to * 2x and * to ** 1x, hdtr in same st as first st, ch1, join with dc to 3rd ch of stch. {48 sts on each side; 4 2-ch cnr sps}

R21: dc over joining dc, *dc in next 48 sts**, (dc, ch2, dc) in 2-ch cnr sp*, rep from * to * 2x and * to ** 1x, dc in same sp as first st, ch1, join with dc to first st. {50 sts on each side; 4 2-ch cnr sps}

R22: dc over joining dc, *dc in next st, 9x [ch3, skip 3 sts, dc in next 2 sts], ch3, skip 3 sts, dc in next st**, (dc, ch2, dc) in 2-ch cnr sp*, rep from * to * 2x and * to ** 1x, dc in same sp as first st, ch1. join with dc to first st. {22 sts, 10 3-ch sps on each side; 4 2-ch cnr sps}

R23: ch3 (stch), *10x [tr in next 2 sts, tr in next 3 sts of R21 behind 3-ch sp], tr in next 2 sts**, (tr, ch2, tr) in 2-ch cnr sp*, rep from * to * 2x and * to ** 1x, tr in same sp as first st, ch1, join with dc to 3rd ch of stch. {54 sts on each side; 4 2-ch cnr sps}

R24: dc over joining dc, *dc in next 54 sts**, (dc, ch2, dc) in 2-ch sp*, rep from * to * 2x and * to ** 1x, dc in same sp as first sts, ch1, join with dc to first st. {56 sts on each side; 4 2-ch cnr sps}

R25: ch3 (stch), *tr in next 56 sts**, (tr, ch2, tr) in 2-ch sp*, rep from * to * 2x and * to ** 1x, tr in same sp as first sts, ch2, join with ss to 3rd ch of stch. Fasten off. {58 sts on each side; 4 2-ch cnr sps}

Size 5 Patterns

Oh so big, but not quite the biggest for this book! I love how big squares mean not many are needed to make a big blanket.

Below are the approximate sizes you will achieve with 3 different yarn weights and hook sizes. The amount of yarn listed on each pattern page is for the middle yarn weight and hook size. The amount of yarn needed for the other yarn weights is on page 177.

🪝	3.5 mm hook	4.5 mm hook	5.5 mm hook
🧶	4 ply/sock/fingering	8 ply/DK/light worsted	10 ply/aran/worsted
⬛	15"	18"	21"

Coterie
page 90

d'Artagnan
page 94

Illudium
page 98

Piazza
page 102

Wreath
page 108

Size 5 Patterns

Colours by Shelley

Colours by Miranda Howard

Coterie

A coterie is an exclusive small group with shared interests or tastes. The Coterie pattern is a small exclusive group of common crochet stitches.

 292 m / 319 yd

Begin with mc.

R1: ch3 (stch), tr, *ch4**, 3tr*, rep from * to * 6x and * to ** 1x, tr, join with ss to 3rd ch of stch. {24 sts, 8 4-ch sps} **Pull mc closed to about 1 cm.**

R2: ch3 (stch), *ch2, skip 1 st, dc in 4-ch sp, ch2, skip 1 st**, tr in next st*, rep from * to *6x and * to ** 1x, join with ss to 3rd ch of stch. {16 sts, 16 2-ch sps}

R3: ch3 (stch), *2tr in 2-ch sp**, tr in next st*, rep from * to * 14x and * to ** 1x, join with ss to 3rd ch of stch. {48 sts}

R4: ch3 (stch), tr in next st, *ch4**, tr in next 3 sts*, rep from * to * 14x and * to ** 1x, tr in next st, join with ss to 3rd ch of stch. {48 sts, 16 4-ch sps}

R5: ch3 (stch), *ch2, skip 1 st, dc in 4-ch sp, ch2, skip 1 st**, tr in next st*, rep from * to *14x and * to ** 1x, join with ss to 3rd ch of stch. {32 sts, 32 2-ch sps}

R6: ch3 (stch), *2tr in 2-ch sp**, tr in next st*, rep from * to * 30x and * to ** 1x, join with ss to 3rd ch of stch. {96 sts}

R7: ch3 (stch), tr in next st, *ch4**, tr in next 3 sts*, rep from * to * 30x and * to ** 1x, tr in next st, join with ss to 3rd ch of stch. {96 sts, 32 4-ch sps}

R8: ch3 (stch), *ch2, skip 1 st, dc in 4-ch sp, ch2, skip 1 st**, tr in next st*, rep from * to * 30x and * to ** 1x, join with ss to 3rd ch of stch. {64 sts, 64 2-ch sps}

Coterie chart
Rounds 1-12

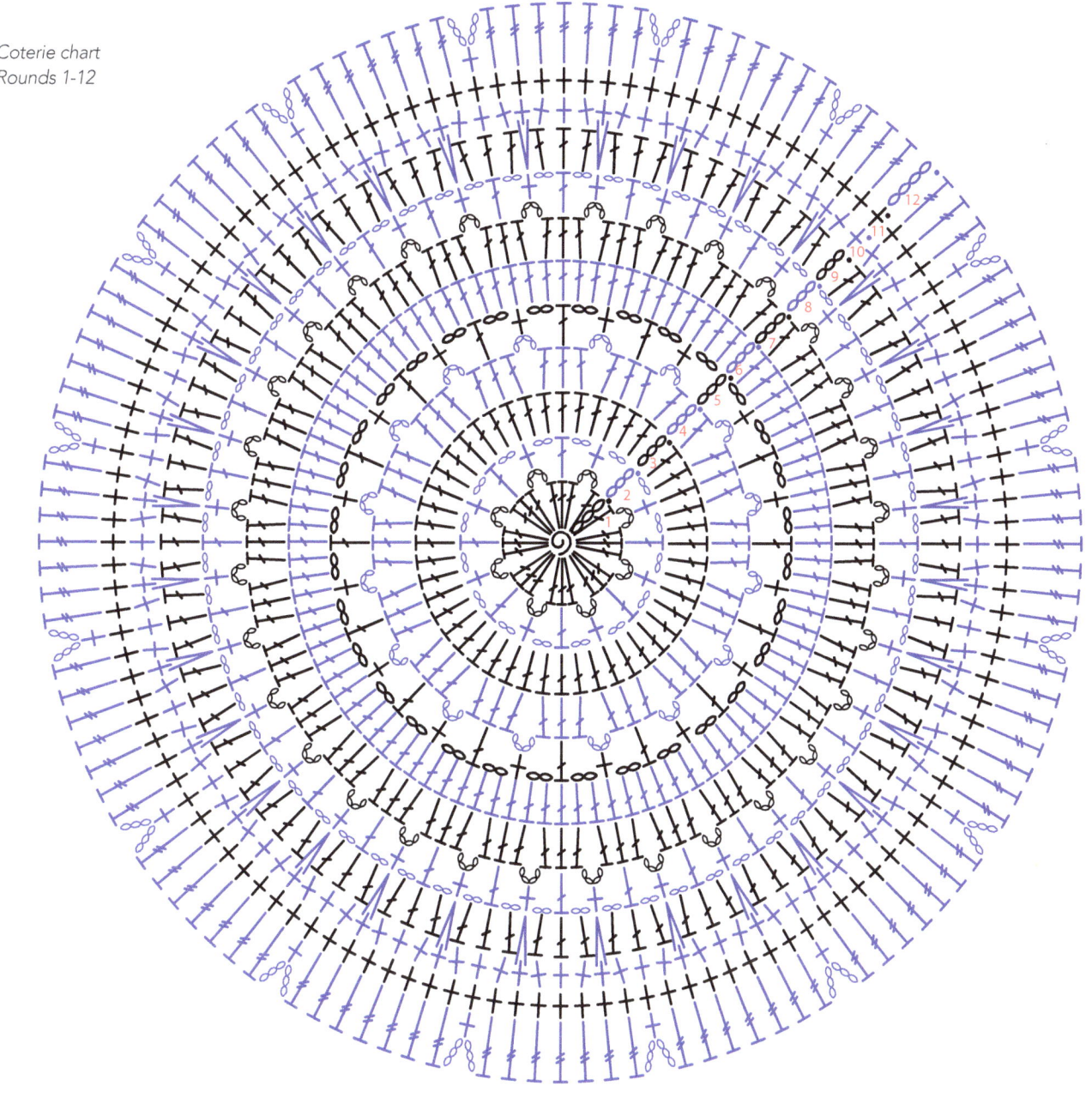

R9: ch3 (stch), *tr in 2-ch sp, skip 1 st, tr in 2-ch sp**, tr in next st*, rep from * to * 30x and * to ** 1x, join with ss to 3rd ch of stch. {96 sts}

R10: dc in same st as ss, dc in next st, *spike dc in skipped st of R8**, dc in next 3 sts*, rep from * to * 30x and * to ** 1x, dc in next st, join with ss to first st. {128 sts}

R11: dc in same st as ss, dc in next 127 sts, join with ss to first st. {128 sts}

R12: ch4 (stch), dtr in next 3 sts, *ch3, dc in next st, ch3**, dtr in next 7 sts*, rep from * to * 14x and * to ** 1x, dtr in next 3 sts, join with ss to 4th ch of stch. {128 sts, 32 3-ch sps}

Coterie chart
Rounds 12-20

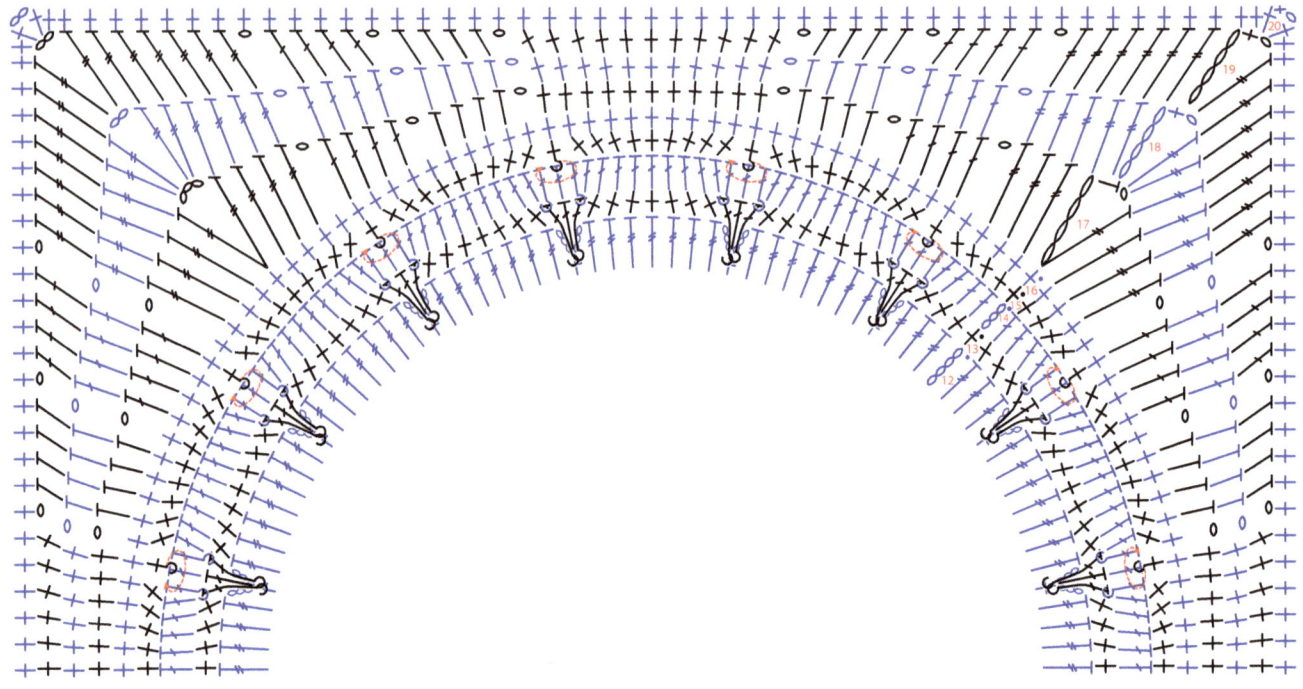

R13: dc in same st as ss, dc in next 3 sts, *skip 3-ch sp, (fptr around, tr in, fptr around) next st, skip 3-ch sp**, dc in next 7 sts*, rep from * to * 14x and * to ** 1x, dc in next 3 sts, join with ss to first st. {160 sts}

R14: ch3 (stch), tr in next 3 sts, *(tr in, fptr around) next st, tr in next st, (fptr around, tr in) next st**, tr in next 7 sts*, rep from * to * 14x and * to ** 1x, tr in next 3 sts, join with ss to 3rd ch of stch. {192 sts}

R15: dc in same st as ss, dc in next 4 sts, *fpdc around next 2 fp sts at the same time skipping st between**, dc in next 9 sts*, rep from * to * 14x and * to ** 1x, dc in next 4 sts, join with ss to first st. {160 sts}

R16: dc in same st as ss, dc in next 159 sts, join with ss to first st. {160 sts}

R17: ch4 (stch), *dtr in next 3 sts, ch1, skip 1 st, tr in next 4 sts, ch1, skip 1 st, htr in next 4 sts, ch1, skip 1 st, dc in next 11 sts, ch1, skip 1 st, htr in next 4 sts, ch1, skip 1 st, tr in next 4 sts, ch1, skip 1 st, dtr in next 3 sts**, (dtr, ch3, dtr) in next st*, rep from * to * 2x and * to ** 1x, dtr in same st as first st, ch1, join with htr to 4th ch of stch. {35 sts, 6 1-ch sps on each side; 4 3-ch cnr sps}

R18: ch4 (stch), dtr over joining htr, *dtr in next 4 sts, ch1, skip 1-ch sp, tr in next 4 sts, ch1, skip 1-ch sp, htr in next 4 sts, ch1, skip 1-ch sp, dc in next 11 sts, ch1, skip 1-ch sp, htr in next 4 sts, ch1, skip 1-ch sp, tr in next 4 sts, ch1, skip 1-ch sp, dtr in next 4 sts**, (2dtr, ch2, 2dtr) in 3-ch cnr sp*, rep from * to * 2x and * to ** 1x, 2dtr in same sp as first sts, ch1, join with dc to 4th ch of stch. {39 sts, 6 1-ch sps on each side; 4 2-ch cnr sps}

R19: ch4 (stch), *dtr in next 6 sts, ch1, skip 1-ch sp, tr in next 4 sts, ch1, skip 1-ch sp, htr in next 4 sts, ch1, skip 1-ch sp, dc in next 11 sts, ch1, skip 1-ch sp, htr in next 4 sts, ch1, skip 1-ch sp, tr in next 4 sts, ch1, skip 1-ch sp, dtr in next 6 sts**, (dtr, ch2, dtr) in 2-ch cnr sp*, rep from * to * 2x and * to ** 1x, dtr in same sp as first st, ch1, join with dc to 4th ch of stch. {41 sts, 6 1-ch sps on each side; 4 2-ch cnr sps}

R20: 2dc over joining dc, *dc in next 7 sts, 2x [dc in 1-ch sp, dc in next 4 sts], dc in 1-ch sp, dc in next 11 sts, 2x [dc in 1-ch sp, dc in next 4 sts], dc in 1-ch sp, dc in next 7 sts**, (2dc, ch2, 2dc) in 2-ch cnr sp*, rep from * to * 2x and * to ** 1x, 2dc in same sp as first sts, ch1, join with dc to first st. {51 sts on each side; 4 2-ch cnr sps}

Coterie chart
Rounds 20-26

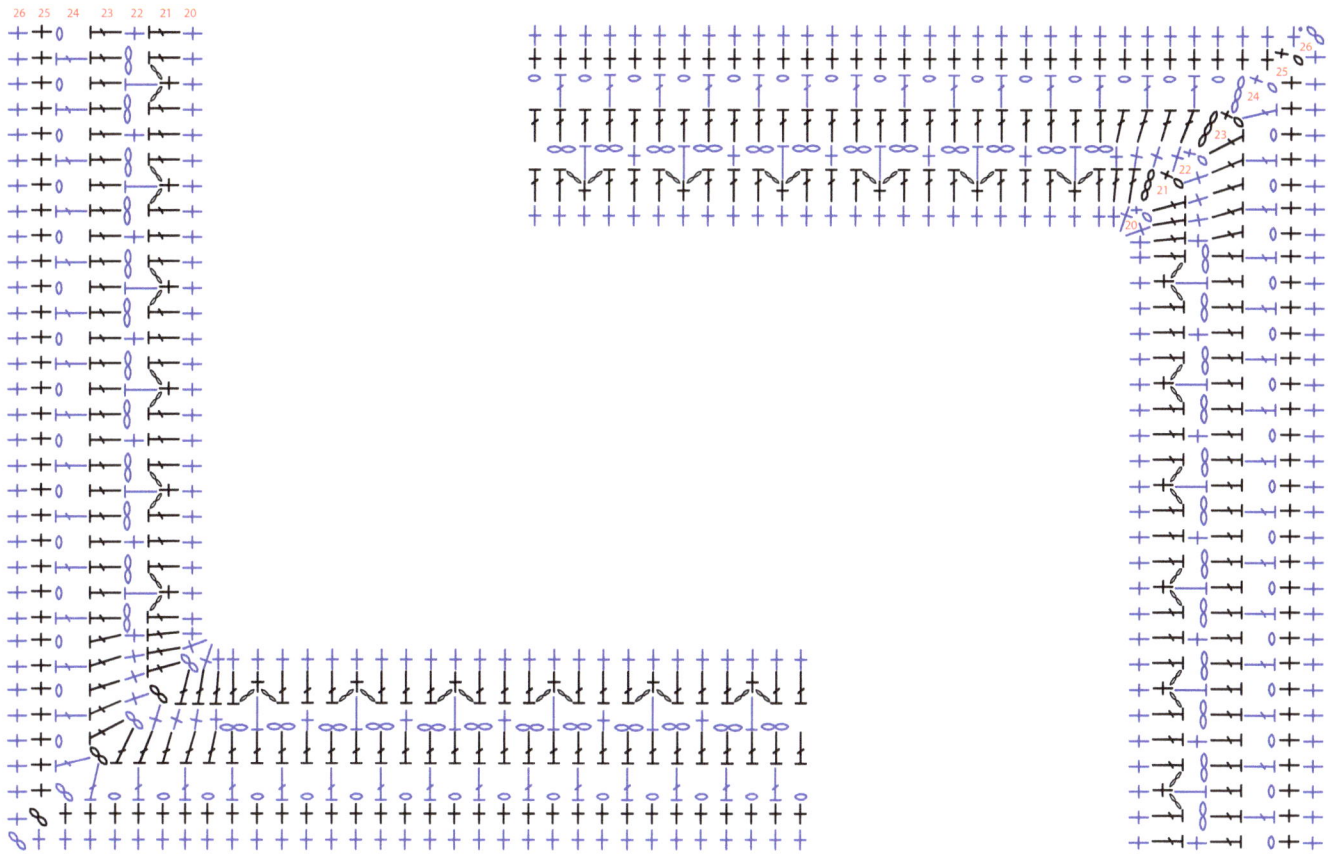

R21: ch3 (stch), *12x [tr in next 3 sts, ch2, dc in next st, ch2], tr in next 3 sts**, (tr, ch2, tr) in 2-ch cnr sp*, rep from * to * 2x and * to ** 1x, tr in same sp as first st, ch1, join with dc to 3rd ch of stch. {53 sts, 24 2-ch sps on each side; 4 2-ch cnr sps}

R22: dc over joining dc, *dc in next 3 sts, 12x [ch2, skip (1 st & 2-ch sp), htr in next st, ch2, skip (2-ch sp & 1 st), dc in next st], dc in next 2 sts**, (dc, ch2, dc) in 2-ch cnr sp*, rep from * to * 2x and * to ** 1x, dc in same sp as first st, ch1, join with dc to first st. {31 sts, 24 2-ch sps on each side; 4 2-ch cnr sps}

R23: ch3 (stch), *tr in next 4 sts, 24x [tr in 2-ch sp, tr in next st], tr in next 3 sts**, (tr, ch2, tr) in 2-ch cnr sp*, rep from * to * 2x and * to ** 1x, tr in same sp as first st, ch1, join with dc to 3rd ch of stch. {57 sts on each side; 4 2-ch cnr sps}

R24: ch3 (stch), *28x [ch1, skip 1 st, tr in next st], ch1, skip 1 st**, (tr, ch2, tr) in 2-ch cnr sp*, rep from * to * 2x and * to ** 1x, tr in same sp as first sp, ch1, join with dc to 3rd ch of stch. {30 sts, 29 1-ch sps on each side; 4 2-ch cnr sps}

R25: dc over joining dc, *29x [dc in next st, dc in 1-ch sp], dc in next st**, (dc, ch2, dc) in 2-ch cnr sp*, rep from * to * 2x and * to ** 1x, dc in same sp as first st, ch1, join with dc to first st. {61 sts on each side; 4 2-ch cnr sps}

R26: dc over joining dc, *dc in next 61 sts**, (dc, ch2, dc) in 2-ch cnr sp*, rep from * to * 2x and * to ** 1x, dc in same sp as first st, ch2, join with ss to first st. Fasten off. {63 sts on each side; 4 2-ch cnr sps}

Colours by Kim Siebenhausen

Colours by Hayley Neubauer

d'Artagnan

Named after one of the characters from The Three Musketeers because of the rapier-like shapes.

  296 m / 324 yd

Begin with mc.

R1: ch3 (stch), 15tr, join with ss to 3rd ch of stch. {16 sts}

R2: ch3 (stch), tr in same st as ss, *skip 1 st, 3tr in next st*, rep from * to * 6x, skip 1 st, tr in same st as first sts, join with ss to 3rd ch of stch. {24 sts}

R3: ch3 (stch), *ch2, fpdtr2tog over next 2 sts, ch2**, tr in next st*, rep from * to * 6x and * to ** 1x, join with ss to 3rd ch of stch. {16 sts, 16 2-ch sps}

R4: dc in same st as ss, *2dc in 2-ch sp, fpdc around next st, 2dc in 2-ch sp**, 2dc in next st*, rep from * to * 6x and * to ** 1x, dc in same st as first st, join with ss to first st. {56 sts}

R5: ch3 (stch), *ch2, skip 1 st**, tr in next st*, rep from * to * 26x and * to ** 1x, join with ss to 3rd ch of stch. {28 sts, 28 2-ch sps}

R6: dc in same st as ss, *2dc in 2-ch sp**, dc in next st*, rep from * to * 26x and * to ** 1x, join with ss to first st. {84 sts}

R7: ch3 (stch), tr in next 83 sts, join with ss to 3rd ch of stch. {84 sts}

R8: ch3 (stch), *skip 1 st**, 2tr in next st*, rep from * to * 40x and * to ** 1x, tr in same st as ss, join with ss to 3rd ch of stch. {84 sts}

R9: First leg of fpdtr2tog is around same st as ss. ch3 (stch), *ch1, fpdtr2tog over next 2 sts, ch1**, tr between last and next sts*, rep from * to * 40x and * to ** 1x, join with ss to 3rd ch of stch. {84 sts, 84 1-ch sps}

d'Artagnan chart
Rounds 1-15

R10: using same st as ss & 1-ch sp, dc2tog, *fpdc around next st, dc in 1-ch sp**, dc2tog over next st & 1-ch sp*, rep from * to * 40x and * to ** 1x, join with ss to first st. {126 sts}

R11: ss to next st, ch3 (stch), *ch2, skip 2 sts**, tr in next st*, rep from * to * 40x and * to ** 1x, join with ss to 3rd ch of stch. {42 sts, 42 2-ch sps}

R12: ch3 (stch), *3tr in 2-ch sp**, tr in next st*, rep from * to * 40x and * to ** 1x, join with ss to 3rd ch of stch. {168 sts}

R13: ch3 (stch), tr in same st as ss, *skip 3 sts**, 3tr in next st*, rep from * to * 40 and * to ** 1x, tr in same st as first sts, join with ss to 3rd ch of stch. {126 sts}

R14: ch3 (stch), *ch1, fpdtr2tog over next 2 sts, ch1**, tr in next st*, rep from * to * 40x and * to ** 1x, join with ss to 3rd ch of stch. {84 sts, 84 1-ch sps}

R15: dc in same st as ss, *dc in 1-ch sp, fpdc around next st, dc in 1-ch sp**, dc in next st*, rep from * to * 40x and * to ** 1x, join with ss to first st. {168 sts}

d'Artagnan chart
Rounds 15-25

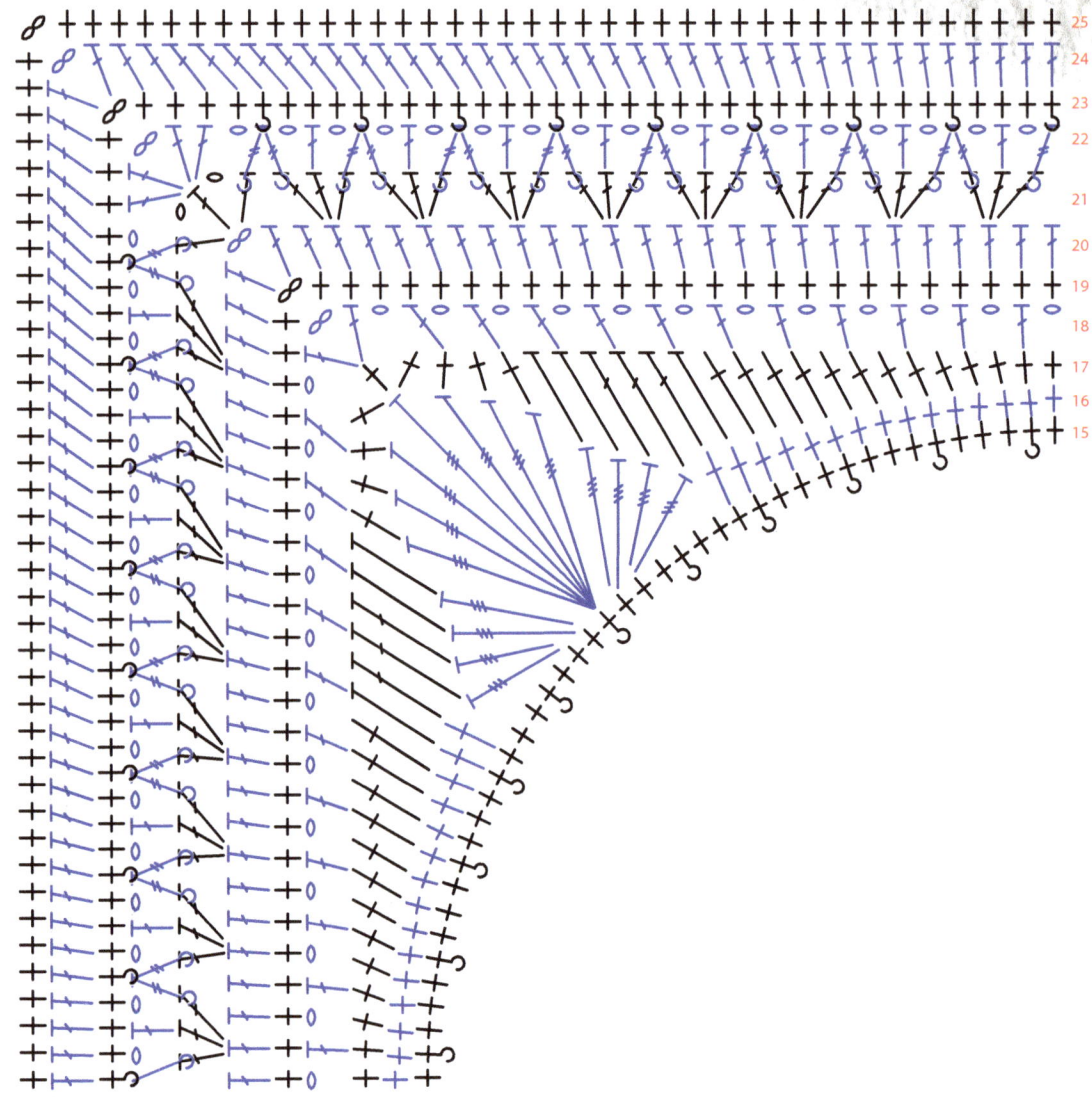

R16: ch5 (stch), 3trtr in same st as ss, *2trtr in next 2 sts, skip 4 sts, dc in next 29 sts, skip 4 sts, 2trtr in next 2 sts**, 7trtr in next st* rep from * to * 2x and * to ** 1x, 3trtr in same st as first sts, join with ss to 5th ch of stch. {37 sts on each side; 4 7-st cnrs}

R17: 2dc in same st as ss, *dc in next 3 sts, htr in next 2 sts, tr in next 3 sts, htr in next st, dc in next 25 sts, htr in next st, tr in next 3 sts, htr in next 2 sts, dc in next 3 sts**, 3dc in next st*, rep from * to * 2x and * to ** 1x, dc in same st as first sts, join with ss to first st. {43 sts on each side; 4 3-st cnrs}

R18: ch3 (stch), *22x [ch1, skip 1 st, tr in next st], ch1, skip 1 st**, (tr, ch2, tr) in next st*, rep from * to * 2x and * to ** 1x, tr in same st as first st, ch1, join with dc to first st. {24 sts, 23 1-ch sps on each side; 4 2-ch cnr sps}

R19: dc over joining dc, *23x [dc in next st, dc in 1-ch sp], dc in next st**, (dc, ch2, dc) in 2-ch cnr sp*, rep from * to * 2x and * to ** 1x, dc in same sp as first st, ch1, join with dc to first st. {49 sts on each side; 4 2-ch cnr sps}

R20: ch3 (stch), *tr in next 49 sts**, (tr, ch2, tr) in 2-ch cnr sp*, rep from * to * 2x and * to ** 1x, tr in same sp as first st, ch1, join with dc to 3rd ch of stch. {51 sts on each side; 4 2-ch cnr sps}

d'Artagnan chart
Beginning of Rounds 15-25

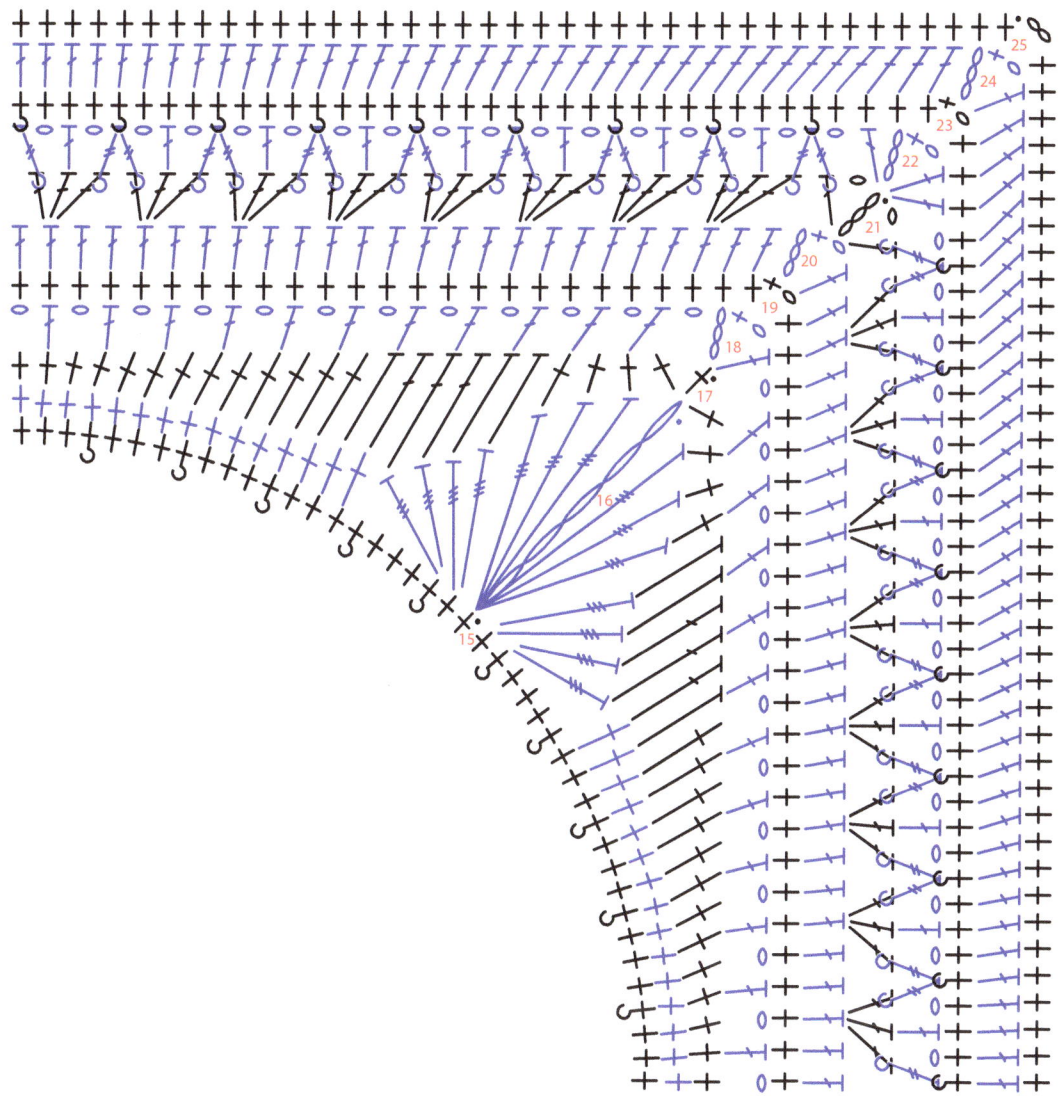

R21: ch3 (stch), ch1, tr over joining dc, *skip 3 sts, 16x [3tr in next st, skip 2 sts]**, (2x [tr, ch1], tr) in 2-ch cnr sp*, rep from * to * 2x and * to ** 1x, tr in same sp as first sts, ch1, join with ss to 3rd ch of stch. {50 sts, 2 1-ch sps on each side; 4 1-st cnrs}

R22: ch3 (stch), tr in same st as ss, *ch1, skip 1-ch sp, 16x [fpdtr2tog over next 2 sts, ch1, tr in next st, ch1], fpdtr2tog over next 2 sts, ch1, skip 1-ch sp**, (2tr, ch2, 2tr) in next st*, rep from * to * 2x and * to ** 1x, 2tr in same st as first sts, ch1, join with dc to 3rd ch of stch. {37 sts, 34 1-ch sps on each side; 4 2-ch cnr sps}

R23: dc over joining dc, *dc in next 2 sts, 17x [dc in 1-ch sp, fpdc around next st, dc in 1-ch sp, dc in next st], dc in next st**, (dc, ch2, dc) in 2-ch cnr sp*, rep from * to * 2x and * to ** 1x, dc in same sp as first st, ch1, join with dc to first st. {73 sts on each side; 4 2-ch sps}

R24: ch3 (stch), *tr in next 73 sts**, (tr, ch2, tr) in 2-ch cnr sp*, rep from * to * 2x and * to ** 1x, tr in same sp as first st, ch1, join with dc to 3rd ch of stch. {75 sts on each side; 4 2-ch cnr sps}

R25: dc over joining dc, *dc in next 75 sts**, (dc, ch2, dc) in 2-ch cnr sp*, rep from * to * 2x and * to ** 1x, dc in same sp as first st, ch2, join with ss to first st. Fasten off. {77 sts on each side; 4 2-ch cnr sps}

Colours by Evangelia V Katsafouros

Colours by Kim Siebenhausen

Illudium

Sounds like a chemical element? But no. See Kaboom on page 120. The Kaboom was meant to have happened because of the "Illudium-Pu Explosive Space Modulator".

  368 m / 403 yd

Begin with mc.

R1: ch3 (stch), 15tr, join with ss to 3rd ch of stch. {16 sts}

R2: ch3 (stch), tr in same st as ss, *ch2, skip 1 st**, 2tr in next st*, rep from * to * 6x and * to ** 1x, join with ss to 3rd ch of stch. {16 sts, 8 2-ch sps}

R3: dc in same st as ss, dc in next st, *dc in 2-ch sp, pc in skipped st of R1 in front of 2-ch sp, dc in same 2-ch sp**, dc in next 2 sts*, rep from * to * 6x and * to ** 1x, join with ss to first st. {40 sts}

R4: ch3 (stch), tr in next 39 sts, join with ss to 3rd ch of stch. {40 sts}

R5: ch3 (stch), tr in same st as ss, *ch2, skip 1 st**, 2tr in next st*, rep from * to * 18x and * to ** 1x, join with ss to 3rd ch of stch. {40 sts, 20 2-ch sps}

R6: dc in same st as ss, dc in next st, *pc in skipped st of R4 in front of 2-ch sp**, dc in next 2 sts*, rep from * to * 18x and * to ** 1x, join with ss to first st. {60 sts}

R7: dc in same st as ss, *ch2, skip 1 st**, dc in next st*, rep from * to * 28x and * to ** 1x, join with ss to first st. {30 sts, 30 2-ch sps}

R8: dc in same st as ss, *3tr in 2-ch sp**, dc in next st*, rep from * to * 28x and * to ** 1x, join with ss to first st. {120 sts}

R9: bptr around R7 st below, *ch3**, bptr around next R7 st*, rep from * to * 28x and * to ** 1x, join with ss to first st. {30 sts, 30 3-ch sps}

*Illudium chart
Rounds 1-16*

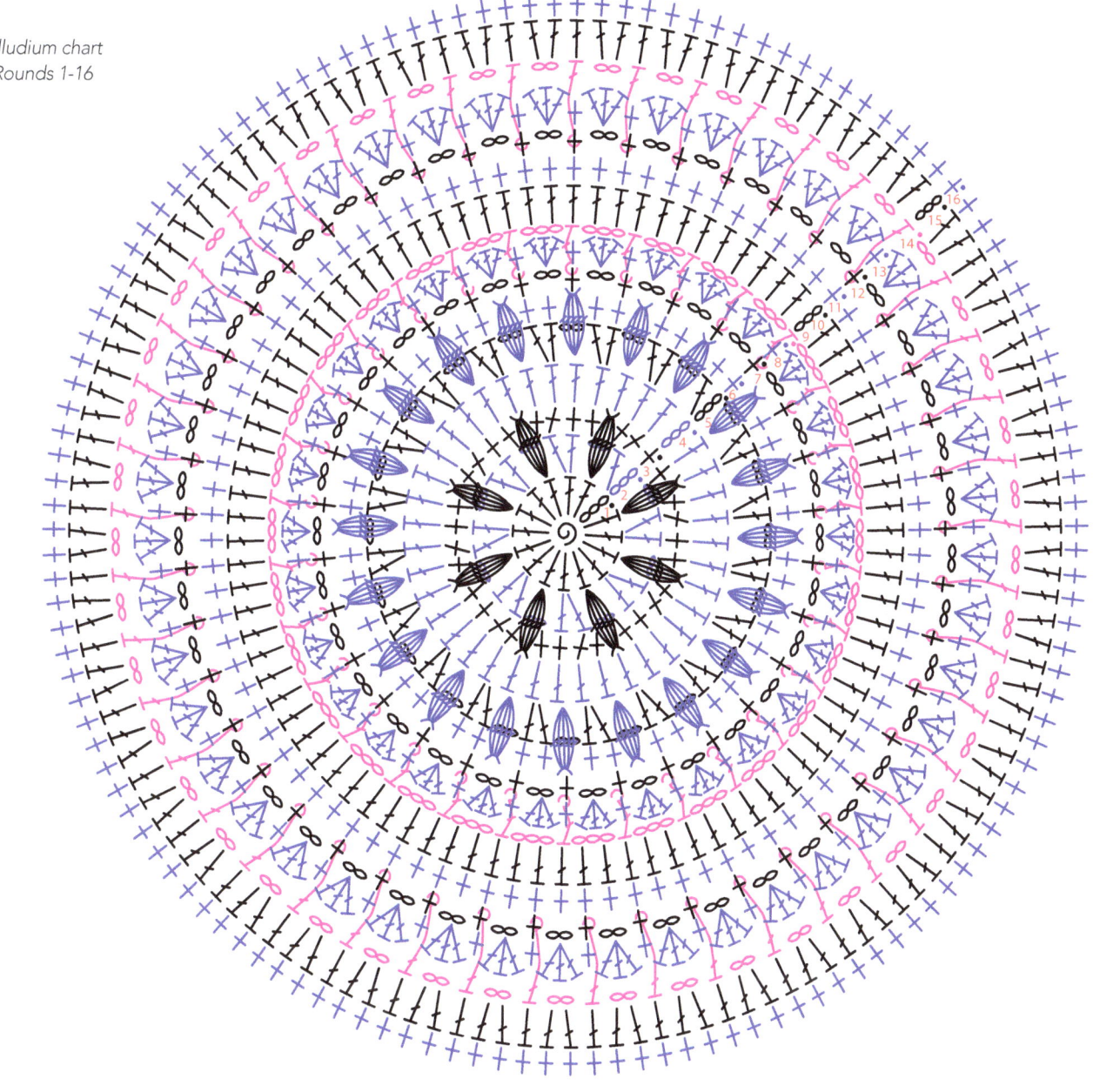

R10: ch3 (stch), *2tr in 3-ch sp**, tr in next st*, rep from * to * 28x and * to ** 1x, join with ss to 3rd st of stch. {90 sts}

R11: dc in same st as ss, dc in next 89 sts, join with ss to first st. {90 sts}

R12: dc in same st as ss, *ch2, skip 1 st**, dc in next st*, rep from * to * 43x and * to ** 1x, join with ss to first st. {45 sts, 45 2-ch sps}

R13: dc in same st as ss, *3tr in 2-ch sp**, dc in next st*, rep from * to * 43x and * to ** 1x, join with ss to first st. {180 sts}

R14: bptr around R12 st below, *ch2**, bptr around next R12 st*, rep from * to * 42x and * to ** 1x, join with ss to first st. {45 sts, 45 2-ch sps}

R15: ch3 (stch), *2tr in 2-ch sp**, tr in next st*, rep from * to * 43x and * to ** 1x, join with ss to 3rd st of stch. {135 sts}

R16: dc in same st as ss, dc in next 134 sts, join with ss to first st. {135 sts}

Illudium chart
Rounds 16–32

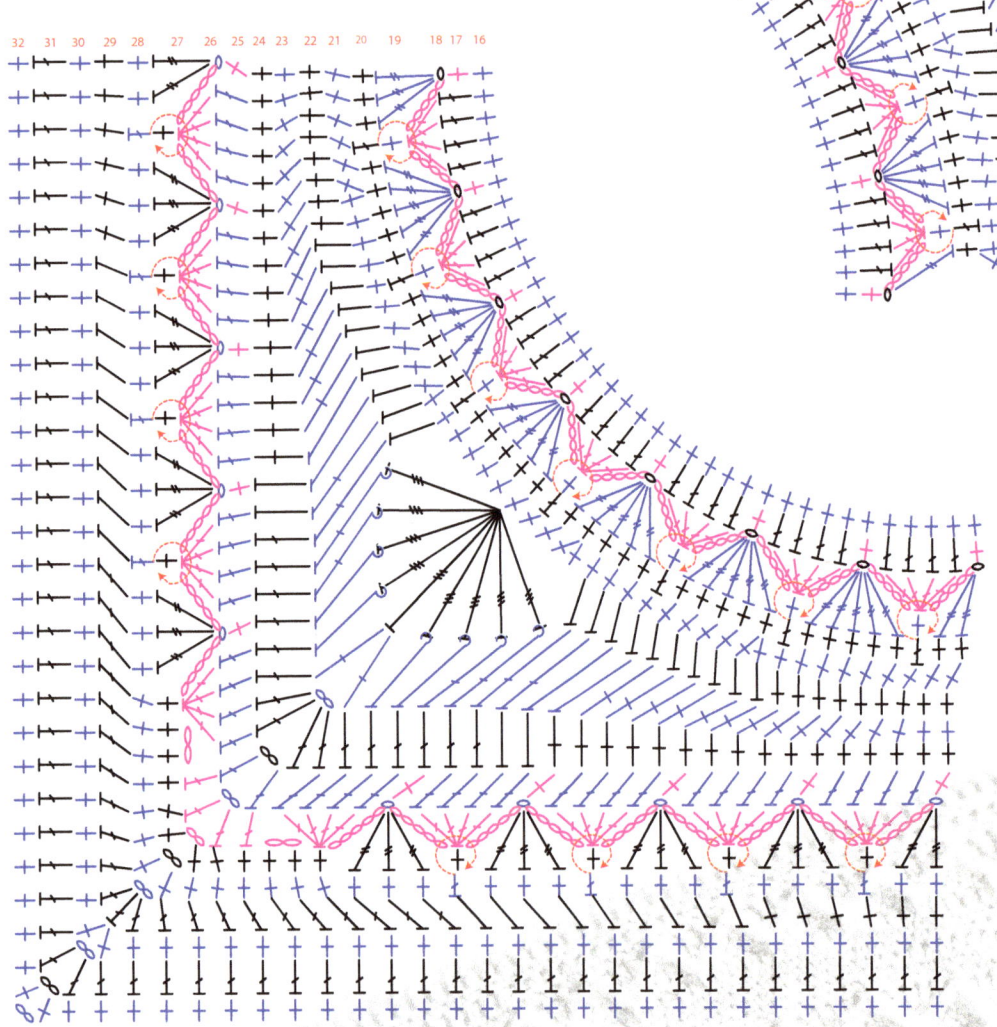

100 • Size 5 Patterns Illudium

R17: ch3 (stch), tr in next 3 sts, *ch1, skip 1 st**, tr in next 4 sts*, rep from * to * 25x and * to ** 1x, join with ss to 3rd ch of stch. {108 sts, 27 1-ch sps}

R18: ch3 (stch), tr3tog over next 3 sts, *ch5, dc in skipped st of R16 in front of 1-ch sp, ch5**, tr4tog over next 4 sts*, rep from * to * 25x and * to ** 1x, join with ss to top of tr3tog. {54 sts, 54 5-ch sps}

R19: dc in same st as ss, *5dtr in 1-ch sp of R17, skip (5-ch sp, 1 st & 5-ch sp)**, dc in next st* rep from * to * 25x and * to ** 1x, join with ss to first st. {162 sts}

R20: ch1, *tr in both 5-ch sps of R18 below at the same time, dc in next 5 sts*, rep from * to * 26x, join with ss to first st. {162 sts}

R21: dc in same st as ss, dc in next 7 sts, *2dc in next st**, dc in next 8 sts*, rep from * to * 16x and * to ** 1x, join with ss to first st. {180 sts}

R22: ch5 (stch), 4trtr in same st as ss, *skip 4 sts, htr in next 10 sts, dc in next 16 sts, htr in next 10 sts, skip 4 sts**, 9trtr in next st*, rep from * to * 2x and * to ** 1x, 4trtr in same st as first sts, join with ss to 5th ch of stch. {36 sts on each side; 4 9-st cnrs}

R23: dc in same st as ss, *bphtr around next 2 sts, bptr around next 2 sts, tr in next 2 sts, htr in next 2 sts, dc in next 28 sts, htr in next 2 sts, tr in next 2 sts, bptr around next 2 sts, bphtr around next 2 sts**, (dc, ch2, dc) in next st*, rep from * to * 2x and * to ** 1x, dc in same st as first st, ch1, join with dc to first st. {46 sts on each side; 4 2-ch cnr sps}

R24: ch3 (stch), tr over joining dc, *tr in next 6 sts, htr in next 2 sts, dc in next 30 sts, htr in next 2 sts, tr in next 6 sts**, (2tr, ch2, 2tr) in 2-ch cnr sp*, rep from * to * 2x and * to ** 1x, 2tr in same sp as first sts, ch1, join with dc to 3rd ch of stch. {50 sts on each side; 4 2-ch cnr sps}

R25: ch3 (stch), *skip 1 st, 9x [tr in next 4 sts, ch1, skip 1 st], tr in next 4 sts**, (tr, ch2, tr) in 2-ch cnr sp*, rep from * to * 2x and * to ** 1x, tr in same sp as first st, ch1, join with dc to 3rd ch of stch. {42 sts, 9 1-ch sps on each side; 4 2-ch cnr sps}

R26: ch3 (stch), *tr in next st, ch2, 9x [tr4tog over next 4 sts, ch5, dc in skipped st of R24 in front of 1-ch sp, ch5], tr4tog over next 4 sts, ch2, tr in next st**, (tr, ch2, tr) in 2-ch cnr sp*, rep from * to * 2x and * to ** 1x, tr in same sp as first st, ch1, join with dc to 3rd ch of stch. {23 sts, 18 5-ch sps, 2 2-ch sps on each side; 4 2-ch cnr sps}

R27: dc over joining dc, *dc in next 2 sts, 2dc in 2-ch sp, 9x [dc in next st, 3dtr in 1-ch sp of R25, skip (5-ch sp, 1 st & 5-ch sp)], dc in next st, 2dc in 2-ch sp, dc in next 2 sts**, (dc, ch2, dc) in 2-ch cnr sp*, rep from * to * 2x and * to ** 1x, dc in same sp as first st, ch1, join with dc to first st. {47 sts on each side; 4 2-ch cnr sps}

R28: dc over joining dc, *dc in next 9 sts, 7x [tr in both 5-ch sps of R26 below at the same time, dc in next 3 sts], tr in both 5-ch sps of R26 below at the same time, dc in next 9 sts**, (dc, ch2, dc) in 2-ch cnr sp*, rep from * to * 2x and * to ** 1x, dc in same sp as first st, ch1, join with dc to first st. {49 sts on each side; 4 2-ch cnr sps}

R29: ch3 (stch), tr over joining dc, *tr in next 10 sts, htr in next 9 sts, dc in next 11 sts, htr in next 9 sts, tr in next 10 sts**, 3tr in 2-ch cnr sp*, rep from * to * 2x and * to ** 1x, tr in same sp as first sts, join with ss to 3rd ch of stch. {49 sts on each side; 4 3-st cnrs}

R30: dc in same st as ss, *dc in next 51 sts**, (dc, ch2, dc) in next st*, rep from * to * 2x and * to ** 1x, dc in same st as first st, ch1, join with dc to first st. {53 sts on each side; 4 2-ch cnr sps}

R31: ch3 (stch), *tr in next 53 sts**, (tr, ch2, tr) in 2-ch cnr sp*, rep from * to * 2x and * to ** 1x, tr in same sp as first st, ch1, join with dc to 3rd ch of stch. {55 sts on each side; 4 2-ch cnr sps}

R32: dc over joining dc, *dc in next 55 sts**, (dc, ch2, dc) in 2-ch cnr sp*, rep from * to * 2x and * to ** 1x, dc in same sp as first st, ch2, join with ss to first st. Fasten off. {57 sts on each side; 4 2-ch cnr sps}

Colours by Evangelia V Katsafouros

Colours by Miranda Howard

Piazza

I see a town square with a fountain in the center, radiating movement outwards, and so Piazza seemed to suit.

  375 m / 411 yd

Refer to both the chart and written pattern to understand better how to make Piazza.

Begin with mc.

R1: ch2 (stch), 11htr, join with ss to top loop of 2nd ch of stch. {12 sts}

R2: ch3 (stch), 2tr in same st as ss, *skip 2 sts**, 5tr in next st*, rep from * to * 2x and * to ** 1x, 2tr in same st as first sts, join with ss to 3rd ch of stch. {4 5-st cnrs}

R3: ch4 (stch), dtr in same st as ss, *tr in next 2 sts, tr between last and next sts, tr in next 2 sts**, 3dtr in next st*, rep from * to * 2x and * to ** 1x, dtr in same st as first sts, join with ss to 4th ch of stch.
{5 sts on each side; 4 3-st cnrs}

R4: dc in same st as ss, *fphtr around next 7 sts**, (dc, ch2, dc) in next st*, rep from * to * 2x and * to ** 1x, dc in same st as first st, ch1, join with dc to first st. {9 sts on each side; 4 2-ch cnr sps}

R5: dc over joining dc, *ch1, 7tr in 4th st of R3 behind R4 sts, ch1**, (dc, ch2, dc) in 2-ch cnr sp*, rep from * to * 2x and * to ** 1x, dc in same sp as first st, ch1, join with dc to first st.
{9 sts, 2 1-ch sps on each side; 4 2-ch cnr sps}

R6: ch3 (stch), 2tr over joining dc, *skip 1 st, dc in 1-ch sp, 3x [spike dc over next st, dc in next st], spike dc over next st, dc in 1-ch sp, skip 1 st**, (3tr, ch1, 3tr) in 2-ch cnr sp*, rep from * to * 2x and * to ** 1x, 3tr in same sp as first sts, join with dc to 3rd ch of stch. {15 sts on each side; 4 1-ch cnr sps}

*Piazza chart
Rounds 1-10*

R7: dc over joining dc, *dc in next 4 sts, ch6, skip 7 sts, dc in next 4 sts**, (dc, ch2, dc) in 1-ch cnr sp*, rep from * to * 2x and * to ** 1x, dc in same sp as first st, ch1, join with dc to first st.
{10 sts, 1 6-ch sp on each side; 4 2-ch cnr sps}

R8: ch3 (stch), tr over joining dc, *tr in next 5 sts, 3dc in 6-ch sp, tr in next 5 sts**, (2tr, ch1, 2tr) in 2-ch cnr sp*, rep from * to * 2x and * to ** 1x, 2tr in same sp as first sts, join with dc to 3rd ch of stch.
{17 sts on each side; 4 1-ch cnr sps}

R9: dc over joining dc, *3x [spike dc over next st, dc in next st], spike dc over next st, skip 1 st, dc in next st, skip 1 st, 3x [spike dc over next st, dc in next st], spike dc over next st**, (dc, ch2, dc) in 1-ch cnr sp*, rep from * to * 2x and * to ** 1x, dc in same sp as first st, ch1, join with dc to first st. {17 sts on each side; 4 2-ch cnr sps}

R10: dc over joining dc, *4x [ch1, skip 1 st, bpdc in 2 loops at back of next spike st], ch1, dc in next st, ch1, 4x [bpdc in 2 loops at back of next spike st, ch1, skip 1]**, dc in 2-ch cnr sp*, rep from * to * 2x and * to ** 1x, join with ss to first st. {9 sts, 10 1-ch sps on each side; 4 1-st cnrs}

Piazza chart
Rounds 10 - 18

104 • Size 5 Patterns - Piazza

R11: ch3 (stch), 3tr in same st as ss, *4x [skip 1-ch sp, dc in next st, skip 1-ch sp, 5tr in next st], skip 1-ch sp, dc in next st, skip 1-ch sp**, 7tr in next st*, rep from * to * 2x and * to ** 1x, 3tr in same st as first sts, join with ss to 3rd ch of stch. {25 sts on each side; 4 7-st cnrs}

R12: dc in same st as ss, *spike dc over next st, dc in next st, spike dc over next st, skip 1 st, tr in next 2 sts, 3tr in next st, tr in next 2 sts, skip 3 sts, dc in lbv of next st, htr in lbv of next st, tr3tog in lbv over next 3 sts, htr in lbv of next st, dc in lbv of next st, skip 3 sts, tr in next 2 sts, 3tr in next st, tr in next 2 sts, skip 1 st, spike dc over next st, dc in next st, spike dc over next st**, (dc, ch2, dc) in next st*, rep from * to * 2x and * to ** 1x, dc in same st as first st, ch1, join with dc to first st. {27 sts on each side; 4 2-ch cnr sps}

R13: dc over joining dc, *2x [ch1, skip 1 st, bpdc in 2 loops at back of next spike st], tr in next 3 sts, 3tr in next st, tr in next 3 sts, dc in next 2 sts, fpdc around next st, dc in next 2 sts, tr in next 3 sts, 3tr in next st, tr in next 3 sts, 2x [bpdc in 2 loops at back of next spike st, ch1, skip 1 st]**, (dc, ch2, dc) in 2-ch cnr sp*, rep from * to * 2x and * to ** 1x, dc in same sp as first st, ch1, join with dc to first st. {29 sts, 4 1-ch sps on each side; 4 2-ch cnr sps}

R14: dc over joining dc, *2x [dc in next st, dc in 1-ch sp], dc in next st, htr in lbv of next 9 sts, dc in next st, skip 1 st, 5tr in next st, skip 1 st, dc in next st, htr in lbv of next 9 sts, 2x [dc in next st, dc in 1-ch sp], dc in next st**, (dc, ch2 dc) in 2-ch cnr sp*, rep from * to * 2x and * to ** 1x, dc in same sp as first st, ch1, join with dc to first st. {37 sts on each side; 4 2-ch cnr sps}

R15: dc over joining dc, *dc in next 6 sts, htr in lbv of next 9 sts, dc in next st, 3x [spike dc over next st, dc in next st], htr in lbv of next 9 sts, dc in next 6 sts**, (dc, ch2, dc) in 2-ch cnr sp*, rep from * to * 2x and * to ** 1x, dc in same sp as first st, ch1, join with dc to first st. {39 sts on each side; 4 2-ch cnr sps}

R16: dc over joining dc, *dc in next 7 sts, htr in lbv of next 9 sts, dc in next st, ch2, skip 2 sts, bpdc in 2 loops at back of next spike st, ch2, skip 2 sts, dc in next st, htr in lbv of next 9 sts, dc in next 7 sts**, dc in 2-ch cnr sp*, rep from * to * 2x and * to ** 1x, join with ss to first st. {35 sts, 2 2-ch sps on each side; 4 1-st cnrs}

R17: ch3 (stch), tr in same st as ss, *ch2, tr3tog over next 3 sts, ch2, tr in next st, ch2, tr3tog over next 3 sts, ch2, skip 2 sts, dc in lbv of next 7 sts, skip 1 st, 2tr in 2-ch sp, tr in next st, 2tr in 2-ch sp, skip 1 st, dc in lbv of next 7 sts, ch2, skip 2 sts, tr3tog over next 3 sts, ch2, tr in next st, ch2, tr3tog over next 3 sts, ch2**, (2tr, ch1, 2tr) in next st*, rep from * to * 2x and * to ** 1x, 2tr in same st as first sts, join with dc to 3rd ch of stch.
{29 sts, 8 2-ch sps on each side; 4 1-ch cnr sps}

R18: dc over joining dc, *dc in next 2 sts, 3x [2dc in 2-ch sp, skip 1 st], 2dc in 2-ch sp, dc in next 19 sts, 3x [2dc in 2-ch sp, skip 1 st], 2dc in 2-ch sp, dc in next 2 sts**, (dc, ch2, dc) in 1-ch cnr sp*, rep from * to * 2x and * to ** 1x, dc in same sp as first st, ch1, join with dc to first st. {41 sts on each side; 4 2-ch cnr sps}

R19: ch3 (stch), *tr in next 41 sts**, (tr, ch2, tr) in 2-ch cnr sp*, rep from * to * 2x and * to ** 1x, tr in same sp as first st, ch1, join with dc to 3rd ch of stch. {43 sts on each side; 4 2-ch cnr sps}

R20: dc over joining dc, *21x [dc in next st, spike dc over next st], dc in next st**, (dc, ch2, dc) in 2-ch cnr sp*, rep from * to * 2x and * to ** 1x, dc in same sp as first st, ch1, join with dc to first st. {45 sts on each side; 4 2-ch cnr sps}

R21: dc over joining dc, *ch1, skip 2 sts, 20x [bpdc in 2 loops at back of next spike st, ch1, skip 1 st], bpdc in 2 loops at back of next spike st, ch1, skip 2 sts**, (dc, ch2, dc) in 2-ch cnr sp*, rep from * to * 2x and * to ** 1x, dc in same sp as first st, ch1, join with dc to first st. {23 sts, 22 1-ch sps on each side; 4 2-ch cnr sps}

R22: dc over joining dc, *22x [dc in next st, dc in 1-ch sp], dc in next st**, (dc, ch2, dc) in 2-ch cnr sp*, rep from * to * 2x and * to ** 1x, dc in same sp as first st, ch1, join with dc to first st. {47 sts on each side; 4 2-ch cnr sps}

R23: ch3 (stch), *tr in next 47 sts**, (tr, ch2, tr) in 2-ch cnr sp*, rep from * to * 2x and * to ** 1x, tr in same sp as first st, ch1, join with dc to 3rd ch of stch. {49 sts on each side; 4 2-ch cnr sps}

R24: dc over joining dc, *dc in next 49 sts**, (dc, ch2, dc) in 2-ch cnr sp*, rep from * to * 2x and * to ** 1x, dc in same sp as first st, ch1, join with dc to first st. {51 sts on each side; 4 2-ch cnr sps}

R25: dc over joining dc, *25x [ch1, skip 1 st, dc in flo of next st], ch1, skip 1 st**, (dc, ch2, dc) in 2-ch cnr sp*, rep from * to * 2x and * to ** 1x, dc in same sp as first st, ch1, join with dc to first st.
{27 sts, 26 1-ch sps on each side; 4 2-ch cnr sps}

R26: ch2 (stch), *htr in next st, 25x [htr in 1-ch sp, tr in blo of R24 st behind R25 sts], htr in 1-ch sp, htr in next st**, (htr, ch2, htr) in 2-ch cnr sp*, rep from * to * 2x and * to ** 1x, htr in same sp as first st, ch1, join with dc to 2nd ch of stch. {55 sts on each side; 4 2-ch cnr sps}

R27: ch2 (stch), *htr in lbv of next 55 sts**, (htr, ch2, htr) in 2-ch cnr sp*, rep from * to * 2x and * to ** 1x, htr in same sp as first st, ch1, join with dc to 2nd ch of stch. {57 sts on each side; 4 2-ch cnr sps}

R28: ch2 (stch), *htr in lbv of next 57 sts**, (htr, ch2, htr) in 2-ch cnr sp*, rep from * to * 2x and * to ** 1x, htr in same sp as first st, ch1, join with dc to 2nd ch of stch. {59 sts on each side; 4 2-ch cnr sps}

R29: dc over joining dc, *29x [ch1, skip 1 st, dc in lbv of next st], ch1, skip 1 st**, (dc, ch2, dc) in 2-ch cnr sp*, rep from * to * 2x and * to ** 1x, dc in same sp as first st, ch1, join with dc to first st.
{31 sts, 30 1-ch sps on each side; 4 2-ch cnr sps}

R30: dc over joining dc, *30x [dc in next st, dc in 1-ch sp], dc in next st**, (dc, ch2, dc) in 2-ch cnr sp*, rep from * to * 2x and * to ** 1x, dc in same sp as first st, ch1, join with dc to first st. {63 sts on each side; 4 2-ch cnr sps}

R31: ch3 (stch), *tr in next 63 sts**, (tr, ch2, tr) in 2-ch sp*, rep from * to * 2x and * to ** 1x, tr in same sp as first sts, ch1, join with dc to 3rd ch of stch. {65 sts on each side; 4 2-ch cnr sps}

R32: dc over joining dc, *dc in next 65 sts**, (dc, ch2, dc) in 2-ch cnr sp*, rep from * to * 2x and * to ** 1x, dc in same sp as first st, ch1, join with dc to first st. {67 sts on each side; 4 2-ch cnr sps}

R33: dc over joining dc, *33x [ch1, skip 1 st, dc in flo of next st], ch1, skip 1 st**, (dc, ch2, dc) in 2-ch cnr sp*, rep from * to * 2x and * to ** 1x, dc in same sp as first st, ch1, join with dc to first st.
{35 sts, 34 1-ch sps on each side; 4 2-ch cnr sps}

R34: ch3 (stch), *tr in next st, 33x [tr in 1-ch sp, tr in blo of R32 st behind], tr in 1-ch sp, tr in next st**, (tr, ch2, tr) in 2-ch cnr sp*, rep from * to * 2x and * to ** 1x, tr in same sp as first st, ch1, join with dc to 3rd ch of stch.
{71 sts on each side; 4 2-ch cnr sps}

R35: dc over joining dc, *dc in next 71 sts**, (dc, ch2, dc) in 2-ch cnr sp*, rep from * to * 2x and * to ** 1x, dc in same sp as first st, ch2, join with ss to first st. Fasten off. {73 sts on each side; 4 2-ch cnr sps}

Piazza chart
Rounds 18 - 35

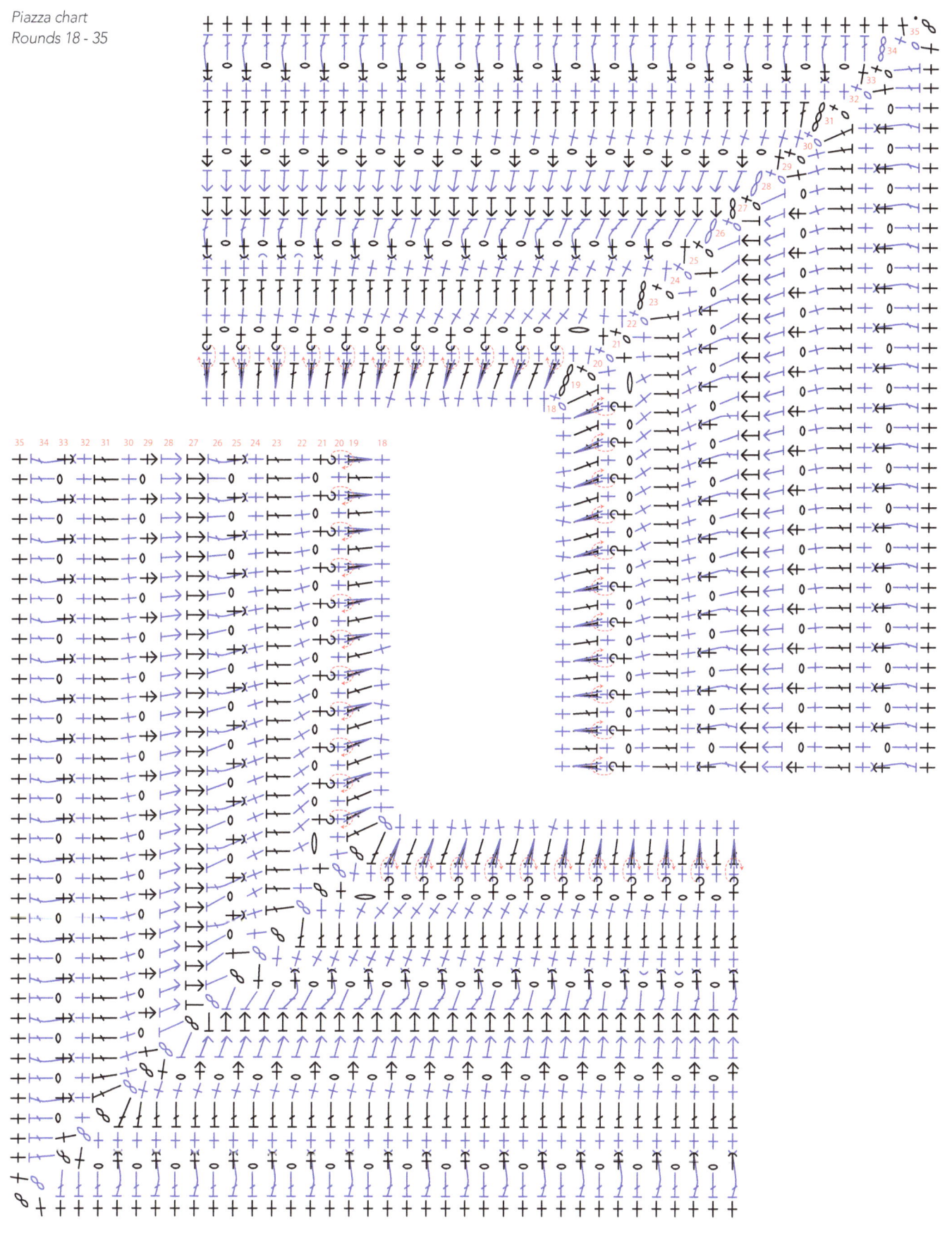

Piazza - Size 5 Patterns • 107

Colours by Jenny Hebbard

Colours by Mell Sappho

Wreath

Named as it reminds me of an arrangement of flowers in a ring.

 396 m / 433 yd

In Round 20, you will see an instruction to "rep from [to ^" in addition to the usual repeats indicated with asterisks.

Begin with mc.

R1: ch3 (stch), 15tr, join with ss to 3rd ch of stch. {16 sts}

R2: ch3 (stch), 4trcl in same st as ss, *ch2, dc in next st, ch2**, 5trcl in next st*, rep from * to * 6x and * to ** 1x, join with ss to top of 4trcl. {16 sts, 16 2-ch sps}

R3: fpdc around (stch & 4trcl), *ch2, skip 2-ch sp, bptr around next st, ch2, skip 2-ch sp**, fpdc around next st*, rep from * to * 6x and * to ** 1x, join with ss to first st. {16 sts, 16 2-ch sps}

R4: ch3 (stch), *2tr in 2-ch sp**, tr in next st*, rep from * to * 14x and * to ** 1x, join with ss to 3rd ch of stch. {48 sts}

R5: ch3 (stch), 4trcl in same st as ss, *ch2, dc in next 2 sts, ch2**, 5trcl in next st*, rep from * to * 14x and * to ** 1x, join with ss to top of 4trcl. {48 sts, 32 2-ch sps}

R6: fpdc around (stch & 4trcl), *ch2, skip 2-ch sp, bptr around next 2 sts at the same time, ch2, skip 2-ch sp**, fpdc around next st*, rep from * to * 14x and * to ** 1x, join with ss to first st. {32 sts, 32 2-ch sps}

R7: ch3 (stch), *tr in 2-ch sp**, tr in next st*, rep from * to * 30x and * to ** 1x, join with ss to 3rd ch of stch. {64 sts}

108 • Size 5 Patterns - Wreath

*Wreath chart
Rounds 1 - 11*

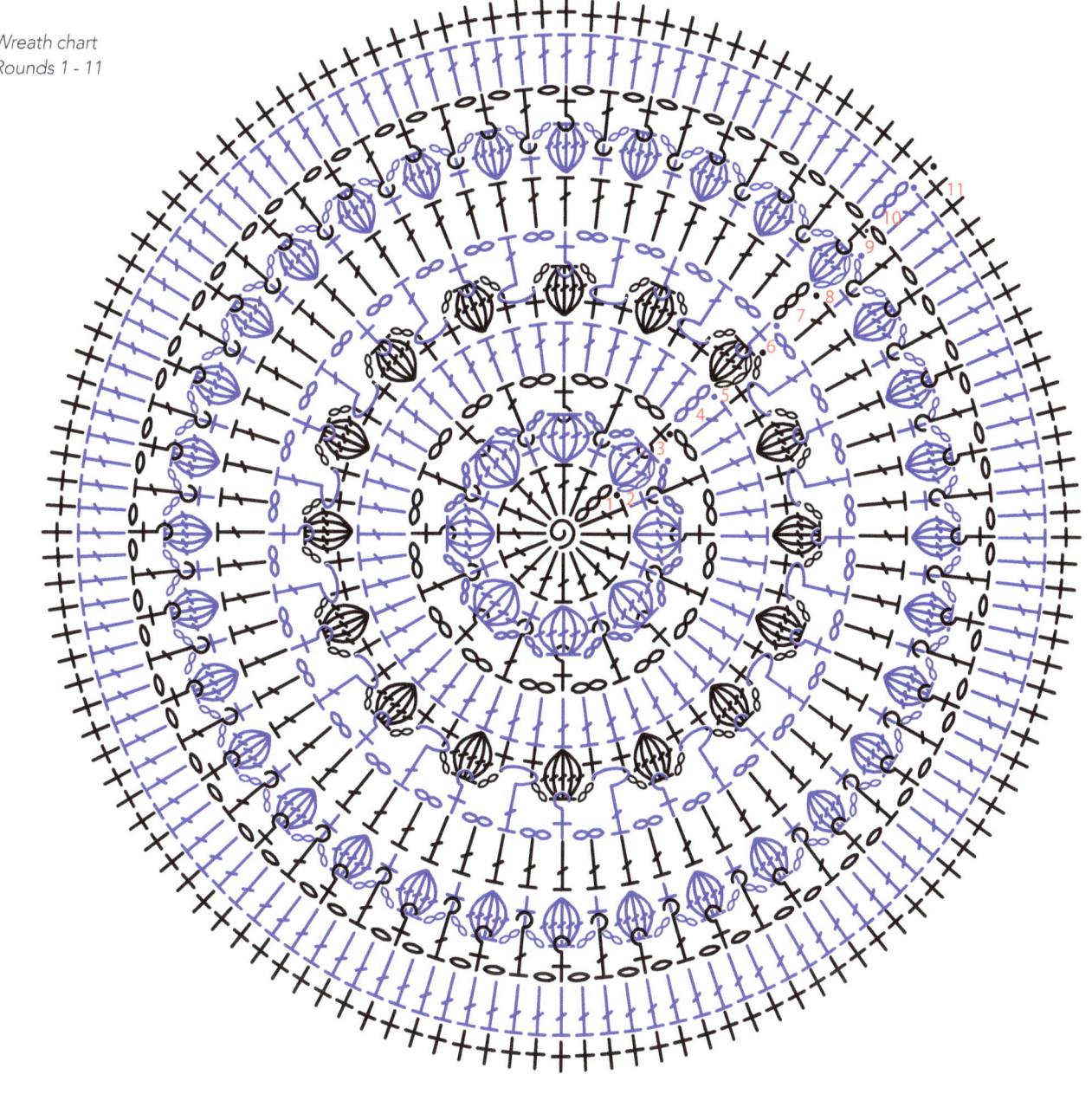

R8: ch3 (stch), 4trcl in same st as ss, *ch2, dc in next st, ch2**, 5trcl in next st*, rep from * to * 30x and * to ** 1x, join with ss to top of 4trcl. {64 sts, 64 2-ch sps}

R9: fpdc around (stch & 4trcl), *ch1, skip 2-ch sp, bptr around next st, ch1, skip 2-ch sp**, fpdc around next st*, rep from * to * 30x and * to ** 1x, join with ss to first st. {64 sts, 64 1-ch sps}

R10: ch3 (stch), *tr in 1-ch sp**, tr in next st*, rep from * to * 62x and * to ** 1x, join with ss to 3rd ch of stch. {128 sts}

R11: dc in same st as ss, dc in next 127 sts, join with ss to first dc. {128 sts}

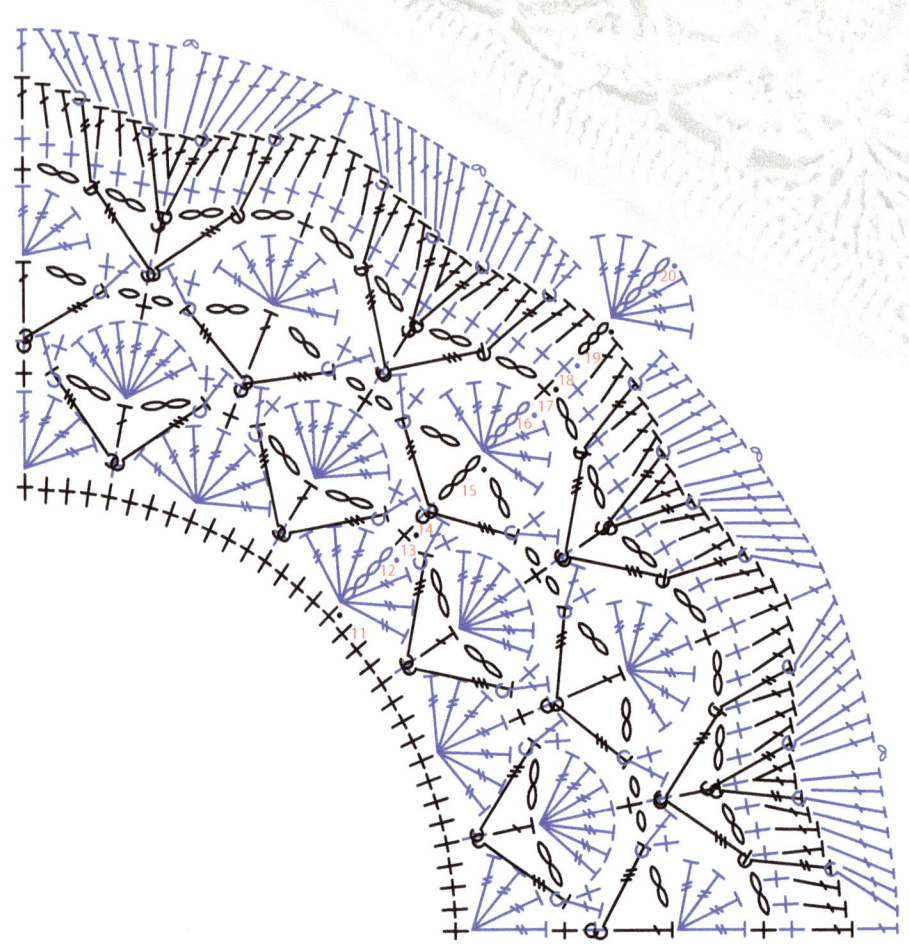

*Wreath chart
Rounds 11 - 20*

R12: ch4 (stch), 3dtr in same st as ss, *skip 3 sts, dc in next st, skip 3 sts**, 7dtr in next st*, rep from * to * 14x and * to ** 1x, 3dtr in same st as ss, join with ss to 4th ch of stch. {128 sts}

R13: dc in same st as ss, *skip 3 sts, (fptrtr around, ch2, tr in, ch2, fptrtr around) next st, skip 3 sts**, dc in next st*, rep from * to * 14x and * to ** 1x, join with ss to first st. {64 sts, 32 2-ch sps}

R14: dc in same st as ss, *(fptr around, dc in) next st, skip 2-ch sp, 7dtr in next st, skip 2-ch sp, (dc in, fptr around) next st**, dc in next st*, rep from * to * 14x and * to ** 1x, join with ss to first st. {192 sts}

R15: ch3 (stch), (ch2, fptrtr around) same st as ss, *ch1, skip 5 sts, dc in next st, ch1, skip 5 sts**, (fptrtr around, ch2, tr in, ch2, fptrtr around) next st*, rep from * to * 14x and * to ** 1x, fptrtr around same st as first sts, ch2, join with ss to 3rd ch of stch. {64 sts, 32 1-ch sps, 32 2-ch sps}

R16: ch4 (stch), 3dtr in same st as ss, *skip 2-ch sp, (dc in, fptr around) next st, skip 1-ch sp, dc in next st, skip 1-ch sp, (fptr around, dc in) next st, skip 2-ch sp**, 7dtr in next st*, rep from * to * 14x and * to ** 1x, 3dtr in same st as first sts, join with ss to 4th ch of stch. {192 sts}

R17: dc in same st as ss, *ch2, skip 5 sts, (fptrtr around, ch2, tr in, ch2, fptrtr around) next st, ch2, skip 5 sts**, dc in next st*, rep from * to * 14x and * to ** 1x, join with ss to first st. {64 sts, 64 2-ch sps}

R18: dc in same st as ss, *2dc in 2-ch sp**, dc in next st*, rep from * to * 62x and * to ** 1x, join with ss to first st. {192 sts}

R19: ch3 (stch), tr in next 2 sts, *fpdtr around R17 st below, tr in next 3 sts, fpdtr around R17 st below, 2tr in next st, fpdtr around same R17 st, tr in next 3 sts, fpdtr around R17 st below**, tr in next 5 sts*, rep from * to * 14x and * to ** 1x, tr in next 2 sts, join with ss to 3rd ch of stch. {272 sts}

R20: ch4 (stch), 3dtr in same st as ss, *3x [skip 2 sts, (fptr around, tr in) next st, tr in next 3 sts, (fptr around, tr in) next st, tr in next st, ch2, tr in next st, (tr in, fptr around) next st, tr in next 3 sts, (tr in, fptr around) next st, skip 2 sts^, tr in next st], rep from [to ^ 1x**, 7dtr in next st*, rep from * to * 2x and * to ** 1x, 3dtr in same st as first sts, join with ss to 4th ch of stch. {67 sts, 4 2-ch sps on each side; 4 7-st cnrs}

Wreath chart
Rounds 19 - 27

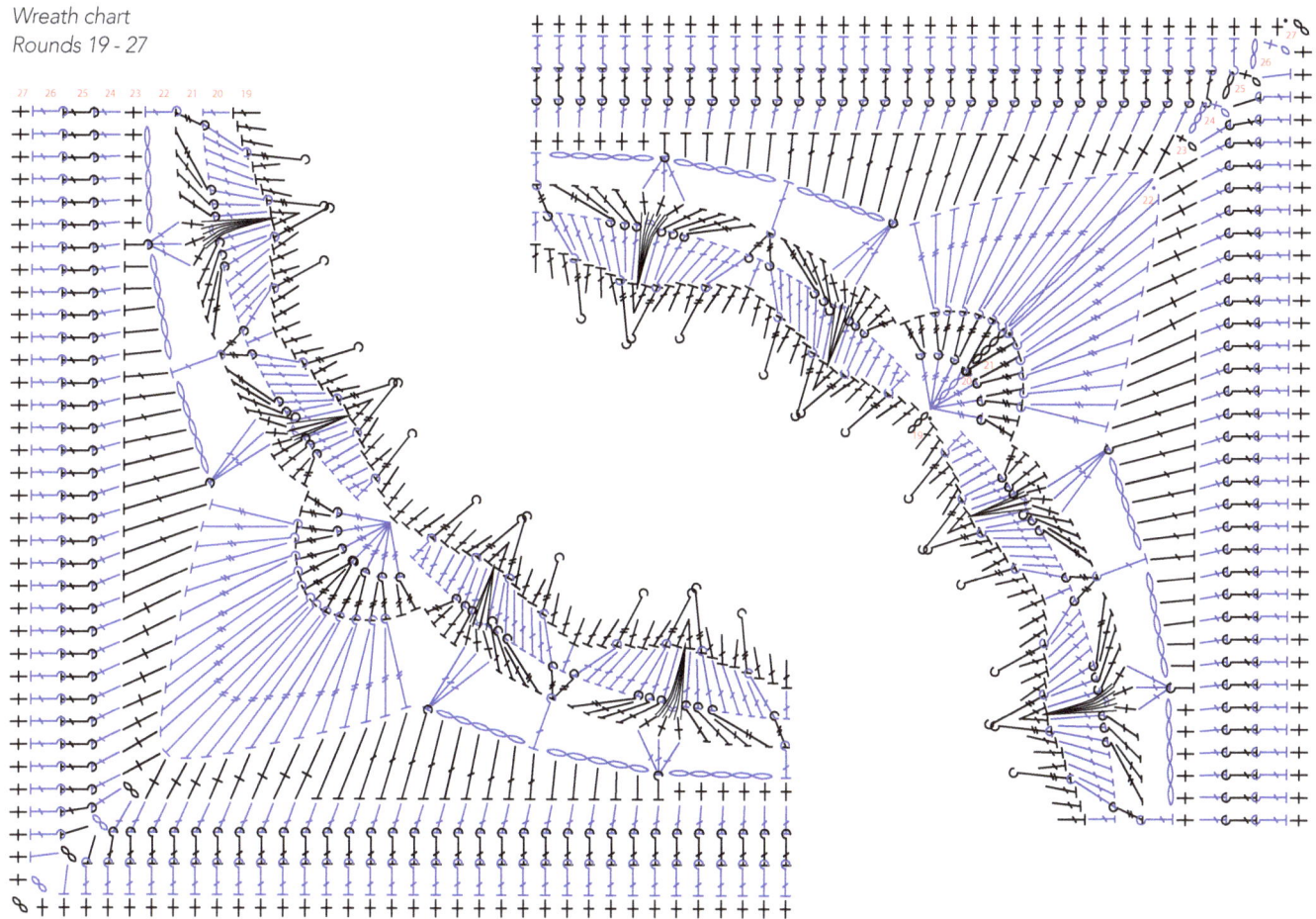

R21: ch4 (stch), fpdtr around same st as ss, *(dtr in, fpdtr around) next 3 sts, skip 5 sts, 3x [(fpdtr around, tr in) next st, fptr around next 2 sts, 3 spike dc sts between R19 sts below, fptr around next 2 sts, (tr in, fpdtr around) next st^, skip 4 sts, fptr2tog around next 3 sts skipping the middle st, skip 4 sts], rep from [to ^ 1x, skip 5 sts, (fpdtr around, dtr in) next 3 sts**, (fpdtr around, dtr in, fpdtr around) next st*, rep from * to * 2x and * to ** 1x, fpdtr around same st as first sts, join with ss to 4th ch of stch. {59 sts on each side; 4 3-st cnrs}

R22: ch4 (stch), fpdtr around same st as ss, *(dtr in, fpdtr around) next 5 sts, skip 6 sts, 3x [tr3tog over next 3 sts, ch5, skip 4 sts, fptr around next st, ch5, skip 4 sts], tr3tog over next 3 sts, skip 6 sts, (fpdtr around, dtr in) next 5 sts**, (fpdtr around, dtr in, fpdtr around) next st*, rep from * to * 2x and * to ** 1x, fpdtr around same st as first sts, join with ss to 4th ch of stch. {27 sts, 6 5-ch sps on each side; 4 3-st cnrs}

R23: dc in same st as ss, *dc in next 7 sts, htr in next 2 sts, tr in next 2 sts, fptr around next st, 5tr in 5-ch sp, tr in next st, 5htr in 5-ch sp, fphtr around next st, 5dc in 5-ch sp, dc in next st, 5dc in 5-ch sp, fphtr around next st, 5htr in 5-ch sp, tr in next st, 5tr in 5-ch sp, fptr around next st, tr in next 2 sts, htr in next 2 sts, dc in next 7 sts**, (dc, ch2, dc) in next st*, rep from * to * 2x and * to ** 1x, dc in same st as first st, ch1, join with dc to first st. {61 sts on each side; 4 2-ch cnr sps}

R24: ch3 (stch), *tr in next 61 sts**, (tr, ch2, tr) in 2-ch cnr sp*, rep from * to * 2x and * to ** 1x, tr in same sp as first st, ch1, join with dc to 3rd ch of stch. {63 sts on each side; 4 2-ch cnr sps}

R25: ch2 (stch), *fptr around next 63 sts**, (htr, ch2, htr) in 2-ch cnr sp*, rep from * to * 2x and * to ** 1x, htr in same sp as first st, ch1, join with dc to 2nd ch of stch. {65 sts on each side; 4 2-ch cnr sps}

R26: ch2 (stch), *fptr around next 65 sts**, (htr, ch2, htr) in 2-ch cnr sp*, rep from * to * 2x and * to ** 1x, htr in same sp as first st, ch1, join with dc to 2nd ch of stch. {67 sts on each side; 4 2-ch cnr sps}

R27: dc over joining dc, *dc in next 67 sts**, (dc, ch2, dc) in 2-ch cnr sp*, rep from * to * 2x and * to ** 1x, dc in same sp as first st, ch2, join with ss to first st. Fasten off. {69 sts on each side; 4 2-ch cnr sps}

Size 6 Patterns

And here we are at the meaty end! The largest patterns I have for you in this book. Well, that is if you keep them as is and don't extend them with the next set of patterns!

Below are the approximate sizes you will achieve with 3 different yarn weights and hook sizes. The amount of yarn listed on each pattern page is for the middle yarn weight and hook size. The amount of yarn needed for the other yarn weights is on page 177.

hook	3.5 mm hook	4.5 mm hook	5.5 mm hook
yarn	4 ply/sock/fingering	8 ply/DK/light worsted	10 ply/aran/worsted
square	17.5"	21"	24.5"

Hope
page 114

Kaboom
page 120

Kim
page 124

Mayan
page 130

Rebecca
page 134

Colours by Evangelia V Katsafouros

Colours by Mell Sappho

Hope

Hope and Shine on page 38 are related patterns that brought a lot of hope. The Shine with Hope pattern raised thousands for charity in 2020.

  442 m / 483 yd

Begin with mc.

R1: ch2 (stch), 15htr, join with ss to 2nd ch of stch. {16 sts}.

R2: ch4 (stch), dtr in same st as ss, 2dtr in next 15 sts, join with ss to 4th ch of stch. {32 sts}

R3: dc in same st as ss, *ch2, skip 1 st**, dc in next st*, rep from * to * 14x and * to ** 1x, join with ss to first st. {16 sts, 16 2-ch sps}

R4: ch3 (stch), tr in same st as ss, *skip 2-ch sp**, 3tr in next st*, rep from * to * 14x and * to ** 1x, tr in same st as first sts, join with ss to 3rd ch of stch. {48 sts}

R5: dc in same st as ss, *ch3, dc in skipped st of R2 in front of R3 & R4 sts, ch3**, dc in middle st of 3-st group*, rep from * to * 14x and * to ** 1x, join with ss to first st. {32 sts, 32 3-ch sps}

R6: ch1, bpdc around same st as ss, *dc in next 2 sts of R4**, bpdc around next st*, rep from * to * 14x and * to ** 1x, join with ss to first st. {48 sts}

R7: ch3 (stch), *ch1**, tr in next st*, rep from * to * 46x and * to ** 1x, join with ss to 3rd ch of stch. {48 sts, 48 1-ch sps}

R8: ch2 (stch), *htr in 1-ch sp**, htr in next st*, rep from * to * 46x and * to ** 1x, join with ss to 2nd ch of stch. {96 sts}

R9: ch4 (stch), dtr in next 95 sts, join with ss to 4th ch of stch. {96 sts}

R10: dc in same st as ss, dc in next 95 sts, join with ss to first st. {96 sts}

Hope chart
Rounds 1 - 10

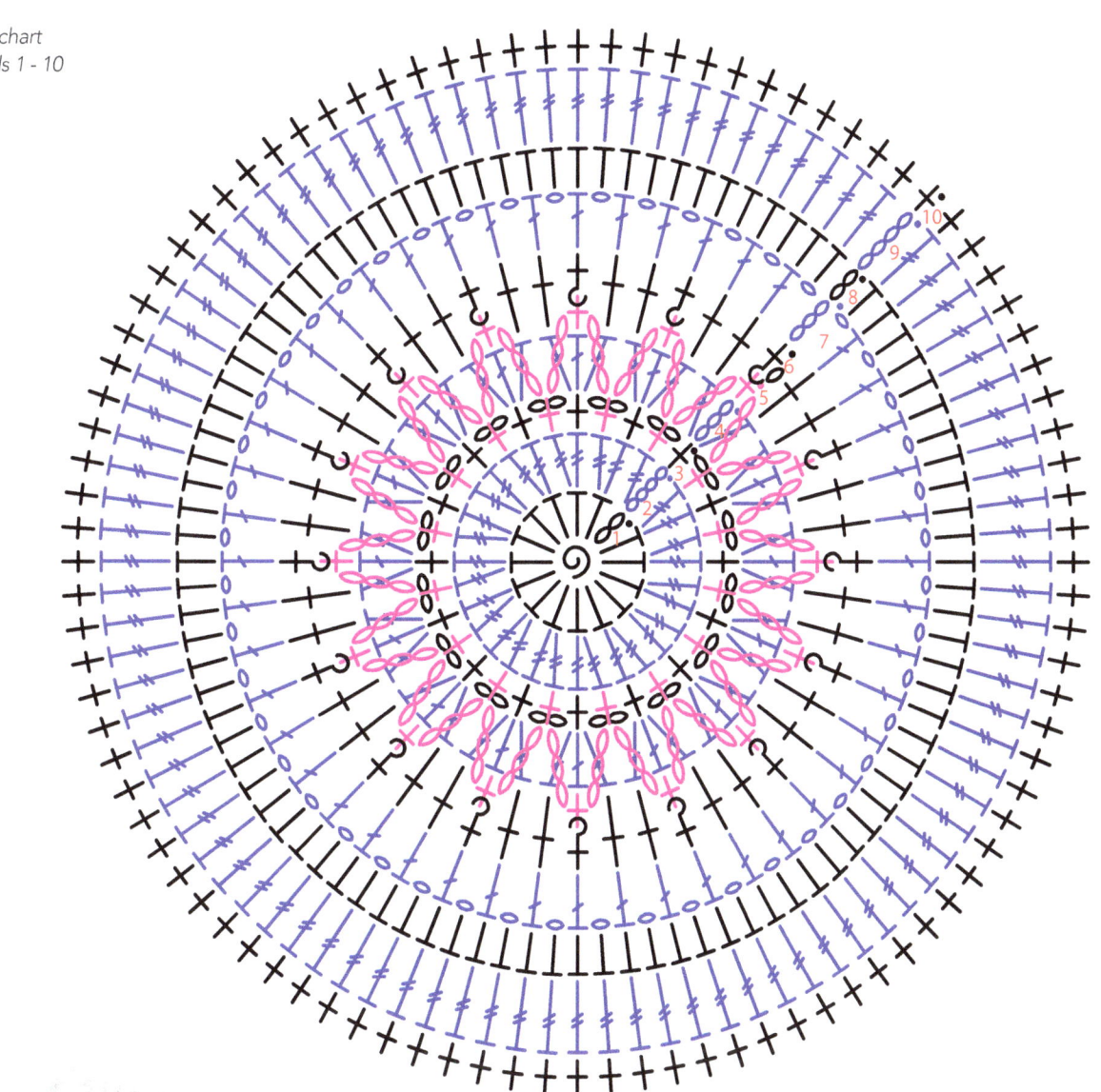

Hope - Size 6 Patterns • 115

Hope chart
Rounds 10 - 20

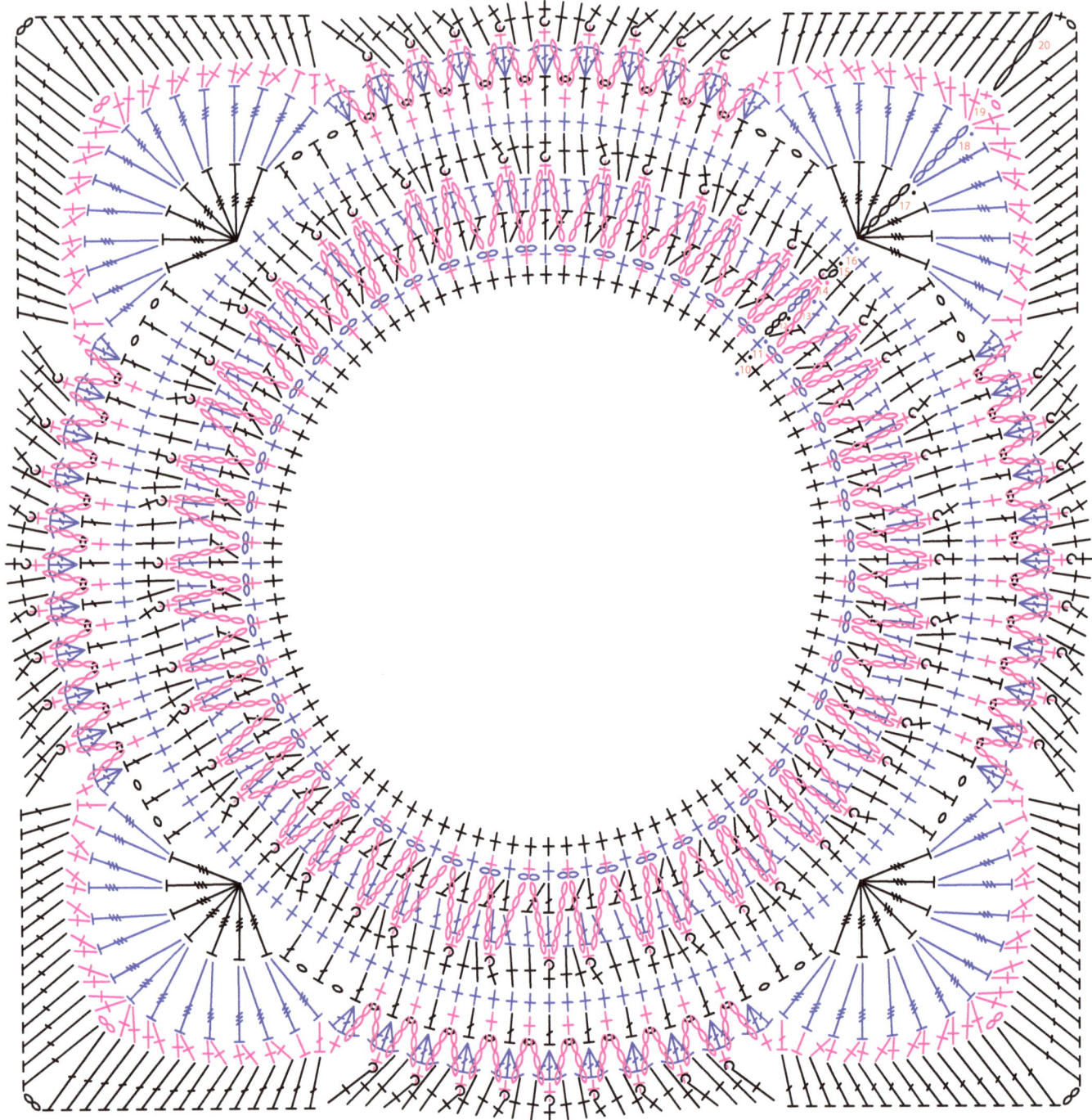

R11: dc in same st as ss, *ch2, skip 1 st**, dc in next st*, rep from * to * 46x and * to ** 1x, join with ss to first st. {48 sts, 48 2-ch sps}

R12: ch3 (stch), *skip 2-ch sp**, 2tr in next st*, rep from * to * 46x and * to ** 1x, tr in same st as first st, join with ss to 3rd ch of stch. {96 sts}

R13: ch3 (stch), tr in next st, *tr between last and next sts**, tr in next 4 sts*, rep from * to * 22x and * to ** 1x, tr in next 2 sts, join with ss to 3rd ch of stch. {120 sts}

R14: dc in same st as ss, *ch5, dc in skipped st of R10 in front of (R11, R12 & R13), ch5, skip 1 st, dc in next st, ch5, dc in skipped st of R10 in front of (R11, R12 & R13), ch5, skip 2 sts**, dc in next st*, rep from * to * 22x and * to ** 1x, join with ss to first st. {96 sts, 96 5-ch sps}

R15: ch1, bpdc around same st as ss, *2dc in next st of R13, bpdc around next st, dc in next 2 sts of R13**, bpdc around next st*, rep from * to * 22x and * to ** 1x, join with ss to first st. {144 sts}

R16: dc in same st as ss, dc in next 143 sts, join with ss to first st. {144 sts}

R17: ch5 (stch), 3trtr in same st as ss, *skip 3 sts, 14x [tr in next st, ch1, skip 1 st], tr in next st, skip 3 sts**, 7trtr in next st*, rep from * to * 2x and * to ** 1x, 3trtr in same st as first sts, join with ss to 5th ch of stch. {15 sts, 14 1-ch sps on each side; 4 7-st cnrs}

R18: ch5 (stch), trtr in same st as ss, *2trtr in next 3 sts, skip (1 st, 1-ch sp, 1 st & 1-ch sp), 10x [3tr in next st, skip 1-ch sp], 3tr in next st, skip (1-ch sp, 1 st, 1-ch sp & 1 st), 2trtr in next 3 sts**, 3trtr in next st*, rep from * to * 2x and * to ** 1x, trtr in same st as first sts, join with ss to 5th ch of stch. {45 sts on each side; 4 3-st cnrs}

R19: 2dc in same st as ss, *2dc in next 5 sts, htr in next st, tr in next st, skip 1 st, dc in next st, 10x [ch3, dc in next skipped st of R16 in front of R17 & 18, ch3, dc in middle st of 3-st group], skip 1 st, tr in next st, htr in next st, 2dc in next 5 sts**, (2dc, ch2, 2dc) in next st*, rep from * to * 2x and * to ** 1x, 2dc in same st as first sts, ch1, join with dc to first st. {49 sts, 20 3-ch sps on each side; 4 2-ch cnr sps}

R20: ch3 (stch), *tr in next 14 sts, skip (1 st, 3-ch sp, 1 st & 3-ch sp), 8x [bpdc around next st, dc in next 2 sts of R18], bpdc around next st, skip (3-ch sp, 1 st, 3-ch sp & 1 st), tr in next 14 sts**, (tr, ch2, tr) in 2-ch cnr sp*, rep from * to * 2x and * to ** 1x, tr in same sp as first st, ch1, join with dc to 3rd ch of stch. {55 sts on each side; 4 2-ch cnr sps}

Hope chart
Rounds 20 - 33

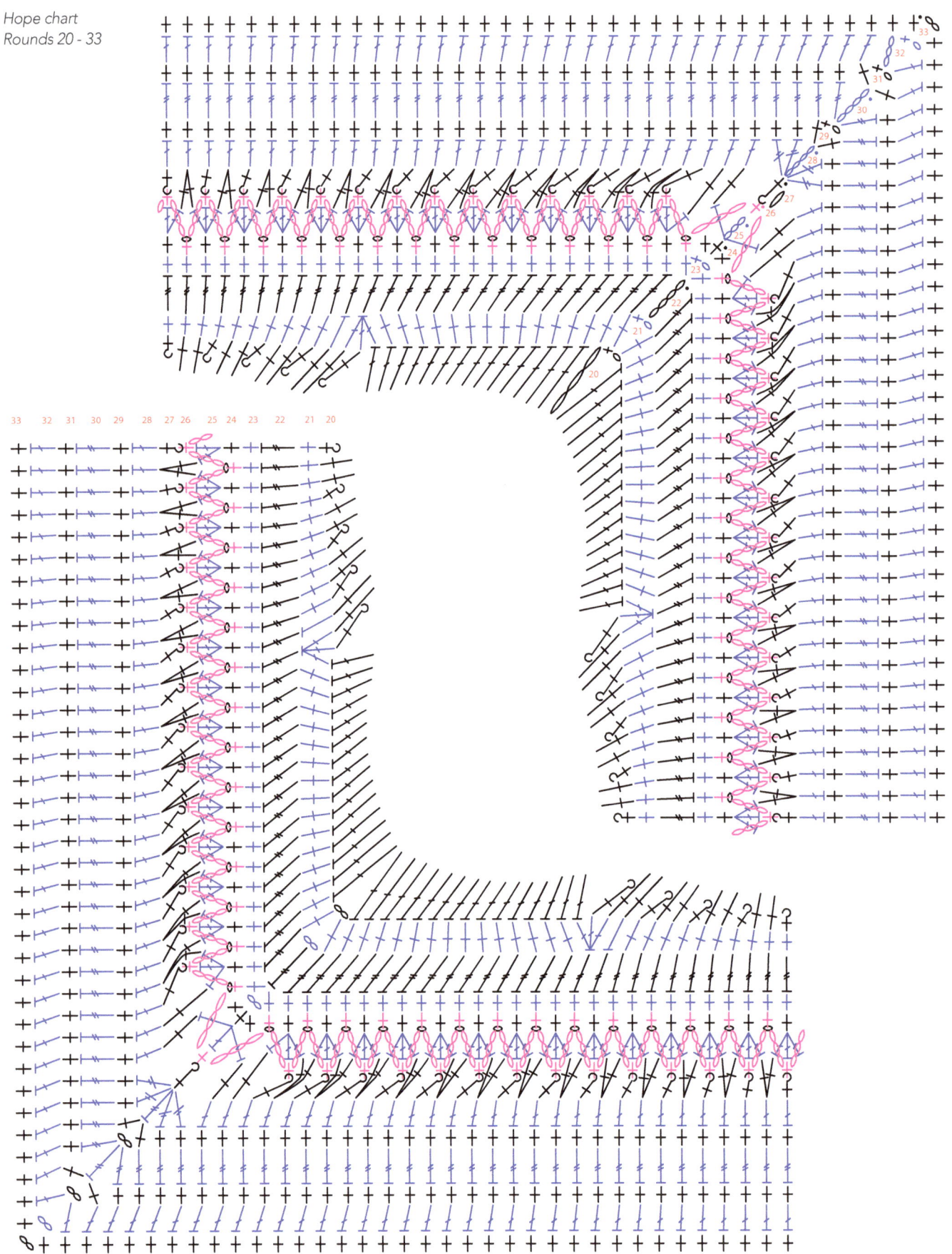

118 • Size 6 Patterns - Hope

R21: dc over joining dc, *dc in next 14 sts, tr3tog over next 3 sts, htr in next st, dc in next 19 sts, htr in next st, tr3tog over next 3 sts, dc in next 14 sts**, (dc, ch2, dc) in 2-ch cnr sp*, rep from * to * 2x and * to ** 1x, dc in same sp as first st, ch1, join with dc to first st. {53 sts on each side; 4 2-ch cnr sps}

R22: ch4 (stch), *dtr in next 53 sts**, dtr in 2-ch cnr sp*, rep from * to * 2x and * to ** 1x, join with ss to 4th ch of stch. {53 sts on each side; 4 1-st cnrs}

R23: dc in same st as ss, *dc in next 53 sts**, (dc, ch2, dc) in next st*, rep from * to * 2x and * to ** 1x, dc in same st as first st, ch1, join with dc to first st. {55 sts on each side; 4 2-ch cnr sps}

R24: 2dc over joining dc, *27x [ch1, skip 1 st, dc in next st], ch1, skip 1 st**, 3dc in 2-ch cnr sp*, rep from * to * 2x and * to ** 1x, dc in same sp as first sts, join with ss to first st. {27 sts, 28 1-ch sps on each side; 4 3-st cnrs}

R25: ch3 (stch), tr in same st as ss, *skip (1 st & 1-ch sp), 27x [3tr in next st, skip 1-ch sp], skip 1 st**, 3tr in next st*, rep from * to * 2x and * to ** 1x, tr in same st as first sts, join with ss to 3rd ch of stch. {81 sts on each side; 4 3-st cnrs}

R26: dc in same st as ss, *ch3, dc in skipped st of R23 in front of R24 & R25 sts, ch3**, dc in middle st of 3-st group*, rep from * to * 110x and * to ** 1x, join with ss to first st. {55 sts, 56 3-ch sps on each side; 4 1-st cnrs}

R27: ch1, bpdc around same st as ss, *dc in next 2 sts of R25, 26x [bpdc around next st, dc2tog over next 2 sts of R25], bpdc around next st, dc in next 2 sts of R25**, bpdc around next st*, rep from * to * 2x and * to ** 1x, join with ss to first st. {57 sts on each side; 4 1-st cnrs}

R28: ch4 (stch), 2hdtr in same st as ss, *tr in next 57 sts**, (2hdtr, dtr, 2hdtr) in next st*, rep from * to * 2x and * to ** 1x, 2hdtr in same st as first sts, join with ss to 4th st of stch. {57 sts on each side; 4 5-st cnrs}

R29: dc in same st as ss, *dc in next 61 sts**, (dc, ch2, dc) in next st*, rep from * to * 2x and * to ** 1x, dc in same st as first st, ch1, join with dc to first st. {63 sts on each side; 4 2-ch cnr sps}

R30: ch4 (stch), dtr over joining dc, *dtr in next 63 sts**, 3dtr in 2-ch cnr sp*, rep from * to * 2x and * to ** 1x, dtr in same sp as first sts, join with ss to 4th ch of stch. {63 sts on each side; 4 3-st cnrs}

R31: dc in same st as ss, *dc in next 65 sts**, (dc, ch2, dc) in next st*, rep from * to * 2x and * to ** 1x, dc in same st as first st, ch1, join with dc to first st. {67 sts on each side; 4 2-ch cnr sps}

R32: ch3 (stch), *tr in next 67 sts**, (tr, ch2, tr) in 2-ch cnr sp*, rep from * to * 2x and * to ** 1x, tr in same sp as first st, ch1, join with dc to 3rd ch of stch. {69 sts on each side; 4 2-ch cnr sps}

R33: dc over joining dc, *dc in next 69 sts**, (dc, ch2, dc) in 2-ch cnr sp*, rep from * to * 2x and * to ** 1x, dc in same sp as first st, ch2, join with ss to first st. Fasten off. {71 sts on each side; 4 2-ch cnr sps}

Colours by Kim Siebenhausen

Colours by Evangelia V Katsafouros

Kaboom

"There was supposed to be an earth-shattering Kaboom". It's a line by one of my favourite cartoon characters, Marvin the Martian. The initial design was a rainbow explosion of colour. And so Kaboom!

  400 m / 438 yd

Begin with mc.

R1: ch3 (stch), 11tr, join with ss to 3rd ch of stch. {12 sts}

R2: dc in same st as ss, *ch3, skip 1 st, dc in next st*, rep from * to * 4x, ch3, skip 1 st, join with ss to first st. {6 sts, 6 3-ch sps}

R3: ch3 (stch), *ch2, puff in 3-ch sp, ch2**, tr in next st*, rep from * to * 4x and from * to ** 1x, join with ss to 3rd ch of stch. {12 sts, 12 2-ch sps}

R4: dc in same st as ss, *2dc in 2-ch sp**, dc in next st*, rep from * to * 10x and from * to ** 1x, join with ss to first st. {36 sts}

R5: ch3 (stch), *ch1, tr in next st*, rep from * to * 34x, ch1, join with ss to 3rd ch of stch. {36 sts, 36 1-ch sps}

R6: ch3 (stch), fptr around same st as ss, *skip 1-ch sp, (tr in, fptr around) next st*, rep from * to * 34x, join with ss to 3rd ch of stch. {72 sts}

R7: dc in same st as ss, dc in next 71 sts, join with ss to first st. {72 sts}

R8: dc in same st as ss, *ch3, skip 2 sts**, dc in next st*, rep from * to * 22x and from * to ** 1x, join with ss to first st. {24 sts, 24 3-ch sps}

R9: ch3 (stch), *3tr in 3-ch sp**, tr in next st*, rep from * to * 22x and from * to ** 1x, join with ss to 3rd ch of stch. {96 sts}

Kaboom chart
Rounds 1- 15

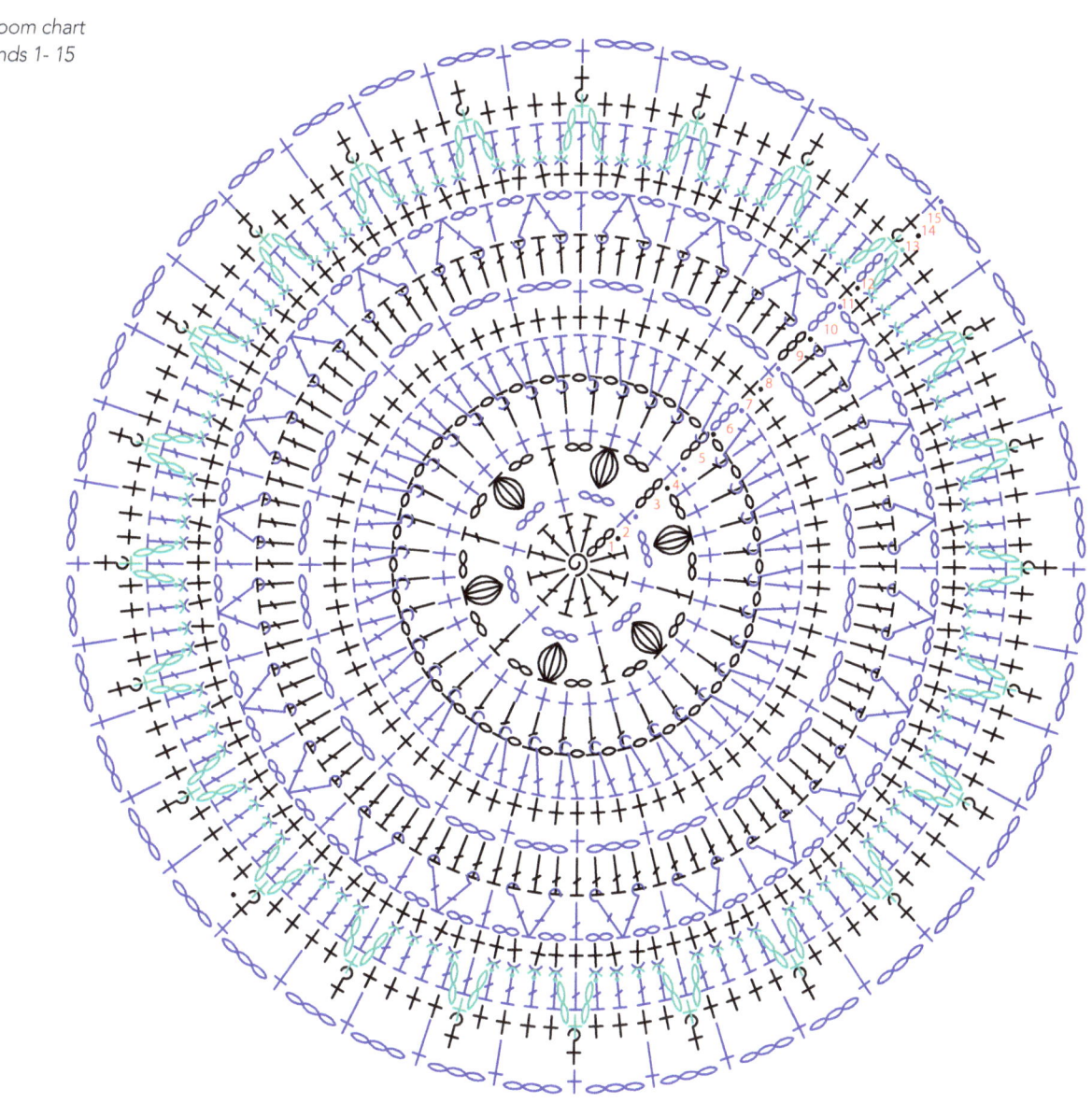

R10: ch3 (stch), *ch2, fptr2tog over next 3 sts skipping the middle st, ch2**, tr in next st*, rep from * to * 22x and from * to ** 1x, join with ss to 3rd ch of stch. {48 sts, 48 2-ch sps}

R11: dc in same st as ss, *2dc in 2-ch sp, skip 1 st, 2dc in 2-ch sp**, dc in next st*, rep from * to * 22x and from * to ** 1x, join with ss to first st. {120 sts}

R12: ch3 (stch), *tr in blo of next 4 sts**, tr in next st*, rep from * to * 22x and from * to ** 1x, join with ss to first st. {120 sts}

R13: dc in same st as ss, *ch2, ss in flo of next 4 sts of R11 below, ch2**, dc in next st*, rep from * to * 22x and from * to ** 1x, join with ss to first st. {24 R13 sts, 96 R11 sts, 48 2-ch sps}

R14: ch1, bpdc around same st as ss, *dc in next 4 sts of R12**, bpdc around next st*, rep from * to * 22x and from * to ** 1x, join with ss to first st. {120 sts}

R15: dc in same st as ss, *ch3, skip 2 sts**, dc in next st*, rep from * to * 38x and from * to ** 1x, join with ss to first st. {40 sts, 40 3-ch sps}

Kaboom charts
Rounds 15-24

R16: ch3 (stch), *ch2, 5tr in 3-ch sp, ch2**, tr in next st*, rep from * to * 38x and from * to ** 1x, join with ss to 3rd ch of stch. {240 sts, 80 2-ch sps}

Will be very ruffled.

R17: dc in same st as ss, *dc in 2-ch sp, dc in both 2-ch sps either side of next 5 sts at the same time, dc in same 2-ch sp**, dc in next st*, rep from * to * 38x and from * to ** 1x, join with ss to first st. {160 sts}

R18: ch3 (stch), *ch1, skip 1 st**, tr in next st*, rep from * to * 78x and from * to ** 1x, join with ss to 3rd ch of stch. {80 sts, 80 1-ch sps}

R19: dc in same st as ss, *fptr2tog around same st last worked into and next st skipping 1-ch sp between, dc in same st last leg was worked around, spike dc over 1-ch sp in skipped st of R17 below**, dc in next st*, rep from * to * 38x and from * to ** 1x, join with ss to first st. {160 sts}

R20: dc in same st as ss, dc in next 159 sts, join with ss to first st. {160 sts}

R21: ch3 (stch), *ch2, tr2tog over the next 3 sts skipping the middle st, ch2**, tr in next st*, rep from * to * 38x and from * to ** 1x, join with ss 3rd ch of stch. {80 sts, 80 2-ch sps}

R22: dc in same st as ss, *2dc in 2-ch sp, skip 1 st, 2dc in 2-ch sp**, dc in next st*, rep from * to * 38x and from * to ** 1x, join with ss to first st. {200 sts}

R23: dc in same st as ss, *ch3, skip 3 sts**, dc in next st*, rep from * to * 48x and from * to ** 1x, join with ss to first st. {50 sts, 50 3-ch sps}

R24: dc in same st as ss, *3dc in 3-ch sp**, dc in next st*, rep from * to * 48x and from * to ** 1x, join with ss to first st. {200 sts}

R25: ch3 (stch), *24x [ch1, skip 1 st, tr in next st], ch1, skip 1 st**, (tr, ch6, tr) in next st*, rep from * to * 2x and from * to ** 1x, tr in same st as first st, ch3, join with tr to 3rd ch of stch. {26 sts, 25 1-ch sps on each side; 4 6-ch cnr sps}

R26: ch3 (stch), 4tr over joining tr, *skip (1 st & 1-ch sp), 23x [dc in next st, spike dc over 1-ch sp in skipped st of R24 below], dc in next st, skip (1-ch sp & 1 st)**, (5tr, ch2, 5tr) in 6-ch cnr sp*, rep from * to * 2x and from * to ** 1x, 5tr in same sp as first sts, ch1, join with dc to 3rd ch of stch. {57 sts on each side; 4 2-ch cnr sps}

R27: dc over joining dc, *dc in next 5 sts, skip 1 st, tr in next 45 sts, skip 1 st, dc in next 5 sts**, (dc, ch2, dc) in 2-ch cnr sp*, rep from * to * 2x and from * to ** 1x, dc in same sp as first st, ch1, join with dc to first st. {57 sts on each side; 4 2-ch cnr sps}

R28: dc over joining dc, *dc in next 4 sts, htr in next 2 sts, tr2tog over next 2 sts, 3x [fptr around next 3 sts, htr in next 3 sts], fptr around next 5 sts, 3x [htr in next 3 sts, fptr around next 3 sts], tr2tog over next 2 sts, htr in next 2 sts, dc in next 4 sts**, (dc, ch2, dc) in 2-ch cnr sp*, rep from * to * 2x and from * to ** 1x, dc in same sp as first st, ch1, join with dc to first st. {57 sts on each side; 4 2-ch cnr sps}

R29: dc over joining dc, *dc in next 5 sts, ch5, skip 3 sts, 2x [fptr around next 3 sts, htr in next 3 sts], fphtr around next 3 sts, dc in next 11 sts, fphtr around next 3 sts, 2x [htr in next 3 sts, fptr around next 3 sts], ch5, skip 3 sts, dc in next 5 sts**, (dc, ch2, dc) in 2-ch cnr sp*, rep from * to * 2x and from * to ** 1x, dc in same sp as first st, ch1, join with dc to first st. {53 sts, 2 5-ch sps on each side; 4 2-ch cnr sps}

R30: dc over joining dc, *dc in next 6 sts, 5htr in 5-ch sp, fptr around next 3 sts, htr in next 3 sts, fphtr around next 3 sts, dc in next 23 sts, fphtr around next 3 sts, htr in next 3 sts, fptr around next 3 sts, 5htr in 5-ch sp, dc in next 6 sts**, (dc, ch2, dc) in 2-ch cnr sp*, rep from * to * 2x and from * to ** 1x, dc in same sp as first st, ch1, join with dc to first st. {65 sts on each side; 4 2-ch cnr sps}

*Kaboom chart
Rounds 24-36*

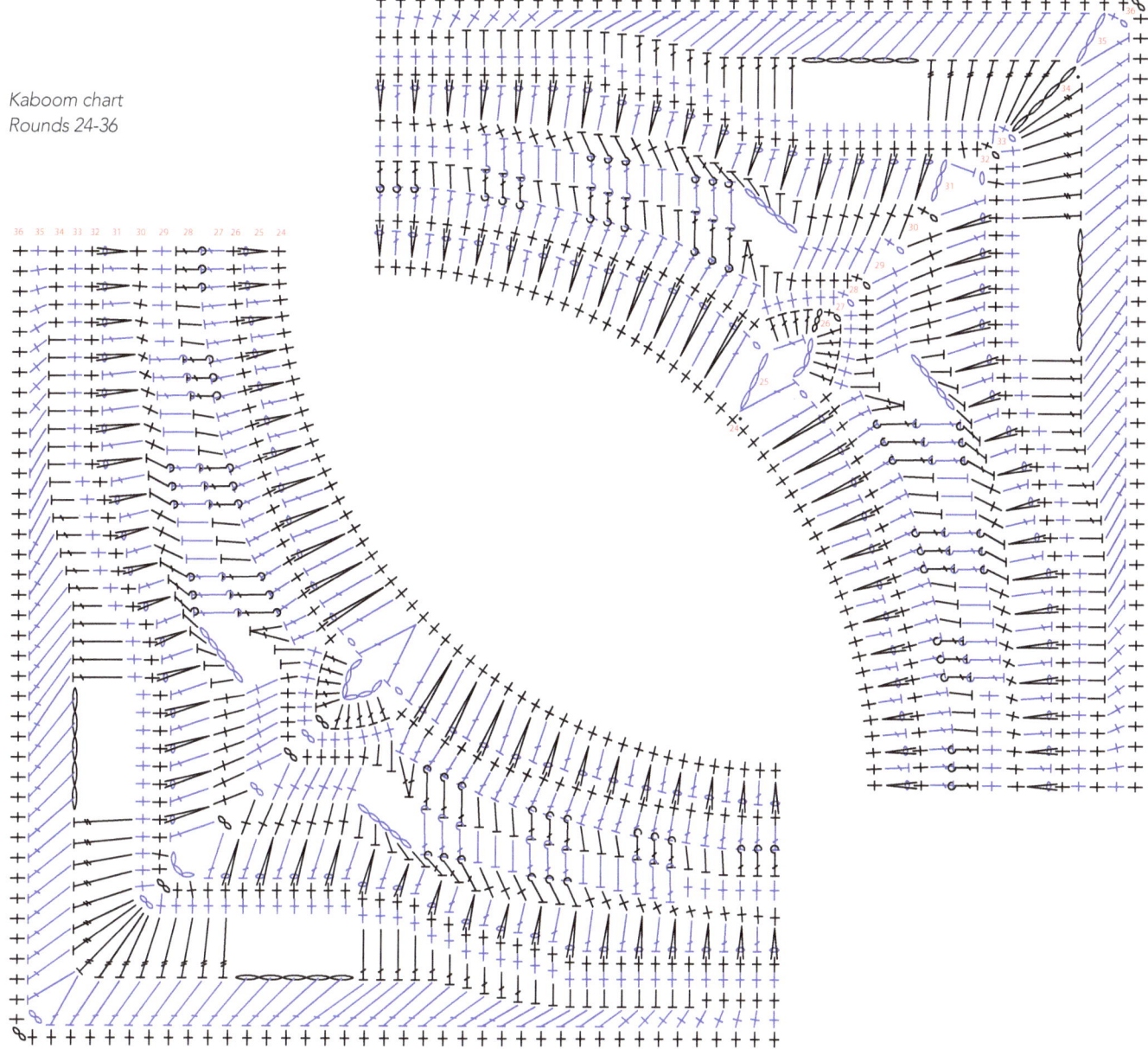

R31: ch3 (stch), *32x [ch1, skip 1 st, tr in next st], ch1, skip 1 st**, (tr, ch3, tr) in 2-ch cnr sp*, rep from * to * 2x and from * to ** 1x, tr in same sp as first st, ch1, join with htr to 3rd ch of stch. {34 sts, 33 1-ch sps on each side; 4 3-ch cnr sps}

R32: 2dc over joining htr, *33x [dc in next st, spike dc over 1-ch sp in skipped st of R30 below], dc in next st**, (2dc, ch2, 2dc) in 3-ch cnr sp*, rep from * to * 2x and from * to ** 1x, 2dc in same sp as first sts, ch1, join with dc to first st. {71 sts on each side; 4 2-ch cnr sps}

R33: dc over joining dc, *dc in next 71 sts**, (dc, ch2, dc) in 2-ch cnr sp*, rep from * to * 2x and from * to ** 1x, dc in same sp as first st, ch1, join with dc to first st. {73 sts on each side; 4 2-ch cnr sps}

R34: ch4 (stch), 2dtr over joining dc, *dtr in next 5 sts, ch5, skip 7 sts, tr in next 10 sts, htr in next 10 sts, dc in next 9 sts, htr in next 10 sts, tr in next 10 sts, ch5, skip 7 sts, dtr in next 5 sts**, 5dtr in 2-ch cnr sp*, rep from * to * 2x and from * to ** 1x, 2dtr in same sp as first sts, join with ss to 4th ch of stch. {59 sts, 2 5-ch sps on each side; 4 5-st cnrs}

R35: ch3 (stch), *tr in next 7 sts, tr in each of next 5 chs, tr in next 10 sts, htr in next 6 sts, dc in next 17 sts, htr in next 6 sts, tr in next 10 sts, tr in each of next 5 chs, tr in next 7 sts**, (tr, ch2, tr) in next st*, rep from * to * 2x and from * to ** 1x, tr in same st as first st, ch1, join with dc to 3rd ch of stch. {75 sts on each side; 4 2-ch cnr sps}

R36: dc over joining dc, *dc in next 75 sts**, (dc, ch2, dc) in 2-ch cnr sp*, rep from * to * 2x and from * to ** 1x, dc in same sp as first st, ch2, join with ss to first st. Fasten off. {77 sts on each side; 4 2-ch cnr sps}

Colours by Miranda Howard

Colours by Kim Siebenhausen

Kim

Kim stands for Kindly, Impressive and Mesmerising and is the largest pattern from my FRAN Blanket (Fetching, Refined, Affable and Noteworthy).

 419 m / 459 yd

Kim will need blocking, particularly if you find a swirl develops.

Begin with mc.

R1: ch3 (stch), 2tr, *ch2, 3tr*, rep from * to * 2x, ch1, join with dc to 3rd ch of stch. {12 sts, 4 2-ch cnr sps}

R2: dc over joining dc, *dc in next 3 sts**, (dc, ch2, dc) in 2-ch cnr sp*, rep from * to * 2x and from * to ** 1x, dc in same sp as first st, ch1, join with dc to first st. {5 sts on each side; 4 2-ch cnr sps}

R3: ch3 (stch), *tr in next 5 sts**, (tr, ch2, tr) in 2-ch cnr sp*, rep from * to * 2x and from * to ** 1x, tr in same sp as first st, ch1, join with dc to 3rd ch of stch. {7 sts on each side; 4 2-ch cnr sps}

R4: dc over joining dc, *dc in next 3 sts, spike dc over next st, dc in next 3 sts**, (dc, ch2, dc) in 2-ch cnr sp*, rep from * to * 2x and from * to ** 1x, dc in same sp as first st, ch1, join with dc to first st. {9 sts on each side; 4 2-ch cnr sps}

R5: ch3 (stch), *4x [ch1, skip 1 st, tr in next st], ch1, skip 1 st**, (tr, ch3, tr) in 2-ch cnr sp*, rep from * to * 2x and from * to ** 1x, tr in same sp as first st, ch1, join with htr to 3rd ch of stch. {6 sts, 5 1-ch sps on each side; 4 3-ch cnr sps}

R6: 2dc over joining htr, *5x [dc in next st, dc in 1-ch sp], dc in next st**, (2dc, ch2, 2dc) in 3-ch cnr sp*, rep from * to * 2x and from * to ** 1x, 2dc in same sp as first sts, ch1, join with dc to first st. {15 sts on each side; 4 2-ch cnr sps}

R7: ch3 (stch), *tr in next 15 sts**, (tr, ch2, tr) in 2-ch cnr sp*, rep from * to * 2x and from * to ** 1x, tr in same sp as first st, ch1, join with dc to 3rd ch of stch. {17 sts on each side; 4 2-ch cnr sps}

Kim chart
Rounds 1-14

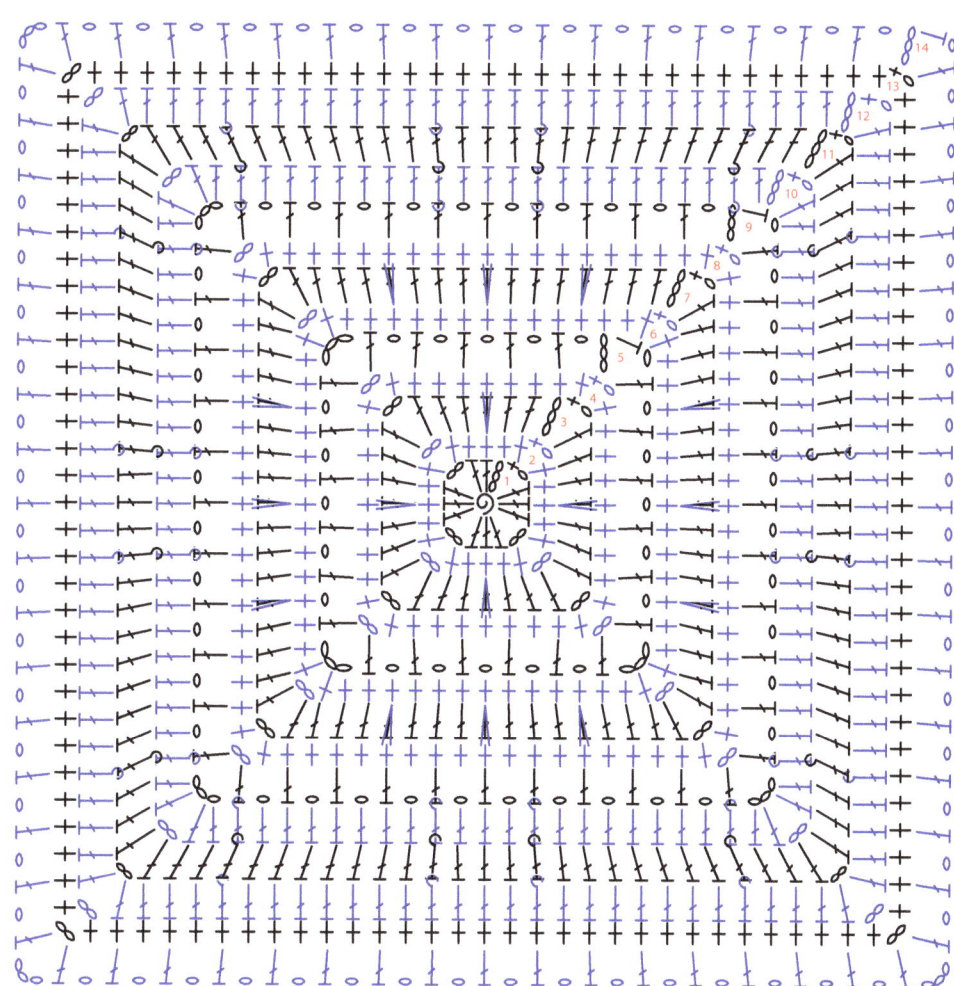

R8: dc over joining dc, *dc in next 4 sts, 2x [spike dc over next st, dc in next 3 sts], spike dc over next st, dc in next 4 sts**, (dc, ch2, dc) in 2-ch cnr sp*, rep from * to * 2x and from * to ** 1x, dc in same sp as first st, ch1, join with dc to first st. {19 sts on each side; 4 2-ch cnr sps}

R9: ch3 (stch), *9x [ch1, skip 1 st, tr in next st], ch1, skip 1 st**, (tr, ch3, tr) in 2-ch cnr sp*, rep from * to * 2x and from * to ** 1x, tr in same sp as first st, ch1, join with htr to 3rd ch of stch. {11 sts, 10 1-ch sps on each side; 4 3-ch cnr sps}

R10: ch3 (stch), tr over joining htr, *fptr around next st, 3x [tr in 1-ch sp, tr in next st], tr in 1-ch sp, fptr around next st, tr in 1-ch sp, tr in next st, tr in 1-ch sp, fptr around next st, 3x [tr in 1-ch sp, tr in next st], tr in 1-ch sp, fptr around next st**, (2tr, ch2, 2tr) in 3-ch cnr sp*, rep from * to * 2x and from * to ** 1x, 2tr in same sp as first sts, ch1, join with dc to 3rd ch of stch. {25 sts on each side; 4 2-ch cnr sps}

R11: ch3 (stch), *tr in next 2 sts, fptr around next st, tr in next 7 sts, fptr around next st, tr in next 3 sts, fptr around next st, tr in next 7 sts, fptr around next st, tr in next 2 sts**, (tr, ch2, tr) in 2-ch cnr sp*, rep from * to * 2x and from * to ** 1x, tr in same sp as first st, ch1, join with dc to 3rd ch of stch. {27 sts on each side; 4 2-ch cnr sps}

R12: ch3 (stch), *tr in next 3 sts, fptr around next st, tr in next 7 sts, fptr around next st, tr in next 3 sts, fptr around next st, tr in next 7 sts, fptr around next st, tr in next 3 sts**, (tr, ch2, tr) in 2-ch cnr sp*, rep from * to * 2x and from * to ** 1x, tr in same sp as first st, ch1, join with dc to 3rd ch of stch. {29 sts on each side; 4 2-ch cnr sps}

R13: dc over joining dc, *dc in next 29 sts**, (dc, ch2, dc) in 2-ch cnr sp*, rep from * to * 2x and from * to ** 1x, dc in same sp as first st, ch1, join with dc to first st. {31 sts on each side; 4 2-ch cnr sps}

R14: ch3 (stch), *15x [ch1, skip 1 st, tr in next st], ch1, skip 1 st**, (tr, ch3, tr) in 2-ch cnr sp*, rep from * to * 2x and from * to ** 1x, tr in same sp as first st, ch1, join with htr to 3rd ch of stch. {17 sts, 16 1-ch sps on each side; 4 3-ch cnr sps}

Kim chart
Rounds 14–28

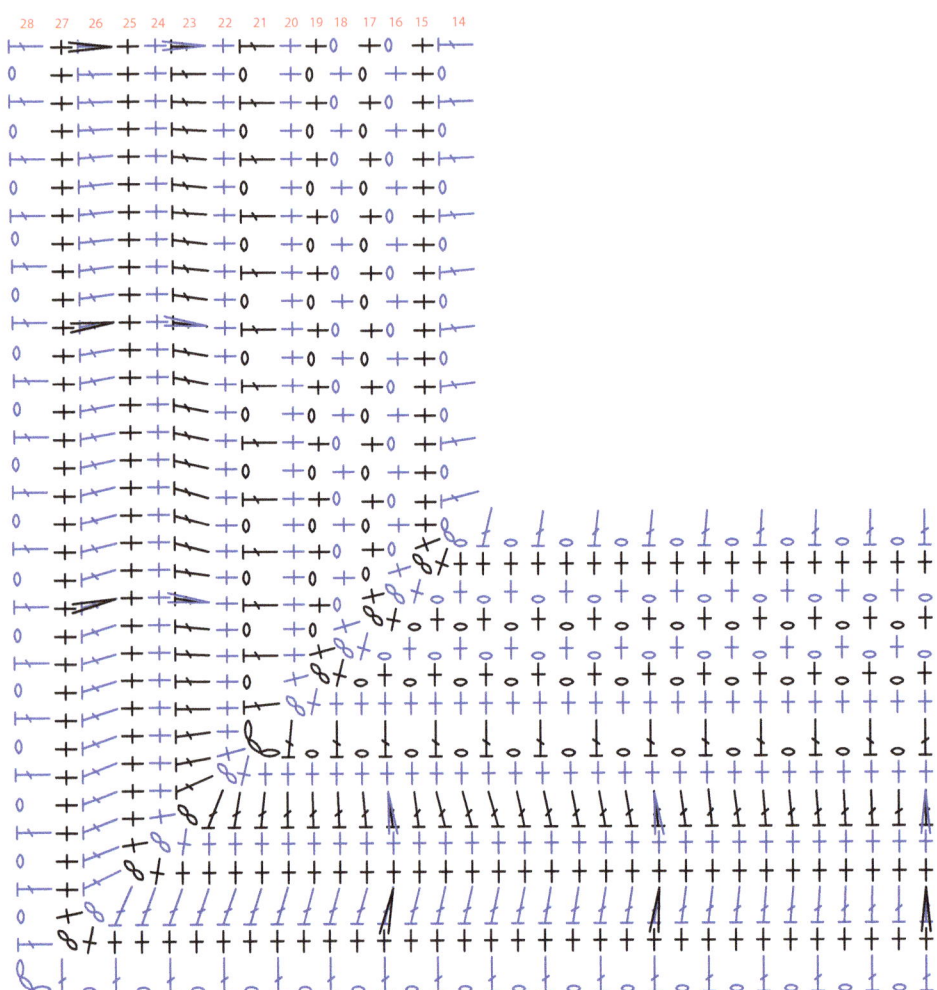

R15: 2dc over joining htr, *16x [dc in next st, dc in 1-ch sp], dc in next st**, (2dc, ch2, 2dc) in 3-ch cnr sp*, rep from * to * 2x and from * to ** 1x, 2dc in same sp as first sts, ch1, join with dc to first st. {37 sts on each side; 4 2-ch cnr sps}

R16: dc over joining dc, *18x [ch1, skip 1 st, dc in next st], ch1, skip 1 st**, (dc, ch2, dc) in 2-ch cnr sp*, rep from * to * 2x and from * to ** 1x, dc in same sp as first st, ch1, join with dc to first st. {20 sts, 19 1-ch sps on each side; 4 2-ch cnr sps}

R17: dc over joining dc, *19x [ch1, skip 1 st, dc in 1-ch sp], ch1, skip 1 st**, (dc, ch2, dc) in 2-ch cnr sp*, rep from * to * 2x and from * to ** 1x, dc in same sp as first st, ch1, join with dc to first st.
{21 sts, 20 1-ch sps on each side; 4 2-ch cnr sps}

R18: dc over joining dc, *20x [ch1, skip 1 st, dc in 1-ch sp], ch1, skip 1 st**, (dc, ch2, dc) in 2-ch cnr sp*, rep from * to * 2x and from * to ** 1x, dc in same sp as first st, ch1, join with dc to first st.
{22 sts, 21 1-ch sps on each side; 4 2-ch cnr sps}

R19: dc over joining dc, *21x [ch1, skip 1 st, dc in 1-ch sp], ch1, skip 1 st**, (dc, ch2, dc) in 2-ch cnr sp*, rep from * to * 2x and from * to ** 1x, dc in same sp as first st, ch1, join with dc to first st.
{23 sts, 22 1-ch sps on each side; 4 2-ch cnr sps}

R20: dc over joining dc, *22x [dc in next st, dc in 1-ch sp], dc in next st**, (dc, ch2, dc) in 2-ch cnr sp*, rep from * to * 2x and from * to ** 1x, dc in same sp as first st, ch1, join with dc to first st. {47 sts on each side; 4 2-ch cnr sps}

R21: ch3 (stch), *23x [ch1, skip 1 st, tr in next st], ch1, skip 1 st**, (tr, ch3, tr) in 2-ch cnr sp*, rep from * to * 2x and from * to ** 1x, tr in same sp as first st, ch1, join with htr to 3rd ch of stch. {25 sts, 24 1-ch sps on each side; 4 3-ch cnr sps}

Kim chart
Beginning of Rounds 14-28

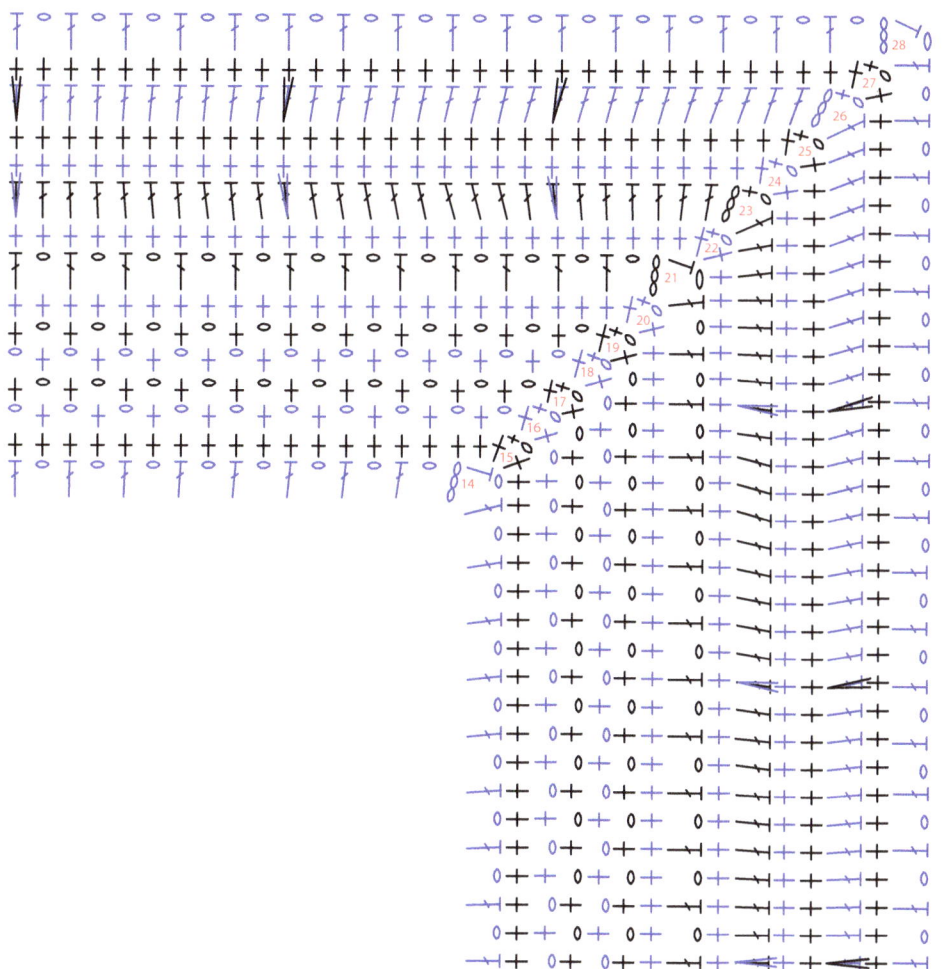

R22: 2dc over joining htr, *24x [dc in next st, dc in 1-ch sp], dc in next st**, (2dc, ch2, 2dc) in 3-ch cnr sp*, rep from * to * 2x and from * to ** 1x, 2dc in same sp as first sts, ch1, join with dc to first st. {53 sts on each side; 4 2-ch cnr sps}

R23: ch3 (stch), *tr in next 53 sts**, (tr, ch2, tr) in 2-ch cnr sp*, rep from * to * 2x and from * to ** 1x, tr in same sp as first st, ch1, join with dc to 3rd ch of stch. {55 sts on each side; 4 2-ch cnr sps}

R24: dc over joining dc, *dc in next 7 sts, 4x [spike dc over next st, dc in next 9 sts], spike dc over next st, dc in next 7 sts**, (dc, ch2, dc) in 2-ch cnr sp*, rep from * to * 2x and from * to ** 1x, dc in same sp as first st, ch1, join with dc to first st. {57 sts on each side; 4 2-ch cnr sps}

R25: dc over joining dc, *dc in next 57 sts**, (dc, ch2, dc) in 2-ch cnr sp*, rep from * to * 2x and from * to ** 1x, dc in same sp as first st, ch1, join with dc to first st. {59 sts on each side; 4 2-ch cnr sps}

R26: ch3 (stch), *tr in next 59 sts**, (tr, ch2, tr) in 2-ch cnr sp*, rep from * to * 2x and from * to ** 1x, tr in same sp as first st, ch1, join with dc to 3rd ch of stch. {61 sts on each side; 4 2-ch cnr sps}

R27: dc over joining dc, *dc in next 10 sts, 4x [spike dc over next st, dc in next 9 sts], spike dc over next st, dc in next 10 sts**, (dc, ch2, dc) in 2-ch cnr sp*, rep from * to * 2x and from * to ** 1x, dc in same sp as first st, ch1, join with dc to first st. {63 sts on each side; 4 2-ch cnr sps}

R28: ch3 (stch), *31x [ch1, skip 1 st, tr in next st], ch1, skip 1 st**, (tr, ch3, tr) in 2-ch cnr sp*, rep from * to * 2x and from * to ** 1x, tr in same sp as first st, ch1, join with htr to 3rd ch of stch. {33 sts, 32 1-ch sps on each side; 4 3-ch cnr sps}

Kim chart
Rounds 28-36

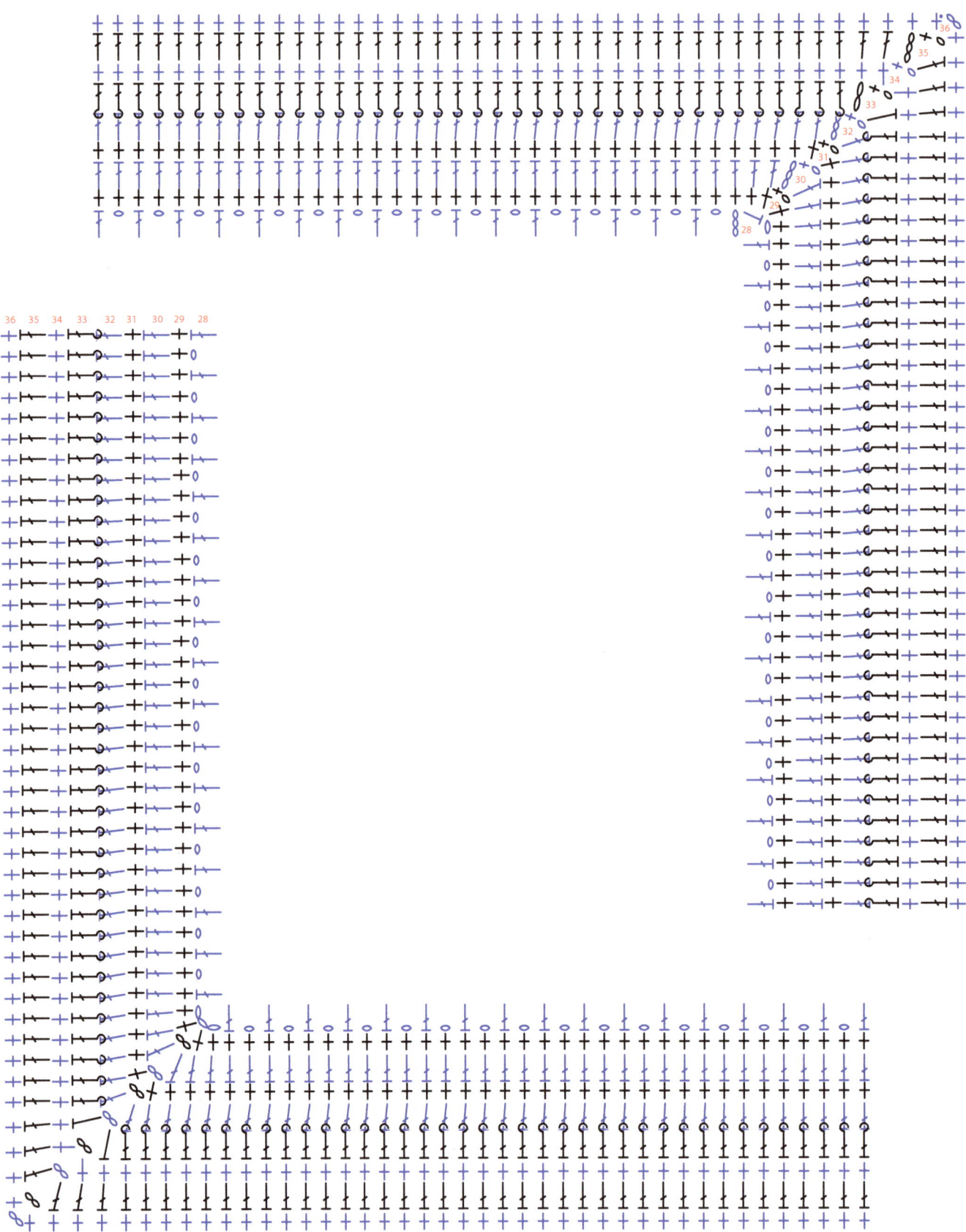

R29: 2dc over joining htr, *32x [dc in next st, dc in 1-ch sp], dc in next st**, (2dc, ch2, 2dc) in 3-ch cnr sp*, rep from * to * 2x and from * to ** 1x, 2dc in same sp as first sts, ch1, join with dc to first st. {69 sts on each side; 4 2-ch cnr sps}

R30: ch3 (stch), *tr in next 69 sts**, (tr, ch2, tr) in 2-ch cnr sp*, rep from * to * 2x and from * to ** 1x, tr in same sp as first st, ch1, join with dc to 3rd ch of stch. {71 sts on each side; 4 2-ch cnr sps}

R31: dc over joining dc, *dc in next 71 sts**, (dc, ch2, dc) in 2-ch cnr sp*, rep from * to * 2x and from * to ** 1x, dc in same sp as first st, ch1, join with dc to first st. {73 sts on each side; 4 2-ch cnr sps}

R32: ch3 (stch), *tr in next 73 sts**, (tr, ch2, tr) in 2-ch cnr sp*, rep from * to * 2x and * to ** 1x, tr in same sp as first st, ch1, join with dc to 3rd ch of stch. {75 sts on each side; 4 2-ch cnr sps}

R33: ch2 (stch), *fptr around next 2 sts, 14x [bptr around next st, fptr around next 4 sts], bptr around next st, fptr around next 2 sts**, (htr, ch2, htr) in 2-ch cnr sp*, rep from * to * 2x and * to ** 1x, htr in same sp as first st, ch1, join with dc to 2nd ch of stch. {77 sts on each side; 4 2-ch cnr sps}

R34: dc over joining dc, *dc in next 77 sts**, (dc, ch2, dc) in 2-ch cnr sp*, rep from * to * 2x and * to ** 1x, dc in same sp as first st, ch1, join with dc to first st. {79 sts on each side; 4 2-ch cnr sps}

R35: ch3 (stch), *tr in next 79 sts**, (tr, ch2, tr) in 2-ch cnr sp*, rep from * to * 2x and * to ** 1x, tr in same sp as first st, ch1, join with dc to 3rd ch of stch. {81 sts on each side; 4 2-ch cnr sps}

R36: dc over joining dc, *dc in next 81 sts**, (dc, ch2, dc) in 2-ch cnr sp*, rep from * to * 2x and * to ** 1x, dc in same sp as first st, ch2, join with ss to first st. Fasten off. {83 sts on each side; 4 2-ch cnr sps}

Colours by Samantha Taylor

Colours by Kim Siebenhausen

Mayan

Named for the similarities in shapes to ancient Mayan structures.

  414 m / 453 yd

Begin with mc.

R1: ch3 (stch), 15tr, join with ss to 3rd ch of stch. {16 sts}

R2: ch3 (stch), *ch1, puff in next st, ch1**, tr in next st*, rep from * to * 6x and * to ** 1x, join with ss to 3rd ch of stch. {16 sts, 16 1-ch sps}

R3: 2dc in same st as ss, *dc in 1-ch sp, skip 1 st, dc in 1-ch sp**, 2dc in next st*, rep from * to * 6x and * to ** 1x, join with ss to first st. {32 sts}

R4: ch3 (stch), *ch3, tr3tog over next 3 sts, ch3**, tr in next st*, rep from * to * 6x and * to ** 1x, join with ss to 3rd ch of stch. {16 sts, 16 3-ch sps}

R5: dc in same st as ss, *3dc in 3-ch sp, fphtr around next st, 3dc in 3-ch sp**, dc in next st*, rep from * to * 6x and * to ** 1x, join with ss to first st. {64 sts}

R6: ch3 (stch), 6tr in same st as ss, *skip 3 sts, dc in next st, skip 3 sts**, 7tr in next st*, rep from * to * 6x and * to ** 1x, join with ss to 3rd ch of stch. {64 sts}

R7: First st is worked a little to the right. *fptr around R5 fp st below, dc in next 3 sts, dc in blo of next st, dc in next 3 sts*, rep from * to * 7x, join with ss to first st. {64 sts}

R8: *fptr around fp st below, tr in next 3 sts, 3tr in next st, tr in next 3 sts*, rep from * to * 7x, join with ss to first st. {80 sts}

R9: *fptr around fp st below, dc in next 3 sts, tr in flo of R6 below, dc in next 3 sts, tr in same flo of R6 below, dc in next 3 sts*, rep from * to * 7x, join with ss to first st. {96 sts}

If making more than one of these squares, make sure you join R16 at the same point to keep the centre orientation the same.

Mayan chart
Rounds 1-15

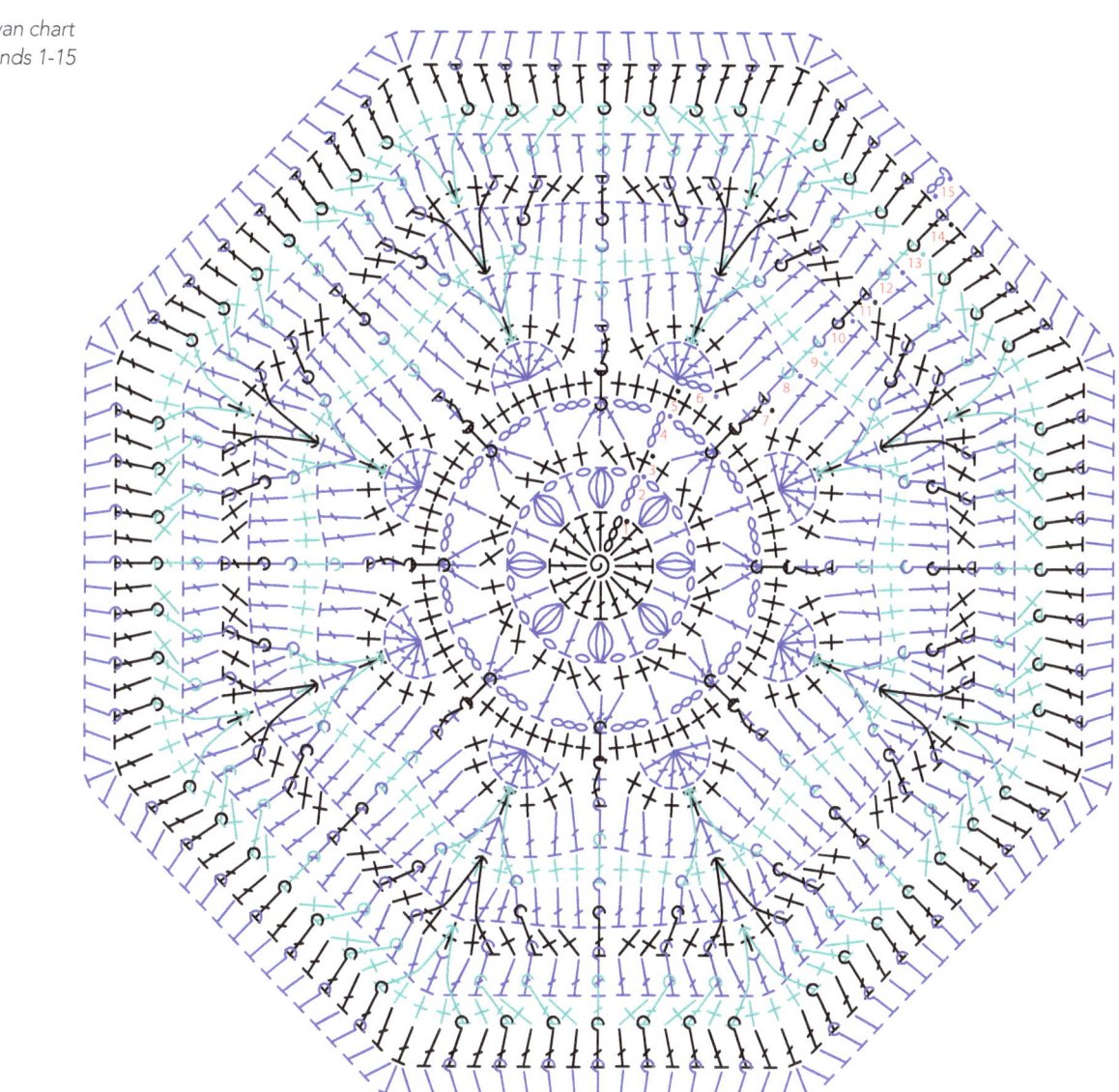

R10: *fptr around fp st below, tr in next 3 sts, (fptr around, tr in) next st, tr in next st, tr in blo of next st, tr in next st, (tr in, fptr around) next st, tr in next 3 sts*, rep from * to * 7x, join with ss to first st. {112 sts}

R11: *fptr around fp st below, skip 1 st, dc in next 2 sts, fptr around next st, dc in next st, tr in flo of R9 below, dc in next 3 sts, tr in same flo of R9 below, dc in next st, fptr around next st, dc in next 2 sts, skip 1 st*, rep from * to * 7x, join with ss to first st. {112 sts}

R12: *fptr around fp st below, tr in next 2 sts, fptr around next st, tr in next st, fptr around next st, tr in next st, tr in blo of next st, tr in next st, fptr around next st, tr in next st, fptr around next st, tr in next 2 sts*, rep from * to * 7x, join with ss to first st. {112 sts}

R13: *fptr around fp st below, skip 1 st, dc in next st, fptr around next st, dc in next st, (fptr around, dc in) next st, tr in flo of R11 below, dc in next 3 sts, tr in same flo of R11, (dc in, fptr around) next st, dc in next st, fptr around next st, dc in next st, skip 1 st*, rep from * to * 7x, join with ss to first st. {128 sts}

R14: *fptr around fp st below, 3x [tr in next st, fptr around next st], tr in next 3 sts, 3x [fptr around next st, tr in next st]*, rep from * to * 7x, join with ss to first st. {128 sts}

R15: ss to next st, ch2 (stch), *3x [fphtr around next st, htr in next st], 3htr in next st, 4x [htr in next st, fphtr around next st]**, htr in next st*, rep from * to * 6x and * to ** 1x, join with inv join to first true st. {144 sts}

Mayan - Size 6 Patterns • 131

Mayan chart
Rounds 15-29

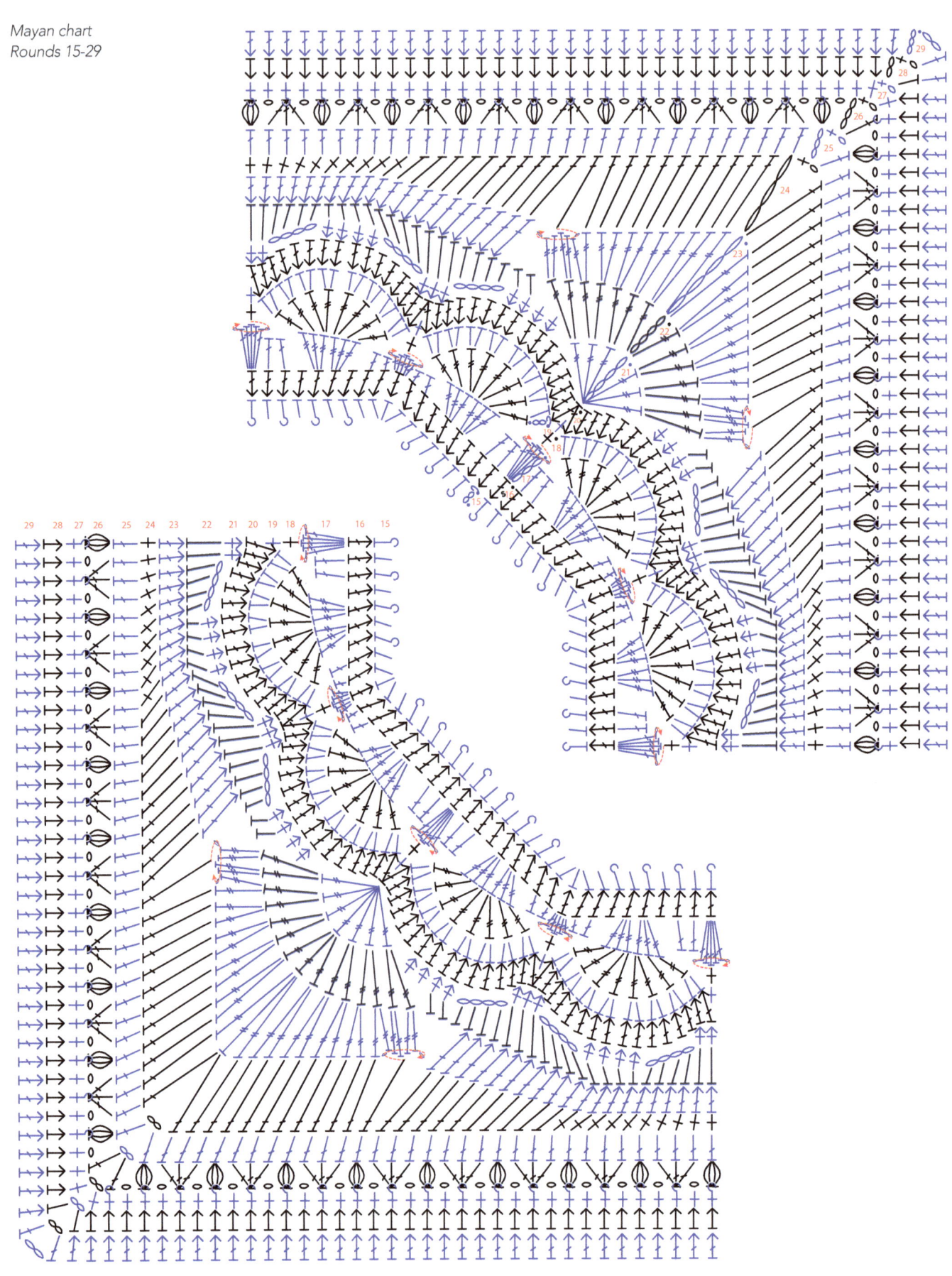

132 • Size 6 Patterns - Mayan

R16: Attach with a stdg tr to the lbv of a fp st directly above one of the sun-like ray points from the centre, tr in lbv of next 143 sts, join with ss to first st. {144 sts}

R17: ch3 (stch), 4tr in same st as ss, *ch1, tr in next 2 sts, skip 1 st, 3dtr in next 2 sts, skip 1 st, tr in next 2 sts, ch1**, 5tr in next st*, rep from * to * 14x and * to ** 1x, join with ss to 3rd ch of stch. {240 sts, 32 1-ch sps}

R18: *dc in both 1-ch sps on either side of the next 5 sts at the same time, skip 2 sts, dtr in next 2 sts, 2dtr in next 2 sts, dtr in next 2 sts, skip 2 sts*, rep from * to * 15x, join with ss to first st. {144 sts}

R19: ss to next st, ch2 (stch), htr in same st, 2htr in next 7 sts, *dc in next st**, 2htr in next 8 sts*, rep from * to * 14x and * to ** 1x, join with inv join to first true st. {272 sts}

R20: Attach with a stdg tr2tog to the lbv of last htr of a 16-st group in a dip directly above one of the sun-like ray points from the centre skipping the next st and finishing in the lbv of the first htr of the next 16-st group, *tr in lbv of next 14 sts**, tr2tog in lbv of next 3 sts skipping the middle st*, rep from * to * 14x and * to ** 1x, join with ss to first st. {240 sts}

R21: ch4 (stch), 3dtr in same st as ss, *skip 5 sts, 3x [dc in lbv of next 4 sts, ch4, skip 4 sts, dc in lbv of next 3 sts, ch4, skip 4 sts], dc in lbv of next 4 sts, skip 5 sts**, 7dtr in next st*, rep from * to * 2x and * to ** 1x, 3dtr in same st as first sts, join with ss to 4th ch of stch. {25 sts, 6 4-ch sps on each side; 4 7-st cnrs}

R22: ch4 (stch), dtr in same st as ss, *2dtr in next 3 sts, skip 2 sts, htr in next 2 sts, 2x [4htr in 4 ch sp, htr in next 3 sts, 4htr in 4 ch sp, htr in next 4 sts], 4htr in 4 ch sp, htr in next 3 sts, 4htr in 4 ch sp, htr in next 2 sts, skip 2 sts, 2dtr in next 3 sts**, 3dtr in next st*, rep from * to * 2x and * to ** 1x, dtr in same st as first sts, join with ss to 4th ch of stch. {57 sts on each side; 4 3-st cnrs}

R23: ch4 (stch), dtr in same st as ss, *2dtr in next 4 sts, (dtr, ch1, dtr) in next st, 2dtr in next 2 sts, ch1, skip 3 sts, tr in lbv of next 39 sts, ch1, skip 3 sts, 2dtr in next 2 sts, (dtr, ch1, dtr) in next st, 2dtr in next 4 sts**, 3dtr in next st*, rep from * to * 2x and * to ** 1x, dtr in same st as first sts, join with ss to 4th ch of stch. {67 sts, 4 1-ch sps on each side; 4 3-st cnrs}

R24: ch3 (stch), *tr in next 10 sts, tr in both 1-ch sps on either side of the next 5 sts at the same time, tr in next 5 sts, htr in next 5 sts, dc in next 19 sts, htr in next 5 sts, tr in next 5 sts, tr in both 1-ch sps on either side of the next 5 sts at the same time, tr in next 10 sts**, (tr, ch2, tr) in next st*, rep from * to * 2x and * to ** 1x, tr in same st as first st, ch1, join with dc to 3rd ch of stch. {63 sts on each side; 4 2-ch cnr sps}

R25: ch3 (stch), *tr in next 63 sts**, (tr, ch2, tr) in 2-ch cnr sp*, rep from * to * 2x and * to ** 1x, tr in same sp as first st, ch1, join with dc to 3rd ch of stch. {65 sts on each side; 4 2-ch cnr sps}

R26: ch3 (stch), *16x [ch1, puff in next st, ch1, tr3tog over next 3 sts], ch1, puff in next st, ch1**, (tr, ch2, tr) in 2-ch cnr sp*, rep from * to * 2x and * to ** 1x, tr in same sp as first st, ch1, join with dc to 3rd ch of stch. {35 sts, 34 1-ch sps on each side; 4 2-ch cnr sps}

R27: dc over joining dc, *dc in next st, 33x [dc in 1-ch sp, fpdc around next st], dc in 1-ch sp, dc in next st**, (dc, ch2, dc) in 2-ch cnr sp*, rep from * to * 2x and * to ** 1x, dc in same sp as first st, ch1, join with dc to first st. {71 sts on each side; 4 2-ch cnr sps}

R28: ch2 (stch), *htr in lbv of next next 71 sts**, (htr, ch2, htr) in 2-ch cnr sp*, rep from * to * 2x and * to ** 1x, htr in same sp as first st, ch1, join with dc to 2nd ch of stch. {73 sts on each side; 4 2-ch cnr sps}

R29: ch3 (stch), *tr in lbv of next 73 sts**, (tr, ch2, tr) in 2-ch cnr sp*, rep from * to * 2x and * to ** 1x, tr in same sp as first st, ch2, join with ss to 3rd ch of stch. Fasten off. {75 sts on each side; 4 2-ch cnr sps}

Colours by Evangelia V Katsafouros

Colours by Hayley Neubauer

Rebecca

Rebecca is one of the 3 patterns named for characters in the book Rebecca by Daphne du Maurier that make up the Manderley Blanket.

 516 m / 564 yd

Begin with mc.

R1: ch3 (stch), 23tr, join with ss to 3rd ch of stch. {24 sts}

R2: ch3 (stch), *ch1, 3trcl in next st, ch1**, tr in next st*, rep from * to * 10x and from * to ** 1x, join with ss to 3rd ch of stch. {24 sts, 24 1-ch sps}

R3: fpdc around same st as ss, *dc in 1-ch sp**, fpdc around next st*, rep from * to * 22x and from * to ** 1x, join with ss to first st. {48 sts}

R4: *Don't work a false st.* ch3 (stch), 6tr in same st as ss, *skip 2 sts, dc in next st, skip 2 sts**, 7tr in next st*, rep from * to * 6x and from * to ** 1x, join with inv join to first true st. {64 sts}

R5: Attach with stdg dc to lbv of the 4th st of any 7-st group, dc in lbv of next st, *htr in lbv of next 2 sts, tr in lbv of next st, htr in lbv of next 2 sts**, dc in lbv of next 3 sts*, rep from * to * 6x and from * to ** 1x, dc in lbv of next st, join with ss to first st. {64 sts}

R6: dc in same st as ss, dc in next 63 sts, join with ss to first st. {64 sts}

R7: ch3 (stch), *ch1, 3trcl in next st, ch1**, tr in next st*, rep from * to * 30x and from * to ** 1x, join with ss to 3rd ch of stch. {64 sts, 64 1-ch sps}

R8: fpdc around same st as ss, *dc in 1-ch sp, skip 1 st, dc in 1-ch sp**, fpdc around next st*, rep from * to * 30x and from * to ** 1x, join with ss to first st. {96 sts}

Rebecca chart
Rounds 1-16

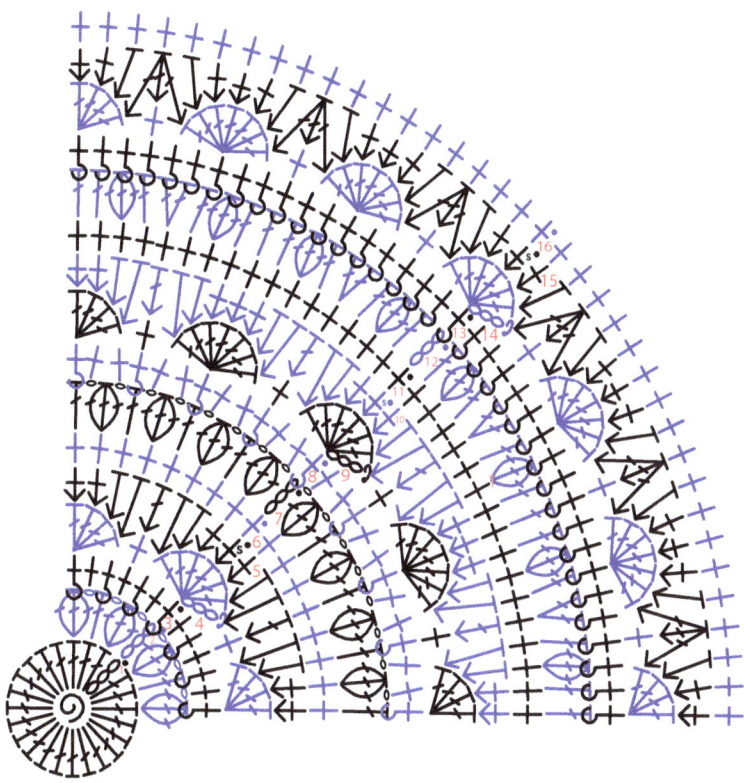

R9: Don't work a false st. ch3 (stch), 6tr in same st as ss, *skip 2 sts, dc in next st, skip 2 sts**, 7tr in next st*, rep from * to * 14x and from * to ** 1x, join with inv join to first true st. {128 sts}

R10: Attach with stdg dc to lbv of the 4th st of any 7-st group, dc in lbv of next st, *htr in lbv of next 2 sts, tr in lbv of next st, htr in lbv of next 2 sts**, dc in lbv of next 3 sts*, rep from * to * 14x and from * to ** 1x, dc in lbv of next st, join with ss to first st. {128 sts}

R11: dc in same st as ss, dc in next 127 sts, join with ss to first st. {128 sts}

R12: ch3 (stch), tr in next st, *3trcl in next st, tr in next st, 2tr in next st, tr in next st, 3trcl in next st**, tr in next 3 sts*, rep from * to * 14x and from * to ** 1x, tr in next st, join with ss to 3rd ch of stch. {144 sts}

R13: fpdc around same st as ss, fpdc around next 143 sts, join with ss to first st. {144 sts}

R14: Don't work a false st. ch3 (stch), 6tr in same st as ss, *skip 2 sts, dc in next st, skip 2 sts**, 7tr in next st*, rep from * to * 22x and from * to ** 1x, join with inv join to first true st. {192 sts}

R15: Attach with stdg dc to lbv of the 4th st of any 7-st group, dc in lbv of next st, *htr in lbv of next st, tr3tog in lbv of next 3 sts, htr in lbv of next st**, dc in lbv of next 3 sts*, rep from * to *22x and from * to ** 1x, dc in lbv of next st, join with ss to first st. {144 sts}

R16: dc in same st as ss, dc in next 143 sts, join with ss to first st. {144 sts}

Rebecca chart
Rounds 16-27

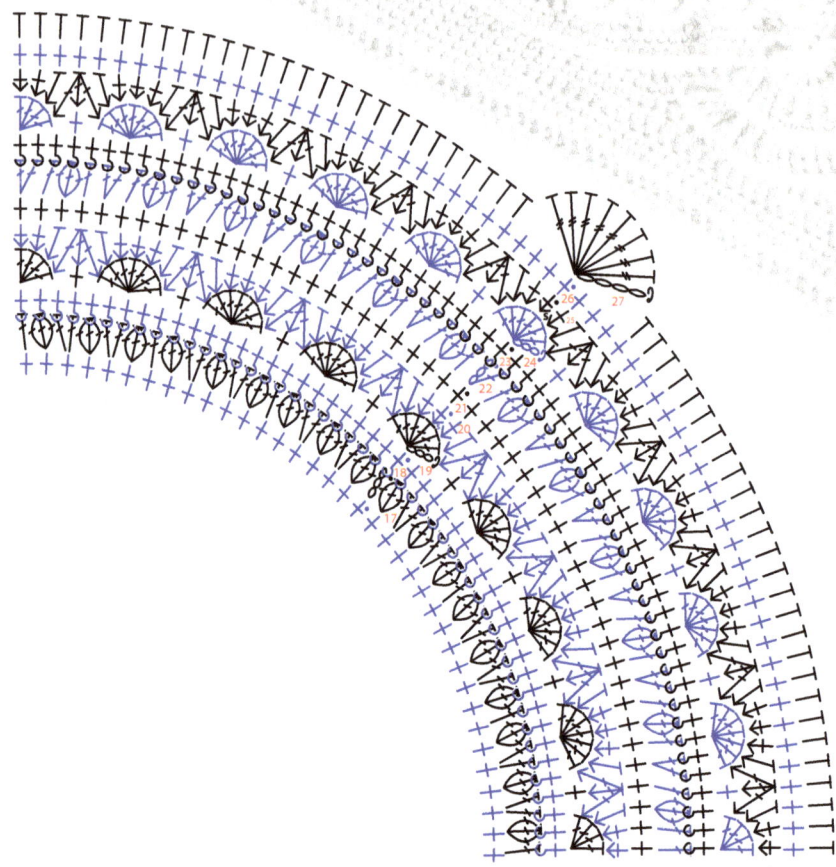

R17: ch3 (stch), *2x [3trcl in next st, 2tr in next st], 3trcl in next st**, tr in next st*, rep from * to * 22x and * to ** 1x, join with ss to 3rd ch of stch. {192 sts}

R18: fpdc around same st as ss, fpdc around next 191 sts, join with ss to first st. {192 sts}

R19: Don't work a false st. ch3 (stch), 6tr in same st as ss, *skip 2 sts, dc in next st, skip 2 sts**, 7tr in next st*, rep from * to * 30x and from * to ** 1x, join with inv join to first true st. {256 sts}

R20: Attach with stdg dc to lbv of the 4th st of a 7-st group, dc in lbv of next st, *htr in lbv of next st, tr3tog in lbv of next 3 sts, htr in lbv of next st**, dc in lbv of next 3 sts*, rep from * to * 30x and from * to ** 1x, dc in lbv of next st, join with ss to first st. {192 sts}

R21: dc in same st as ss, dc in next 191 sts, join with ss to first st. {192 sts}

R22: ch3 (stch), tr in next st, *3trcl in next st, tr in next st**, 2tr in next st, tr in next st*, rep from * to * 46x and * to ** 1x, tr in same st as first st, join with ss to 3rd ch of stch. {240 sts}

R23: fpdc around same st as ss, fpdc around next 239 sts, join with ss to first st. {240 sts}

R24: Don't work a false st. ch3 (stch), 6tr in same st as ss, *skip 2 sts, dc in next st, skip 2 sts**, 7tr in next st*, rep from * to * 38x and from * to ** 1x, join with inv join to first true st. {320 sts}

R25: Attach with stdg dc to lbv of the 4th st of a 7-st group, dc in lbv of next st, *htr in lbv of next st, tr3tog in lbv of next 3 sts, htr in lbv of next st**, dc in lbv of next 3 sts*, rep from * to * 38x and from * to ** 1x, dc in lbv of next st, join with ss to first st. {240 sts}

R26: dc in same st as ss, dc in next 239 sts, join with ss to first st. {240 sts}

R27: Don't work a false st. ch4 (stch), 8dtr in same st as ss, *skip 3 sts, htr in next 53 sts, skip 3 sts**, 9dtr in next st*, rep from * to * 2x and from * to ** 1x, join with inv join to first true st. {53 sts on each side; 4 9-st cnrs}

Rebecca chart
Rounds 27-35

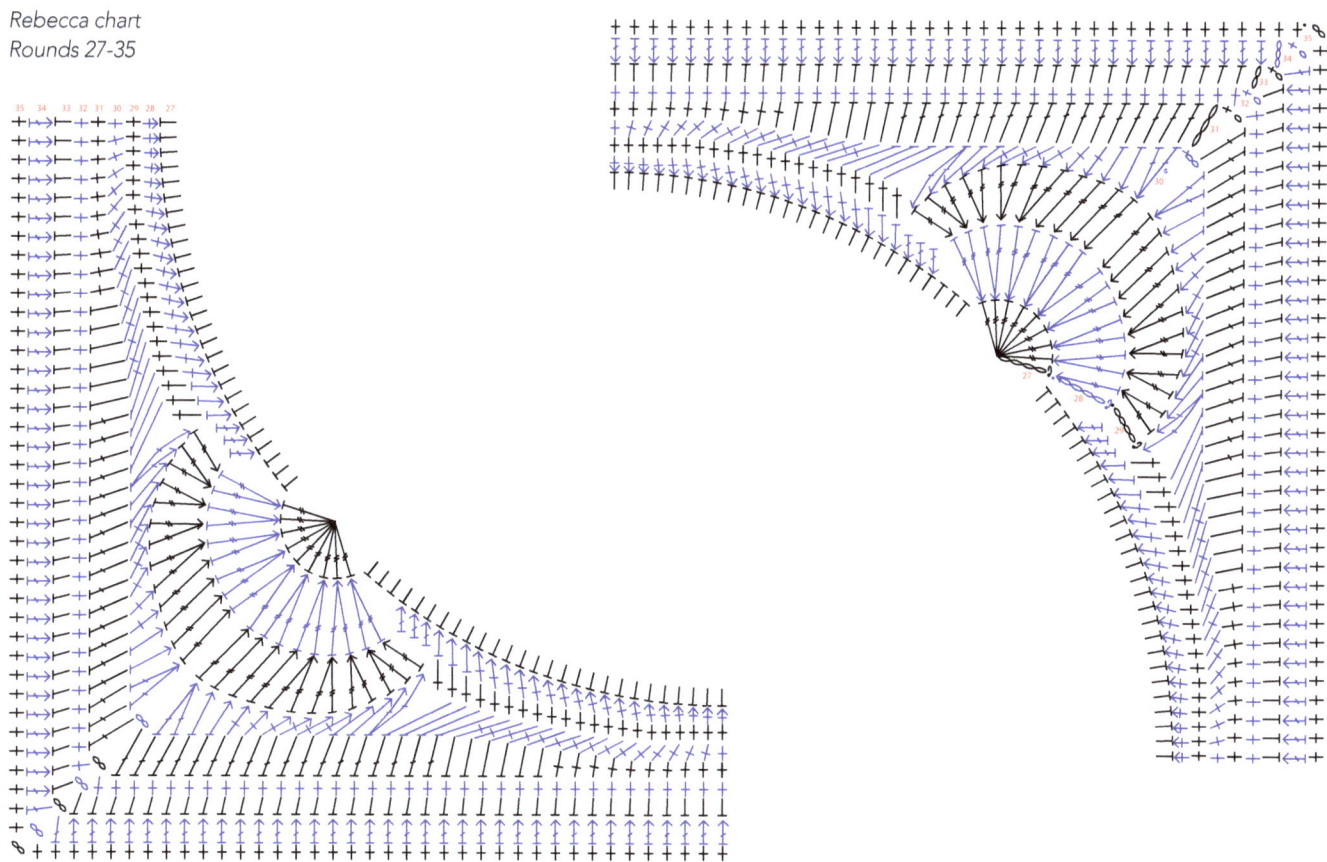

R28: Don't work a false st. Attach with ss to lbv of the first st of any 9-st cnr, ch4 (stch), dtr in same lbv, 2dtr in lbv of next 8 sts, *skip 3 sts, tr in lbv of next 3 sts, htr in lbv of next 3 sts, dc on lbv of next 35 sts, htr in lbv of next 3 sts, tr in lbv of next 3 sts, skip 3 sts**, 2dtr in lbv of next 9 sts*, rep from * to * 2x and from * to ** 1x, join with inv join to first true st. {47 sts on each side; 4 18-st cnrs}

R29: Don't work a false st. Attach with ss to lbv of the first st of any 18-st cnr, ch4 (stch), *2dtr in lbv of next 4 sts, dtr in lbv of next 8 sts, 2dtr in lbv of next 4 sts, dtr in lbv of next st, skip 3 sts, dc in next 41 sts, skip 3 sts**, dtr in lbv of next st*, rep from * to * 2x and * to ** 1x, join with inv join to first true st. {41 sts on each side; 4 26-st cnrs}

R30: Attach with stdg tr to lbv of the 14th st of any 26-st cnr, tr in same lbv, *htr in lbv of next 2 sts, dc in lbv of next 6 sts, htr in lbv of next 2 sts, tr2tog in lbv of next 2 sts, skip 1 st, htr in next 4 sts, dc in next 31 sts, htr in next 4 sts, skip 1 st, tr2tog in lbv of next 2 sts, htr in lbv of next 2 sts, dc in lbv of next 6 sts, htr in lbv of next 2 sts, 2tr in lbv of next st**, ch2, 2tr in lbv of next st*, rep from * to * 2x and * to ** 1x, ch1, join with dc to first st. {65 sts on each side; 4 2-ch cnr sps}

R31: ch3 (stch), *tr in next 17 sts, htr in next 6 sts, dc in next 19 sts, htr in next 6 sts, tr in next 17 sts**, (tr, ch2, tr) in 2 ch cnr sp*, rep from * to * 2x and * to ** 1x, tr in same sp as first st, ch1, join with dc to 3rd ch of stch. {67 sts on each side; 4 2-ch cnr sps}

R32: dc over joining dc, *dc in next 67 sts**, (dc, ch2, dc) in 2-ch sp*, rep from * to * 2x and * to ** 1x, dc in same sp as first st, ch1, join with dc to first st. {69 sts on each side; 4 2-ch cnr sps}

R33: ch2 (stch), *htr in next 69 sts**, (htr, ch2, htr) in 2-ch cnr sp*, rep from * to * 2x and * to ** 1x, htr in same sp as first st, ch1, join with dc to 2nd ch of stch. {71 sts on each side; 4 2-ch cnr sps}

R34: ch3 (stch), *tr in lbv of next 71 sts**, (tr, ch2, tr) in 2-ch cnr sp*, rep from * to * 2x and * to ** 1x, tr in same sp as first st, ch1, join with dc to 3rd ch of stch. {73 sts on each side; 4 2-ch cnr sps}

R35: dc over joining dc, *dc in next 73 sts**, (dc, ch2, dc) in 2-ch sp*, rep from * to * 2x and * to ** 1x, dc in same sp as first st, ch2, join with ss to first st. Fasten off. {75 sts on each side; 4 2-ch cnr sps}

Extension and Border Patterns

Each of these patterns can be used to add one increment to any pattern making them the next size up. You can also use them around a section of a project as in the Conglomeration Blanket on page 170.

These patterns can also be used as a border for a finished blanket or other project.

You can use any of them for a square or project with any stitch count. If you are using one that has a base of an even or odd numbered stitch count, and you need the opposite, simply skip the first stitch of each side in the first round and all will be well.

- **To use as an extension** to increase a pattern to the next size increment, end the last round of the pattern with ch1, join with dc.
- **If using as borders** of projects with many squares joined, add a round of double crochet first, working a stitch in every stitch, 2-chain corner space and join.

Floret
with Bounds extension

Nymph
with Periphery extension

Persnickety
with Enclave extension

Borderline

One increment extension for any st count

R1:

If extending a pattern: dc over joining dc,

If adding as a border: Attach with stdg dc to any 2-ch cnr sp,

*dc in each st along side**, (dc, ch2, dc) in 2-ch cnr sp*, rep from * to * 2x and * to ** 1x, dc in same sp as first st, ch1, join with dc to first st.

R2: dc over joining dc, *dc in blo of each st along side**, (dc, ch2, dc) in 2-ch cnr sp*, rep from * to * 2x and * to ** 1x, dc in same sp as first st, ch1, join with dc to first st.

R3: ch3 (stch), *tr in blo of each st along side**, (tr, ch2, tr) in 2-ch cnr sp*, rep from * to * 2x and * to ** 1x, tr in same sp as first st, ch1, join with dc to 3rd ch of stch.

R4: dc over joining dc, *dc in blo of each st along side**, (dc, ch2, dc) in 2-ch cnr sp*, rep from * to * 2x and * to ** 1x, dc in same sp as first st, ch1, join with dc to first st.

R5: dc over joining dc, *dc in blo of each st along side**, (dc, ch2, dc) in 2-ch cnr sp*, rep from * to * 2x and * to ** 1x, dc in same sp as first st, ch1, join with dc to first st.

R6: dc over joining dc, *dc in each st along side**, (dc, ch2, dc) in 2-ch cnr sp*, rep from * to * 2x and * to ** 1x, dc in same sp as first st, ch2, join with ss to first st. Fasten off.

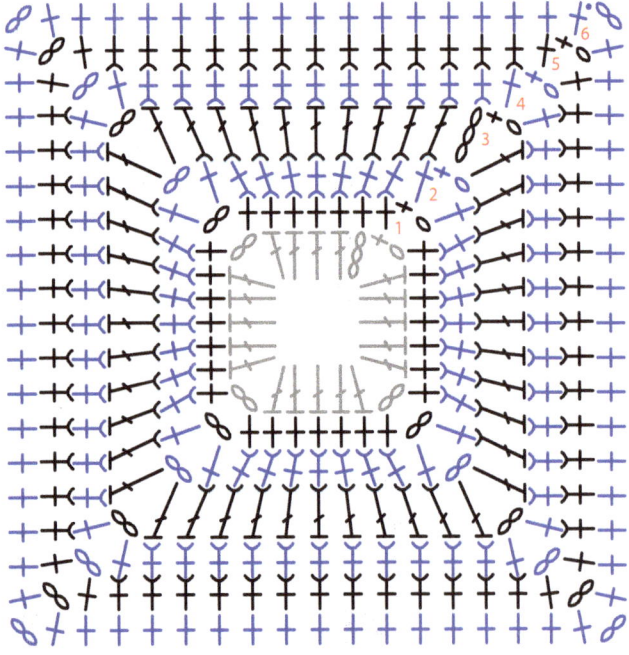

Bounds

One increment extension for odd numbered stitch count

R1:

If extending a pattern: ch3 (stch),

If adding as a border: Attach with stdg tr to any 2-ch cnr sp,

 *along side x [ch1, skip 1 st, tr in next st], ch1, skip 1 st**, (tr, ch2, tr) in 2-ch cnr sp*, rep from * to * 2x and * to ** 1x, tr in same sp as first st, ch1, join with dc to 3rd ch of stch.

R2: dc over joining dc, *along side x [dc in next st, tr in st skipped in R1 in front of 1-ch sp], dc in next st**, (dc, ch2, dc) in 2-ch cnr sp*, rep from * to * 2x and * to ** 1x, dc in same sp as first st, ch1, join with dc to first st.

R3: ch3 (stch), htr over joining dc, *htr in next 2 sts, 2trcl in each of the 1-ch sps of R1, htr in last 2 sts**, (htr, tr, htr) in 2-ch cnr sp*, rep from * to * 2x and * to ** 1x, htr in same sp as first sts, join with ss to 3rd ch of stch.

R4: dc in same st as ss, *dc in next st, dc2tog over next 2 sts, 2dc in each st along side until 3 sts remain, dc2tog over next 2 sts, dc in next st**, (dc, ch2, dc) in next st*, rep from * to * 2x and * to ** 1x, dc in same st as first st, ch1, join with dc to first st.

R5: ch2 (stch), *htr in each st along side**, (htr, ch2, htr) in 2-ch cnr sp*, rep from * to * 2x and * to ** 1x, htr in same sp as first st, ch1, join with dc to 2nd ch of stch.

R6: dc over joining dc, *dc in each st along side**, (dc, ch2, dc) in 2-ch cnr sp*, rep from * to * 2x and * to ** 1x, dc in same sp as first st, ch2, join with ss to first st. Fasten off.

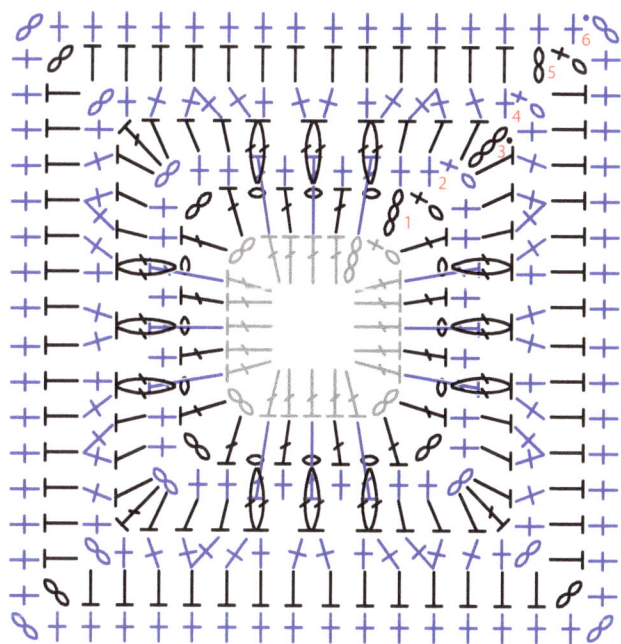

Bounds - Extension and Border Patterns • 141

Enclave

One increment extension for odd numbered stitch count

R1:

If extending a pattern: ch3 (stch),

If adding as a border: Attach with stdg tr to any 2-ch cnr sp,

*along side x [ch1, skip 1 st, tr in next st], ch1, skip 1 st**, (tr, ch2, tr) in 2-ch cnr sp*, rep from * to * 2x and * to ** 1x, tr in same sp as first st, ch1, join with dc to 3rd ch of stch.

R2: dc over joining dc, *along side until 1 st remains x [bpdc around next st, puff in skipped st of round before last in front of previous round], bpdc around last st**, (dc, ch2, dc) in 2-ch cnr sp*, rep from * to * 2x and * to ** 1x, dc in same sp as first st, ch1, join with dc to first st.

R3: dc over joining dc, *dc2tog over next 2 sts, along side until 3 sts remain x [ch1, skip 1 st, dc in next st], ch1, skip 1 st, dc2tog over next 2 sts**, (dc, ch2, dc) in 2-ch cnr sp*, rep from * to * 2x and * to ** 1x, dc in same sp as first st, ch1, join with dc to first st.

R4: ch3 (stch), *tr in next 2 sts, along side until 1 st remains x [tr in 1-ch sp, tr in next st], tr in next st**, (tr, ch2, tr) in 2-ch cnr sp*, rep from * to * 2x and * to ** 1x, tr in same sp as first st, ch1, join with dc to 3rd ch of stch.

R5: dc over joining dc, *dc in each st along side**, (dc, ch2, dc) in 2-ch cnr sp*, rep from * to * 2x and * to ** 1x, dc in same sp as first st, ch1, join with dc to first st.

R6: dc over joining dc, *dc in each st along side**, (dc, ch2, dc) in 2-ch cnr sp*, rep from * to * 2x and * to ** 1x, dc in same sp as first st, ch2, join with ss to first st. Fasten off.

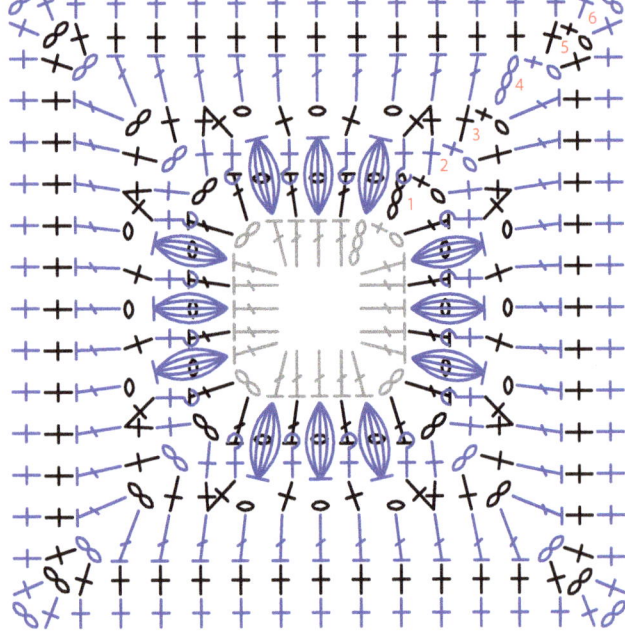

Periphery

One increment extension for even numbered stitch count

R1:

If extending a pattern: ch3 (stch),

If adding as a border: Attach with stdg tr to any 2-ch cnr sp,

*along side x [skip 1 st, tr in next st, tr in skipped st]**, tr in 2-ch cnr sp*, rep from * to * 2x and * to ** 1x, join with ss to 3rd ch of stch.

R2: ch3 (stch), *ch1, skip 1 st, along side until 3 sts remain x [tr between last and next sts, ch1, skip 2 sts], tr between last and next sts, ch1, skip last st of side**, (tr, ch2, tr) in next st*, rep from * to * 2x and * to ** 1x, tr in same st as first st, ch1, join with dc to 3rd ch of stch.

R3: dc over joining dc, *along side until 1 st remains x [dc in next st, dc in 1-ch sp], dc in next st**, (dc, ch2, dc) in 2-ch cnr sp*, rep from * to * 2x and * to ** 1x, dc in same sp as first st, ch1, join with dc to first st.

R4: ch3 (stch), tr over joining dc, *tr in each st along side**, 3tr in 2-ch cnr sp*, rep from * to * 2x and * to ** 1x, tr in same sp as first sts, join with ss to 3rd ch of stch.

R5: dc in same st as ss, *starting with next st, dc in each st along side ending with a st in the first st of a 3-st cnr**, (dc, ch2, dc) in middle of a 3-st cnr*, rep from * to * 2x and * to ** 1x, dc in same st as first st, ch2, join with ss to first st. Fasten off.

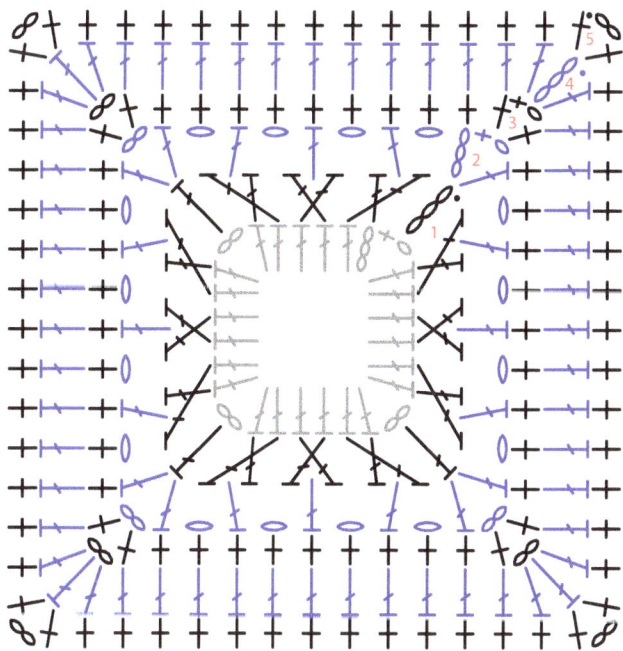

Periphery - Extension and Border Patterns

Selvedge

One increment extension for even numbered stitch count

R1:

If extending a pattern: ch3 (stch),

If adding as a border: Attach with stdg tr to any 2-ch cnr sp,

*along side x [ch1, tr2tog over next 2 sts], ch1**, (tr, ch2, tr) in 2-ch cnr sp*, rep from * to * 2x and * to ** 1x, tr in same sp as first st, ch1, join with dc to 3rd ch of stch.

R2: dc over joining dc, *dc in next st, along side until 1 1-ch sp & 1 st remain x [dc in 1-ch sp, fpdc around next st], dc in 1-ch sp, dc in last st of side**, (dc, ch2, dc) in 2-ch cnr sp*, rep from * to * 2x and * to ** 1x, dc in same sp as first st, ch1, join with dc to first st.

R3: dc over joining dc, *dc in next 2 sts, along side until 3 sts remain x [spike dc over next st, dc in next st], spike dc over next st, dc in next 2 sts**, (dc, ch2, dc) in 2-ch cnr sp*, rep from * to * 2x and * to ** 1x, dc in same sp as first st, ch1, join with dc to first st.

R4: ch3 (stch), *tr in next st, along side until 2 sts remain x [skip 1 st, 2tr in next st], skip 1 st, tr in next st**, (tr, ch2, tr) in 2-ch cnr sp*, rep from * to * 2x and * to ** 1x, tr in same sp as first st, ch1, join with dc to 3rd ch of stch.

R5: dc over joining dc, *along side x [dc in next st, dc between last and next sts, skip 1 st]**, (dc, ch2, dc) in 2-ch cnr sp*, rep from * to * 2x and * to ** 1x, dc in same sp as first st, ch1, join with dc to first st.

R6: dc over joining dc, *dc in every st along side**, (dc, ch2, dc) in 2-ch cnr sp*, rep from * to * 2x and * to ** 1x, dc in same sp as first st, ch2, join with ss to first st. Fasten off.

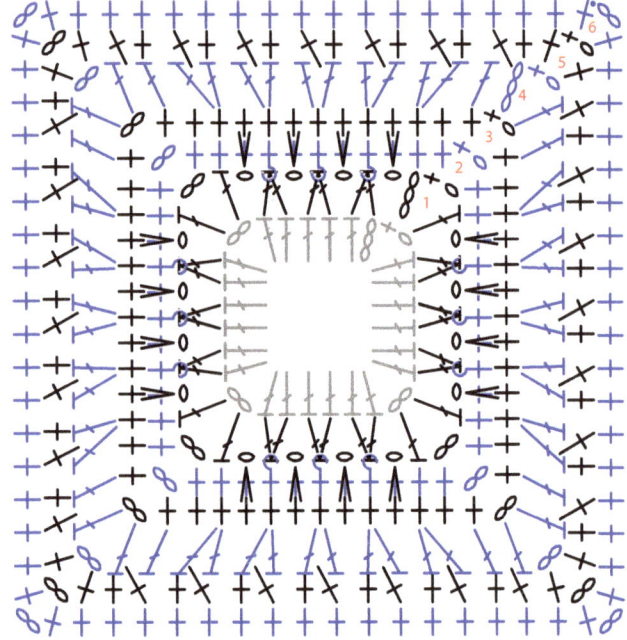

144 • Extension and Border Patterns - Selvedge

Verge

One increment extension for any stitch count

R1:

If extending a pattern: dc over joining dc,

If adding as a border: Attach with stdg dc to any 2-ch cnr sp,

*dc in each st along side**, (dc, ch4, dc) in 2-ch cnr sp*, rep from * to * 2x and * to ** 1x, dc in same sp as first st, ch2, join with htr to first st.

R2: ch3 (stch), 3tr over joining htr, *skip 3 sts, dc in each st along side until 3 sts remain, skip last 3 sts of side**, 7tr in 4-ch cnr sp*, rep from * to * 2x and * to ** 1x, 3tr in same sp as first sts, join with ss to 3rd ch of stch.

R3: dc in same st as ss, *bpdc around next 3 sts, dc in each st along side until 3 sts remain, bpdc around last 3 sts**, (dc, ch2, dc) in next st*, rep from * to * 2x and * to ** 1x, dc in same st as first st, ch1, join with dc to first st.

R4: ch2 (stch), *htr in lbv of each st along side**, (htr, ch2, htr) in 2-ch cnr sp*, rep from * to * 2x and * to ** 1x, htr in same sp as first st, ch1, join with dc to 2nd ch of stch.

R5: ch2 (stch), *htr in lbv of each st along side**, (htr, ch2, htr) in 2-ch cnr sp*, rep from * to * 2x and * to ** 1x, htr in same sp as first st, ch1, join with dc to 2nd ch of stch.

R6: dc over joining dc, *dc in each st along side**, (dc, ch2, dc) in 2-ch cnr sp*, rep from * to * 2x and * to ** 1x, dc in same sp as first st, ch2, join with ss to first st. Fasten off.

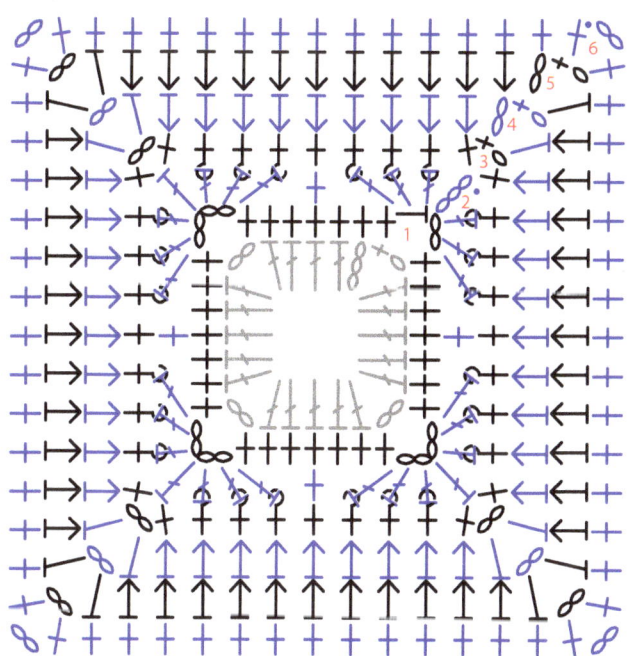

Verge - Extension and Border Patterns • 145

Projects

Summer Fiesta Necklace
page 148

Dessi Cowl or Headband
page 149

Bloom Scarf
page 150

Shine Tote
page 152

Panache Poncho
page 153

Envelop Baby Blanket
page 154

Rapier Blanket
page 156

Marvin, the Blanket
page 158

Medley Blanket
page 160

Manderley Blanket
page 163

Pastiche Blanket
page 166

Conglomeration Blanket
page 170

Summer Fiesta Necklace

A great little project, perfect for gifting.

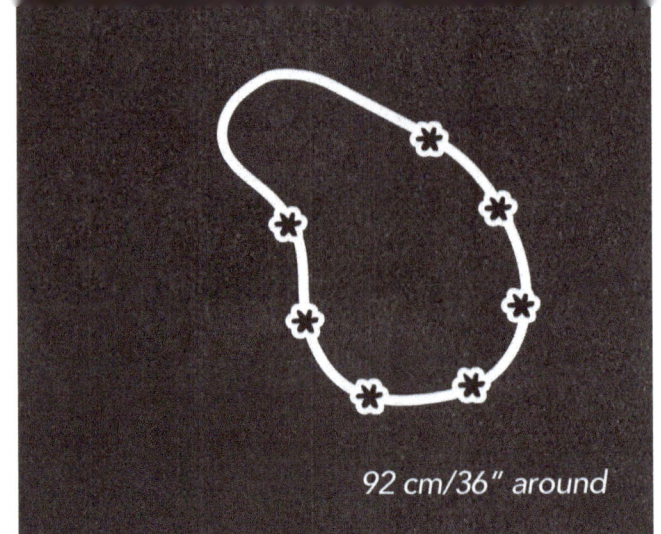

92 cm/36" around

 Aubade, pg 26

 Great Ocean Road Woollen Mill Summer Fiesta

Fibre: 70% merino wool, 30% linen
Weight: 3 ply/light fingering
Yardage: 230 metres/252 yards per 50 grams
Colour: Ocean Blue
Number of skeins: 1
Amount used: 5 grams - 23 metres/26 yards

 3 mm

How to make:

Begin with mc, *work the first 3 rounds of the Aubade pattern**, ch 20, ss into 4th ch from hook to create a ring to work into*, repeat from * to * 5x and from * to ** 1x, ch 100, join with ss to the petal of the first flower opposite the chain to the second flower. Fasten off.

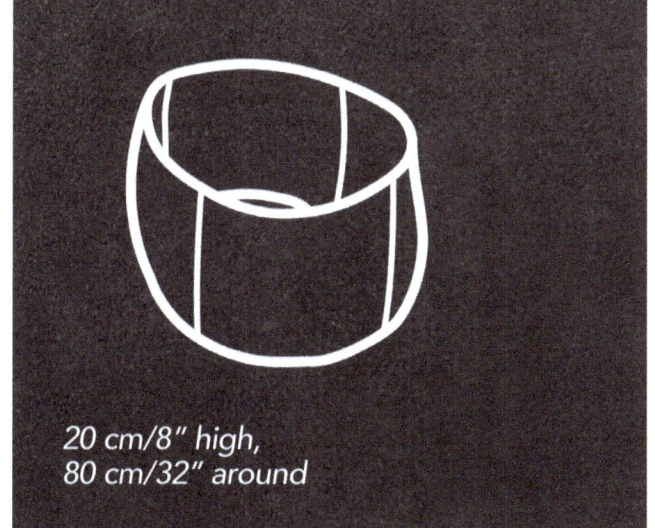

20 cm/8" high, 80 cm/32" around

Dessi Cowl or Headband

You decide how you wear it! Named after the alpaca called Des whose fleece the yarn was spun from.

 Caboodle, pg 28

 Great Ocean Road Woollen Mill Alpaca

Fibre: 100% alpaca
Weight: 5 ply/sport
Yardage: 240 metres/262 yards per 100 grams
Colour: Toffee
Number of skeins: 1
Amount used: 95 grams - 228 metres/250 yards

 4 mm

How to make:

Make 4 squares. Using the zipper join on page 12, join into a strip of 4 squares, then join the ends together.

Dessi Cowl or Headband - Projects • 149

Bloom Scarf

Perfect for slow colour change yarns.

Bellis, pg 16
Flare, pg 50

Bendigo Woollen Mills Multicoloured Sock

Fibre: 70% wool, 30% nylon
Weight: 4 ply/sock/fingering
Yardage: 400 metres/438 yards per 100 grams
Colour: Pot Pourri
Number of balls: 2
Amount used: 180 grams - 720 metres/ 788 yards

4 mm

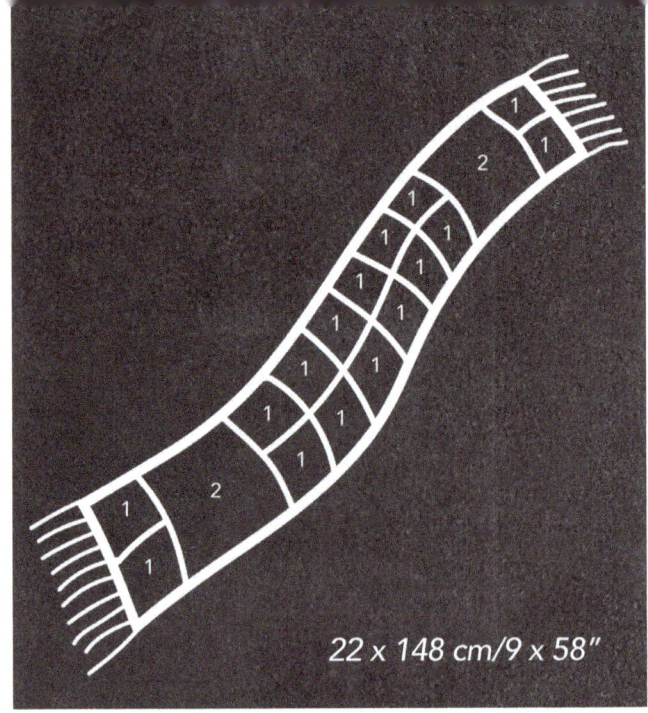

22 x 148 cm/9 x 58"

How to make:

Make 16 Bellis[1] and 2 Flare[2] squares.

Join according to schematic using the dc on back join from page 12.

Fringe

Cut 94 lengths of yarn approximately 20 cm long and using crochet hook, attach one strand to each st and 2-ch cnr sp on short edges. Insert your hook into the end st, fold the length of yarn in half and pull the middle of the yarn through with your hook, then pull both ends through the loop. Pull tight.

Shine Tote

A quick make with super chunky yarn!

 Shine, pg 38

 Homelea Bliss Chunky

Fibre: 100% merino wool
Weight: Super Chunky
Yardage: 60 metres/66 yards per 300 grams
Colours: Donkey and Grey
Number of skeins: 1 Donkey, 2 Grey
Amount used:
- Donkey 145 grams - 29 metres/32 yards
- Grey 390 grams - 78 metres/86 yards

 15 mm

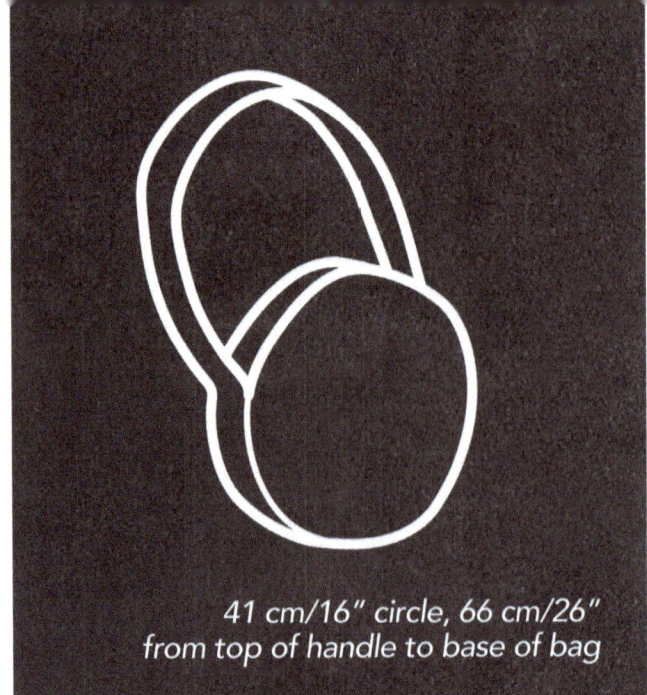

41 cm/16" circle, 66 cm/26" from top of handle to base of bag

How to make:

Make 2 circles

Using Grey, begin with mc, work the first 4 rounds of the Shine pattern, do not cut yarn.

R5: Attach Donkey with stdg dc to the middle st of any 3-st group, work R5, cut yarn.

R6: Continue with Grey working first bpdc around the R5 dc in the middle of a 3-st group of R4. Do not cut yarn.

Repeat to make a second circle.

Make strap

Using Grey, ch 70. Making sure chain is not twisted, join with ss to first ch, ch2 (stch), htr in next 69 sts, join with ss to top loop of 2nd ch of stch. Fasten off.

Hold strap wrong side down next to right side up of a circle, place the join where the circle yarn ends. Using yarn from circle, 17x [ss into next st and one strand of ch of strap], ss into next 14 sts of circle only, skip 36 sts of strap, 17x [ss into next st and one strand of ch of strap], join with ss to first st. Fasten off.

Repeat for other side, but this time work into the 2 loops of the htr of the strap.

Panache Poncho

Relive your childhood with a modern take on the poncho. See page 146 for another way to wear it.

 Hope, pg 114

 Purl Box Eden's Blend

Fibre: 70% Blue faced Leicester wool, 20% silk, 10% Cashmere
Weight: 4 ply/sock/fingering
Yardage: 400 metres/438 yards per 100 grams
Colour: Ghost Walk
Number of skeins: 4
Amount used: 330 grams - 1,320 metres/1,444 yards used

 4 mm

How to make:

Make 4 Hope squares. Join the squares following the schematic using the dc on back join from page 12.

Repeating the last 2 rows of each square before joining will add 3 cm/1.2" to the overall size of the poncho. For a larger size poncho, repeat these rows as many times as necessary.

Neckline edge

R1: Attach with a stdg tr to the first st after the 2-ch sp of the back "V" join, tr in next 70 sts, *tr5tog over (2-ch sp, join, 2-ch sp, join & 2-ch sp)*, tr in next 71 sts, rep from * to * 1x, join with ss to first st. {144 sts}

R2: dc in same st as ss, *dc in next 69 sts*, dc3tog over next 3 sts, rep from * to * 1x, dc2tog over next 2 sts, join with ss to first st. Fasten off. {140 sts}

Neck opening width 28 cm/11", Elbow corner to corner 82 cm/33", Bottom of V to bottom point 53 cm/21"

Envelop Baby Blanket

The perfect sized baby blanket for a cot or pram.

Foundation, pg 20
Borderline Extension, pg 140

Bendigo Woollen Mills Cotton

Fibre: 100% cotton

Weight: 4 ply/sock/fingering

Yardage: 670 metres/733 yards per 200 grams

Colours: French Navy and Parchment

Number of balls: 2 French Navy, 2 Parchment

Amount used:
- French Navy 270 grams - 905 metres/ 990 yards
- Parchment 230 grams - 770 metres/843 yards

4 mm

How to make:

Using French Navy, make 20 Foundation squares. Using Parchment, add the Borderline extension to each square.

Using French Navy, make 1 Foundation square repeating Rounds 8 and 9 eight times, then end with R10. Using Parchment, add the Borderline extension.

Join with Parchment using the dc on back through blo join on page 12, following the schematic.

Border

Attach French Navy with a stdg dc to any 2-ch cnr sp, *dc in each st on side, working a dc in each 2-ch sp and join**, (dc, ch2, dc) in 2-ch cnr sp*, rep from * to * 2x and * to ** 1x, dc in same sp as first st, ch1, join with dc to first st.

Add the Borderline extension as the border.

79 x 120 cm/31 x 47"

Rapier Blanket

Made by Kim Siebenhausen who chose the colours as well.

 d'Artagnan, pg 94

 Scheepjes Catona

Fibre: 100% cotton
Weight: 4 ply/sock/fingering
Yardage: 125 metres/136 yards per 50 grams
Colours: Topaz 179, Ginger Gold 383, Petrol Blue 400, Old Lace 130, English Tea 404
Number of balls: 6 Topaz, 5 Ginger Gold, 2 Petrol Blue, 4 Old Lace, 5 English Tea
Amount used:

- Topaz 272 grams - 680 metres/744 yards
- Ginger Gold 204 grams - 510 metres/558 yards
- Petrol Blue 92 grams - 230 metres/252 yards
- Old Lace 174 grams - 435 metres/476 yards
- English Tea 244 grams - 610 metres/668 yards

 3.5 mm

Colours used: Rounds

Topaz: 1, 6, 13-14, 20, 25
Ginger Gold: 2-3, 21-22
Petrol Blue: 4, 10, 15, 23
Old Lace: 5, 7, 11, 16-18
English Tea: 8-9, 12, 19, 24

110 cm/41" square

How to make:

Make 9 d'Artagnan squares and join them into a 3 x 3 rectangle using Topaz and zipper join on page 12.

Border

R1: Attach Topaz with a stdg dc to any 2-ch cnr sp, *dc in each st on side, working a dc in each 2-ch sp and join**, (dc, ch2, dc) in 2-ch cnr sp*, rep from * to * 2x and * to ** 1x, dc in same sp as first st, ch2, join with ss to first st. Fasten off.

R2: Attach Ginger Gold with a stdg tr to any 2-ch cnr sp, *tr in each st on side**, (tr, ch2, tr) in 2-ch cnr sp*, rep from * to * 2x and * to ** 1x, tr in same sp as first st, ch2, join with ss to first st. Fasten off.

R3: Attach Topaz with a stdg dc to any 2-ch cnr sp, *dc in each st on side**, (dc, ch2, dc) in 2-ch cnr sp*, rep from * to * 2x and * to ** 1x, dc in same sp as first st, ch1, join with dc to first st.

R4: dc over joining dc, *dc in each st on side**, (dc, ch2, dc) in 2-ch cnr sp*, rep from * to * 2x and * to ** 1x, dc in same sp as first st, ch2, join with ss to first st. Fasten off.

Marvin, the Blanket

Marvin, the Blanket was made by Samantha Taylor. The colours are loosely based on those chosen initially by Kim Siebenhausen in a different yarn.

Kaboom, pg 120
Illudium, pg 98,
Periphery Extension, pg 143

Bendigo Woollen Mills Luxury

Fibre: 100% machine washable wool
Weight: 8 ply/DK/light worsted
Yardage: 400 metres/438 yards per 200 grams
Colours: Stone, Cream, Cerise, Boysenberry, Baby Mint, Leaf
Number of balls: 2 Stone, 1 each of Cream, Cerise, Boysenberry, Baby Mint, Leaf
Amount used:
- Stone 370 grams - 740 metres/810 yards
- Cream 190 grams - 380 metres/416 yards
- Cerise 80 grams - 160 metres/175 yards
- Boysenberry 120 grams - 240 metres/263 yards
- Baby Mint 95 grams - 190 metres/208 yards
- Leaf 60 grams - 120 metres/132 yards

4 mm

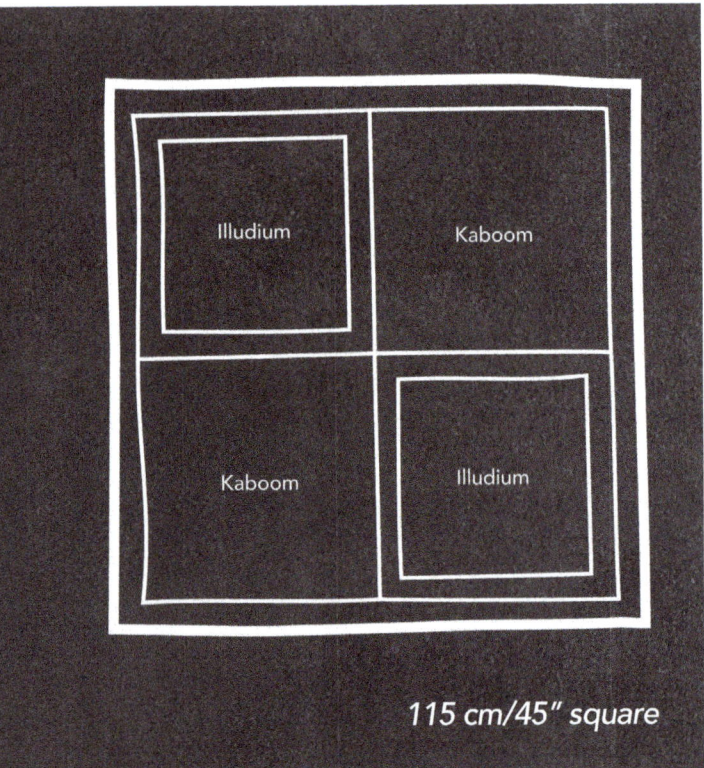

Kaboom
Colours used: Rounds

Stone: 1-2, 4, 7-8, 11-15, 18-20, 25-30
Baby Mint: 3, 33-34
Cream: 5-6, 31-32
Cerise: 9-10
Leaf: 16-17, 35
Boysenberry: 21-24, 36

Illudium + Periphery extension
Colours used: Rounds

Stone 1-2, 4-5, 9-11, 14-17, 21-25, 29-32, 35
Cerise 3, 36
Cream 6, 18 20, 33 34
Leaf 7-8
Boysenberry 12-13, 37
Baby Mint 26-28

How to make:

Make 2 Kaboom squares. Make 2 Illudium squares, adding the Periphery extension.

Join the squares following the schematic using Boysenberry and the dc on back join from page 12.

Border

Attach Boysenberry with a stdg dc to any 2-ch cnr sp, *dc in each st on side, working a dc in each 2-ch sp and join**, (dc, ch2, dc) in 2-ch cnr sp*, rep from * to * 2x and * to ** 1x, dc in same sp as first st, ch1, join with dc to first st.

Add the Periphery extension on page 143 using the same colour order as used to extend Illudium.

Marvin the Blanket - Projects

Medley Blanket

A patchwork of three different sized squares made into a lap blanket.

 Size 1 squares
Bellis, pg 16
Blossom, pg 17
Danvers, pg 18
Foundation, pg 20
Millpond Mini, pg 21
Nosegay, pg 22
Valance, pg 23

Size 2 squares
Aubade, pg 26
Caboodle, pg 28
Inflorescence, pg 30
The Pretender, pg 34

Size 5 Squares
Illudium, pg 98
Wreath, pg 108

Selvedge Extension, pg 144

 Bendigo Woollen Mills Cotton

Fibre: 100% cotton
Weight: 8 ply/DK/light worsted
Yardage: 485 metres/530 yards per 200 grams
Colours: Parchment
Number of balls: 6
Amount used: 1,167 grams - 2,830 metres/ 3,095 yards

 4.5 mm

130 cm /51" square

How to make:

Make 4 each of the size 1 squares. Make 2 each of the size 2 squares. Make 1 each of the size 5 squares.

Join the squares following the schematic using the dc on back join on page 12.

Border

Attach yarn with a stdg dc to any 2-ch cnr sp, *dc in each st on side, working a dc in each 2-ch sp and join**, (dc, ch2, dc) in 2-ch cnr sp*, rep from * to * 2x and * to ** 1x, dc in same sp as first st, ch1, join with dc to first st.

Add the Selvedge extension from page 144 as the border.

Manderley Blanket

Last night I dreamt I went to Manderley again. This blanket was inspired by the grand estate in the classic book Rebecca by Daphne du Maurier.

Danvers, pg 18
Maxim, pg 73
Rebecca, pg 134

Bendigo Woollen Mills Cotton

Fibre: 100% cotton
Weight: 8 ply/DK/light worsted
Yardage: 485 metres/530 yards per 200 grams
Colours: Parchment
Number of balls: 8
Amount used: 1,588 grams - 3,850 metres/ 4,211 yards

4.5 mm

148 cm/58" square

How to make:

Make 24 Danvers squares. Make 12 Maxim squares ending at Round 20. Make 1 Rebecca square ending at Round 32.

Join as shown in the schematic using the dc on back join from page 12.

Border

R1: Attach with a stdg dc to any 2-ch cnr sp, *dc in each st on side, working a dc in each 2-ch sp and join**, (dc, ch2, dc) in 2-ch cnr sp*, rep from * to * 2x and * to ** 1x, dc in same sp as first st, ch1, join with dc to first st.

R2: ch2 (stch), 2htr over joining dc, *htr in each st on side**, 3htr in 2-ch cnr sp*, rep from * to * 2x and * to ** 1x, join with inv join to first true st.

R3: Attach with stdg tr to lbv of the middle st of any 3-st cnr, *tr in lbv of each st on side**, (tr, ch2, tr) in lbv of middle st of a 3-st cnr*, rep from * to * 2x and * to ** 1x, tr in same lbv as first st, ch1, join with dc to first st.

R4: dc over joining dc, *dc in each st on side**, (dc, ch2, dc) in 2-ch cnr sp*, rep from * to * 2x and * to ** 1x, dc in same sp as first st, ch2, join with ss to first st. Fasten off.

Pastiche Blanket

A mix of four different sized squares in my signature blues.

 Size 1 squares
Bellis, pg 16
Blossom, pg 17
Danvers, pg 18
Floret, pg 19
Foundation, pg 20
Millpond Mini, pg 21
Nosegay, pg 22
Valance, pg 23

Size 3 squares
Dendrite, pg 45
Flare, pg 50
Meander, pg 54
Vault, pg 60

Size 4 Squares
Giantess, pg 69
Melbourne, pg 76
Nymph, pg 78
Paradigm, pg 85

Size 5 Squares
Coterie, pg 90
d'Artagnan, pg 94
Illudium, pg 98
Wreath, pg 108

Selvedge Extension, pg 144

 Bendigo Woollen Mills Cotton

Fibre: 100% cotton
Weight: 10 ply/aran/worsted
Yardage: 360 metres/394 yards per 200 grams
Colours: French Navy, Blue Ice, Ice, Parchment
Number of balls: 2 French Navy, 2 Blue Ice, 3 Ice, 4 Parchment
Amount used:
- French Navy 256 grams - 460 metres/504 yards
- Blue Ice 356 grams - 640 metres/700 yards
- Ice 514 grams - 925 metres/1,012 yards
- Parchment 772 grams - 1,390 metres/1,521 yards

 5.5 mm

Pattern	Colour	Rounds	Pattern	Colour	Rounds
Bellis	French Navy	1-2	Meander	French Navy	1-8
	Blue Ice	3-4		Blue Ice	9-14
	Ice	5-6		Ice	15-16
	Parchment	7-8		Parchment	17-20
Blossom	French Navy	1	Vault	French Navy	1-4
	Blue Ice	2-3		Blue Ice	5-7
	Ice	4-8		Ice	8-16
	Parchment	9-10		Parchment	17-19
Danvers	French Navy	1	Giantess	French Navy	1-6
	Blue Ice	2-4		Blue Ice	7-13
	Ice	5-6		Ice	14-17
	Parchment	7-8		Parchment	18-22
Floret	French Navy	1-2	Melbourne	French Navy	1-8
	Blue Ice	3-4		Blue Ice	9-12
	Ice	5-7		Ice	13-16
	Parchment	8-10		Parchment	17-19
Foundation	French Navy	1-3	Nymph	French Navy	1-11
	Blue Ice	4-5		Blue Ice	12-16
	Ice	6-7		Ice	17-19
	Parchment	8-10		Parchment	20-28
Millpond Mini	French Navy	1	Paradigm	French Navy	1-9
	Blue Ice	2-5		Blue Ice	10-17
	Ice	6-7		Ice	18-22
	Parchment	8-10		Parchment	23-25
Nosegay	French Navy	1-3	Coterie	French Navy	1-4
	Blue Ice	4-5		Blue Ice	5-9
	Ice	6-8		Ice	10-16
	Parchment	9-10		Parchment	17-26
Valance	French Navy	1-2	d'Artagnan	French Navy	1-6
	Blue Ice	3-4		Blue Ice	7-13
	Ice	5-6		Ice	14-19
	Parchment	7-8		Parchment	20-25
Dendrite	French Navy	1-5	Illudum	French Navy	1-8
	Blue Ice	6-11		Blue Ice	9-18
	Ice	12-13		Ice	19-25
	Parchment	14-15		Parchment	26-32
Flare	French Navy	1-6	Wreath	French Navy	1-11
	Blue Ice	7-12		Blue Ice	12-17
	Ice	13-15		Ice	18-22
	Parchment	16-19		Parchment	23-27

163 x 193 cm/64 x 76"

How to make:

Make one of each square, changing colours as shown in the table on page 167.

Join with Parchment as shown in the schematic, using the dc on back join from page 12.

Border

Attach Parchment with a stdg dc to any 2-ch cnr sp, *dc in each st on side, working a dc in each 2-ch sp and join**, (dc, ch2, dc) in 2-ch cnr sp*, rep from * to * 2x and * to ** 1x, dc in same sp as first st, ch1, join with dc to first st.

Using Parchment, add the Selvedge extension from page 144 as the border.

Conglomeration Blanket

A huge undertaking, Conglomeration uses each of the 40 squares at least once, demonstrating the multitude of ways the squares can be patchworked together.

 All
Periphery, pg 143

 Bendigo Woollen Mills Cotton

Fibre: 100% cotton
Weight: 8 ply/DK/light worsted
Yardage: 485 metres/530 yards per 200 grams
Colours: Parchment
Number of balls: 18
Amount used: 3,464 grams - 8,400 metres/ 9,187 yards

4.5 mm

Pattern	No.	Rounds
Bellis, pg 16	2	All
Blossom, pg 17	2	All
Danvers, pg 18	2	All
Floret, pg 19	3	All
Foundation, pg 20	2	All
Millpond Mini, pg 21	2	All
Nosegay, pg 22	2	All
Valance, pg 23	2	All
Aubade, pg 26	2	All
Caboodle, pg 28	1	All
Inflorescence, pg 30	1	All
Persnickety, pg 32	1	All
The Pretender, pg 34	1	All
Quarter, pg 36	1	All
Shine, pg 38	1	All
Bushel, pg 42	1	All
Dendrite, pg 45	2	All
Diadem, pg 47	1	All
Flare, pg 50	1	All
Flourish, pg 52	1	All
Meander, pg 54	1	All
Millpond Squared, pg 57	1	All
Vault, pg 60	1	All
Bob, pg 66	1	All

Pattern	No.	Rounds
Giantess, pg 69	1	All
Maxim, pg 73	1	All
Melbourne, pg 76	1	All
Nymph, pg 78	1	All
Pagoda, pg 82	1	All
Paradigm, pg 85	1	All
Coterie, pg 90	1	All
d'Artagnan, pg 94	1	All
Illudium, pg 98	1	All
Piazza, pg 102	1	All
Wreath, pg 108	1	All
Hope, pg 114	1	All
Kaboom, pg 120	1	All
Kim, pg 124	1	All
Mayan, pg 130	1	All
Rebecca, pg 134	1	All

1-increment squares	No.	Rounds
(F) Foundation, pg 20	3	1-4
(B) Bushel, pg 42	3	1-4
(M) Melbourne, pg 76	3	1-3
(K) Kim, pg 124	4	1-4

How to make:

Make the squares as per the table.

Join them using the dc on back join following the schematic. Use the Periphery extension on page 143 to extend the bottom section.

Border

R1: Attach yarn with a stdg dc to any 2-ch cnr sp, *dc in each st on side, working a dc in each 2-ch sp and join**, (dc, ch2, dc) in 2-ch cnr sp*, rep from * to * 2x and * to ** 1x, dc in same sp as first st, ch1, join with dc to first st.

R2: ch3 (stch), *tr in each st on side**, (tr, ch2, tr) in 2-ch cnr sp*, rep from * to * 2x and * to ** 1x, tr in same sp as first st, ch2, join with ss to 3rd ch of stch.

221 x 270 cm/87 x 106"

Glossary

Abbreviations

	cnr	corner	
	R	round	
	rep	repeat	
	sp/s	space/s	
	st/s	stitch/es	
	stch	starting chain	Used in place of the first st in a round. Is included in stitch count.
	stdg	standing	Attach yarn to your hook with a slip knot then work the stitch indicated as normal.
	yo	yarn over	Wrap yarn over hook from back to front.

Stitches

•	ss	slip stitch	Insert hook into st or sp indicated, yo and pull through st or sp and loop on hook.
o	ch	chain	Yarn over, pull through loop on hook.
+	dc	double crochet	Insert hook into st or sp indicated, yo, pull loop to front, yo, pull through both loops on hook.
T	htr	half treble crochet	Wrap yarn around hook, insert hook into st or sp indicated, yo, pull loop to front (3 loops on hook), yo, pull through all 3 loops on hook.
┼	tr	treble crochet	Wrap yarn around hook, insert hook into st or sp indicated, yo, pull loop to front (3 loops on hook), 2x [yo, pull through 2 loops on hook].
╪	hdtr	half double treble crochet	Wrap yarn around hook twice, insert hook into st or sp indicated, yo, pull loop to front (4 loops on hook), yo, pull through 2 loops (3 loops on hook), yo, pull through all 3 loops on hook.
╪	dtr	double treble crochet	Wrap yarn around hook twice, insert hook into st or sp indicated, yo, pull loop to front (4 loops on hook), 3x [yo, pull through 2 loops].
╪	trtr	triple treble crochet	Wrap yarn around hook three times, insert hook into st or sp indicated, yo, pull loop to front (5 loops on hook), 4x [yo, pull through 2 loops].

Techniques

	Abbr	Name	Description
	blo	back loop only	Insert hook into the back loop only of the st indicated.
	flo	front loop only	Insert hook into the front loop only of the st indicated.
	bp	back post	Insert hook around the post of the st indicated from the back. Can be applied to any st.
	fp	front post	Insert hook around the post of the st indicated from the front. Can be applied to any st.
		in front	The bend in the post of the stitch shows it is worked in front of previous round/s.
		behind	The bend in the post of the stitch shows it is worked behind previous round/s.
	cl	cluster	Numerous sts worked together as one st in the st or sp indicated. Begin the type of st indicated as many times as instructed. Work each st of the cl up to before the last yo and pull through 2 loops on hook, then yo and pull though all loops on hook. Could be any number of any kind of st. e.g. 4trcl, 5dtrcl, 3htrcl and worked as fp or bp.
	inv join	invisible join	Cut yarn after completing last st of round. Pull tail up through the last st, thread tail onto needle, insert needle under "v" of first true st of the round and back through the centre of the last st, and through the lbv of the last st. Pull tight enough to form a "v" on top of the stch, weave end away.
	lbv	loop behind v	The third loop or back bump of a st on the back. It's located under the back loop of a st. Any st can be worked into lbv, including cl and tog sts.
	mc	magic circle	Method used to begin a square. Wrap yarn around a few fingers, forming a loop, insert your hook into the centre and pull the working yarn through, ch1 to secure. Work R1 sts into the ring, pull the tail to close the ring once all sts have been made and secure by weaving the end in well.
	beg pc	beginning popcorn	ch3 (stch) and 4 treble crochet sts worked in the same st or sp, gathered together once all sts are made by removing hook, inserting it into the top of the stch and joining it to the last st of the group with a ss.
	pc	popcorn	5 treble crochet sts worked in the same st or sp, gathered together once all sts are made by removing hook, inserting it into the first st of the group and joining it to the last st of the group with a ss.
	puff	puff stitch	5x [yo, insert hook into st or sp indicated, pull loop to front] (11 loops on hook), yo, pull through all loops on hook.
		at the same time	Shows where to place your hook when gathering sts from a previous round into one.
	spike	spike st	Insert hook into st or sp indicated, usually in a round more than 1 round prior to the current round, pull up a long loop level with the current round and work st as normal. Can be any st e.g. spike dc, spike tr.
	tog	together	Numerous sts worked together as one st over a number of sts or sps as indicated. Work the specified number of sts up to before the last yo and pull through 2 loops on hook, then yo and pull though all loops on hook. "tog" will be followed by "over next # sts". It can be done with different numbers and types of sts. e.g. tr5tog over next 5 sts, dc2tog over next 2 sts. Can be worked as fp or bp.
		turn	Turn the square and work on the other side.

Yarn

I used predominantly Australian yarns to make the granny squares and projects in this book, as that is where I am located. You are not bound by that of course!

Matching Yarn

You should be able to find yarns local to you that will give a similar result. The best way to substitute a yarn is to compare the yarn and yardage information I have provided with the yarn you want to use. Yarnsub.com is a great website that compares yarns from all around the world, doing the work for you. It gives each yarn alternative a percentage score of how closely it matches what you are looking at replacing.

If the metres/yards per gram is similar to what I used, you can use my yardage calculations. If your yarn of choice has fewer metres/yards per gram, you will need more. If it has more, you will need less.

Using a Totally Different Yarn

You can use totally different yarn types and weights (even hook sizes) and the patterns will still work. Using a different yarn weight and hook size will change the amount of yarn used. They will also be different sizes of course, but most of the time with granny squares, that does not matter.

Over the page is a table showing the approximate amount of yarn used in 3 yarn weights for each of the 40 granny square patterns.

Weight 1 is 4 ply/sock/fingering, 335 metres per 100 grams (3.5 mm hook).

Weight 2 is 8 ply/DK/light worsted, 242.5 metres per 100 grams (4.5 mm hook).

Weight 3 is 10 ply/aran/worsted, 180 metres per 100 grams (5.5 mm hook).

Using more than one colour

You can of course decide on your own colour changes. There are so many possibilities. If you want to know which yarns and colours have been used for each round, as shown in the examples on each pattern page, you will find a list on my website. See the Helpful Links page for the link to download the alternate colour information.

	Pattern name	Weight 1	Weight 2	Weight 3
Size 1	Bellis	30 m/34 yd	36 m/40 yd	43 m/48 yd
	Blossom	40 m/44 yd	47 m/52 yd	56 m/62 yd
	Danvers	30 m/34 yd	36 m/40 yd	43 m/48 yd
	Floret	32 m/36 yd	38 m/42 yd	46 m/50 yd
	Foundation	30 m/34 yd	35 m/39 yd	42 m/47 yd
	Millpond Mini	35 m/39 yd	41 m/46 yd	50 m/55 yd
	Nosegay	36 m/40 yd	42 m/47 yd	51 m/56 yd
	Valance	36 m/40 yd	42 m/47 yd	50 m/55 yd
Size 2	Aubade	67 m/73 yd	78 m/86 yd	94 m/103 yd
	Caboodle	74 m/81 yd	87 m/96 yd	104 m/115 yd
	Inflorescence	90 m/99 yd	106 m/117 yd	127 m/140 yd
	Persnickety	89 m/98 yd	105 m/115 yd	126 m/138 yd
	The Pretender	70 m/77 yd	82 m/90 yd	98 m/108 yd
	Quarter	67 m/73 yd	78 m/86 yd	94 m/103 yd
	Shine	66 m/71 yd	77 m/85 yd	93 m/102 yd
Size 3	Bushel	139 m/153 yd	164 m/179 yd	196 m/215 yd
	Dendrite	128 m/141 yd	151 m/166 yd	181 m/199 yd
	Diadem	130 m/143 yd	153 m/168 yd	183 m/201 yd
	Flare	130 m/143 yd	153 m/168 yd	183 m/201 yd
	Flourish	127 m/140 yd	150 m/164 yd	180 m/197 yd
	Meander	169 m/185 yd	198 m/217 yd	238 m/261 yd
	Millpond Squared	144 m/159 yd	170 m/186 yd	204 m/224 yd
	Vault	120 m/132 yd	141 m/155 yd	169 m/185 yd
Size 4	Bob	212 m/232 yd	250 m/273 yd	299 m/328 yd
	Giantess	211 m/231 yd	248 m/272 yd	298 m/327 yd
	Maxim	211 m/231 yd	248 m/272 yd	297 m/326 yd
	Melbourne	131 m/144 yd	154 m/169 yd	185 m/203 yd
	Nymph	249 m/273 yd	293 m/321 yd	352 m/386 yd
	Pagoda	186 m/204 yd	219 m/240 yd	262 m/288 yd
	Paradigm	197 m/216 yd	232 m/254 yd	278 m/304 yd
Size 5	Coterie	248 m/272 yd	292 m/319 yd	350 m/383 yd
	d'Artagnan	252 m/276 yd	296 m/324 yd	355 m/389 yd
	Illudium	313 m/343 yd	368 m/403 yd	442 m/483 yd
	Piazza	319 m/349 yd	375 m/411 yd	451 m/493 yd
	Wreath	336 m/368 yd	396 m/433 yd	475 m/520 yd
Size 6	Hope	375 m/411 yd	442 m/483 yd	530 m/580 yd
	Kaboom	340 m/373 yd	400 m/438 yd	480 m/526 yd
	Kim	356 m/390 yd	419 m/459 yd	503 m/551 yd
	Mayan	352 m/386 yd	414 m/453 yd	497 m/544 yd
	Rebecca	438 m/480 yd	516 m/564 yd	619 m/677 yd

Project Planner

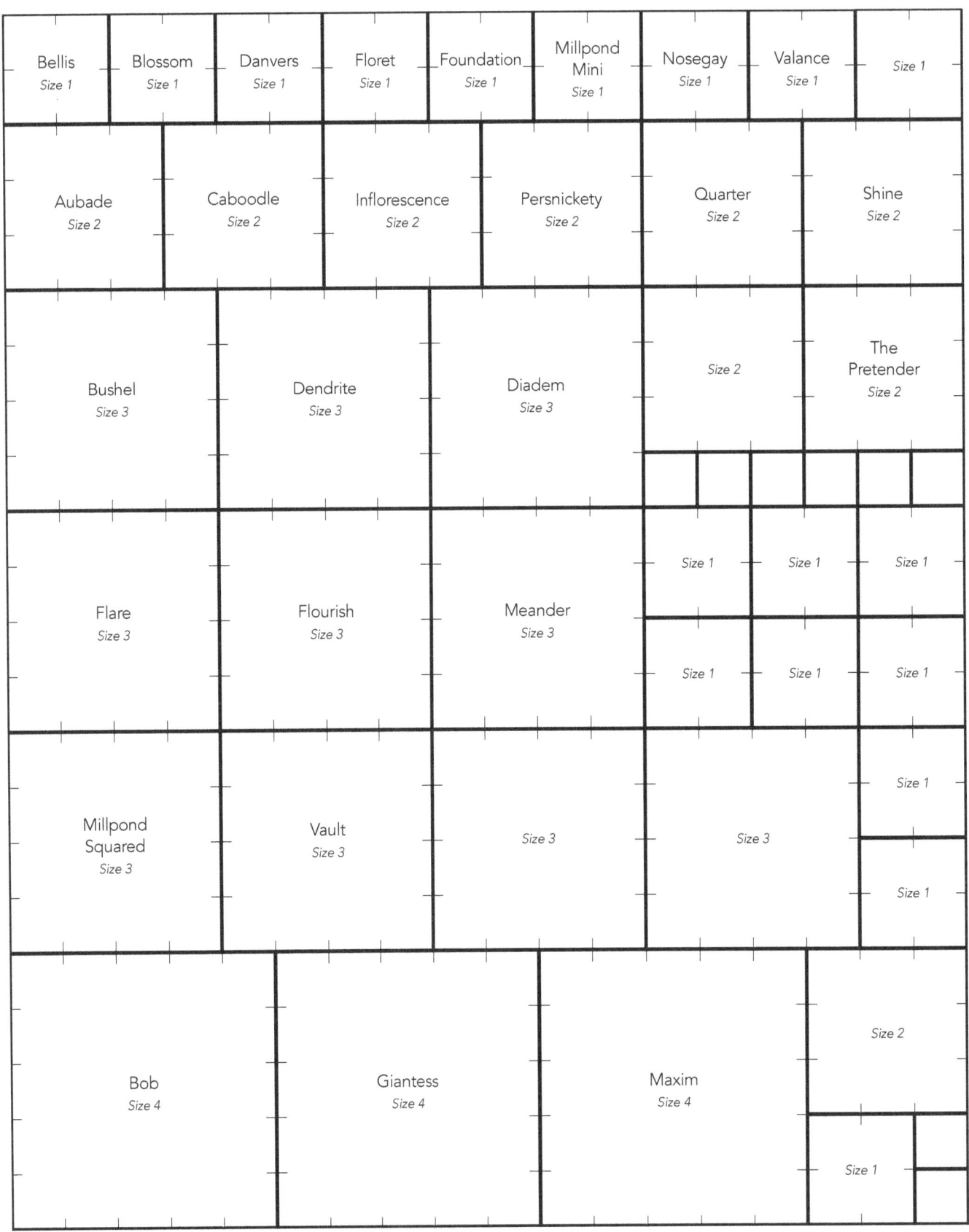

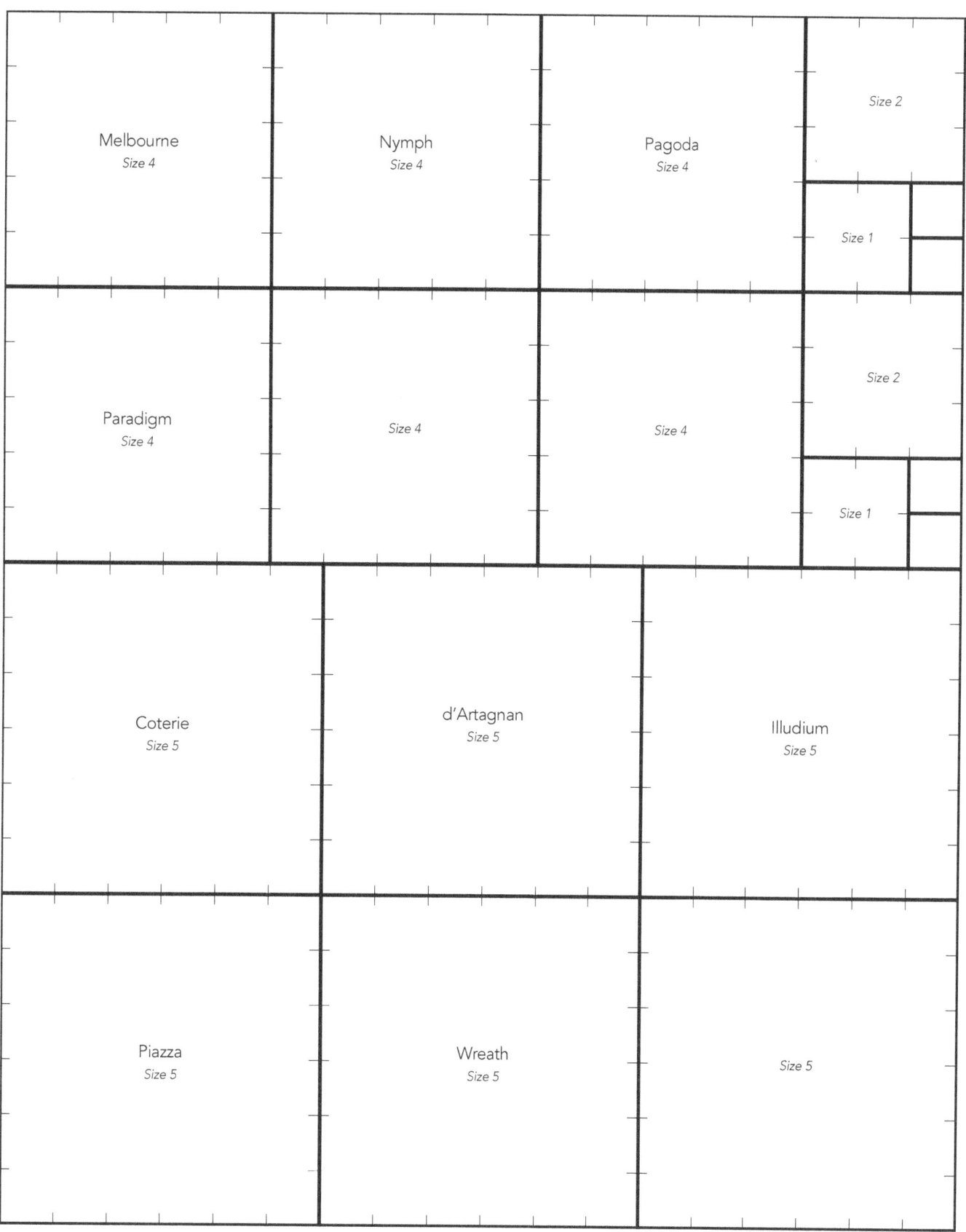

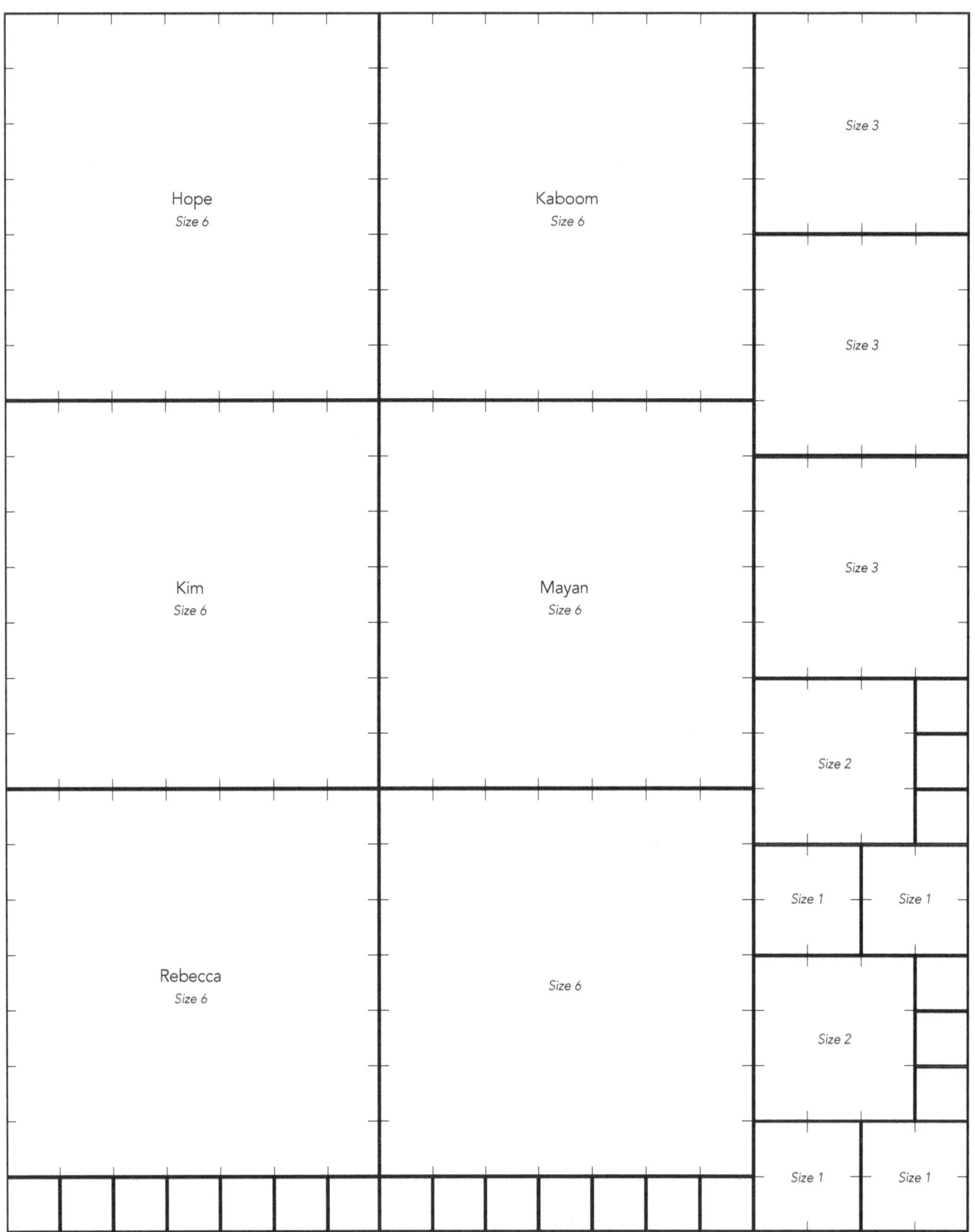

Helpful Links

Do you need a little bit more help with anything or some more information? Head to this page on my blog where you can access lots of help: https://shelleyhusbandcrochet.com/GSPHelp

On that page, you will find links to explanations of:

- How to read my patterns
- Seamless crochet tips
- How to work a stitch over a joining stitch

There are also links to my YouTube channel for:

- Stitch and Technique Playlist (short videos of most stitches and techniques used in the book)
- Seamless Crochet Tips (joining with a stitch and working over a joining stitch)
- How to work a standing stitch
- How to work a false stitch instead of a starting chain
- How to work a magic circle (and weave in the end well)
- A simple join (dc join)

The last thing you will find there are downloads:

- Project planner
- Alternate colour yarn details (yarn used and which rounds for which colours)

If you are still having any trouble, please don't hesitate to reach out. You can email me from my website, shelleyhusbandcrochet.com.

Digital download

Scan the QR code to download the digital version of Granny Square Patchwork.

Thank You

Writing a book is a team effort. Once again, my trusty team of helpers have outdone themselves, helping my crochet dream come to life.

Thanks, Michelle Lorimer, for your graphic design. You understood exactly my vision and made it happen.

Thank you, Jo O'Keefe, for the awesome photography of the projects. Thank you to the wonderful Grace Rowsthorn for modelling the projects for me.

Thank you, SiewBee Pond, for your fabulous technical editing and proofreading as always. Thanks to Amy Gunderson, for being a trooper making all the complex charts so well.

Terrii Lanham checked all the charts for me. Thank you, Terrii.

Thank you, Kim Siebenhausen for making the Rapier Blanket and Samantha Taylor, for making Marvin, the Blanket for me.

My pattern testing team were incredible as usual, testing all the patterns over and over again. They really do give so much time (and yarn!) to testing my patterns. Thank you, Anna Lawson, Anna Moore, Barbara Roberts, Bonita Dunne, Chantelle Daigneault, Chris Wilkins, Hayley Roma, Jennifer French, Jenny Hebbard, Judy Hartwig, Kalpana Chitharanjan, Kathy Mant, Keri-An Richards, Lyn Merton, Marion Van Steveninck, Meghan McKenna, Melissa Russell, Monica Dague, Nicole Hooper, Paulina Smith, Pauline Vos, Rita Spaulding, Ruth Bracey, Samantha Taylor, Sharon Lee, Shona Campbell, Stephanie Ann, Tammy Renwick-Patterson, Tammy Thompson, Teresa Johnson, Terrii Lanham, Tharana Rasheed, Ursula Uphof and Yralmy Pereira.

I had the help of some fabulous crocheters to come up with the alternate colour ways you see for each pattern. Thank you, Chelsea Butler, Cheryl Shields, Chris Wilkins, Evangalina Katsafouros, Hayley Neubauer, Jenny Hebbard, Jo Waring, Kim Siebenhausen, Mell Sappho, Miranda Howard and Yralmy Pereira.

Thank you to Bendigo Woollen Mills for supplying the yarn for me to make most of what you see in this book.

And lastly, thank you for choosing my book. I hope it brings you as much joy to make from as it brought me in creating it for you.

xx Shelley

About the Author

Shelley Husband is a prolific crochet pattern designer, publishing 10 books bursting with modern takes on the traditional granny square. Her first book, Granny Square Flair, won the best crochet book of 2019 in the UK.

Shelley has a real passion for designing seamless crochet patterns with the aim of teaching others through encouragingly supported patterns to create timeless, classic crochet heirlooms.

Based in Narrawong in South West Victoria, Australia, when not designing and publishing new patterns, Shelley teaches crochet in person around Australia, and throughout the world via her online presence.

You can find Shelley online on her website shelleyhusbandcrochet.com.

More Books

Looking for more books by Shelley Husband?

Granny Square Academy

Learn all there is to know about making granny squares, including how to read patterns.

Granny Square Academy 2

Expand your granny square knowledge with instructions for more advanced stitches and techniques.

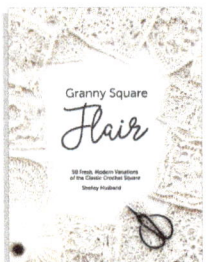

Granny Square Flair

50 written and charted granny square patterns and 11 project ideas to make with them.

Beneath the Surface

A beginner friendly pattern, with lots of extra support including video links.

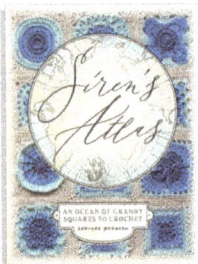

Siren's Atlas

64 written and charted granny square patterns for adventurous crocheters.

Dotty Spotty

Classic circle-to-square granny square fun.

Nimue Crochet Blanket

A crochet quest of epic proportions with very detailed help including video links.

The Cove

A pick your path pattern inspired by coastal adventures.

Corners and Curves

45 Granny Square patterns for crocheters ready to play with colours, corners and curves.

Buy my books direct from me in my shop or online at most online book retailers around the world.

Visit my pattern shop for digital patterns galore.

shop.shelleyhusbandcrochet.com

www.ingramcontent.com/pod-product-compliance
Lightning Source LLC
Chambersburg PA
CBHW061806290426
44109CB00031B/2946